I *Believe* IN HEAVEN

REAL STORIES FROM THE BIBLE, HISTORY AND TODAY

CECIL MURPHEY
& TWILA BELK

Regal

For more information and
special offers from Regal Books, email us at
subscribe@regalbooks.com

Published by Regal
From Gospel Light
Ventura, California, U.S.A.
www.regalbooks.com
Printed in the U.S.A.

Library of Congress Cataloging-in-Publication Data
Murphey, Cecil. I believe in heaven : real stories from the Bible, history,
and today / Cecil Murphey and Twila Belk.
pages cm
Includes bibliographical references and index.
ISBN 978-0-8307-6636-9 (trade paper : alk. paper)
1. Heaven—Christianity. I. Title.
BT846.3.M87 2013
236'.24dc22
2013006794

Rights for publishing this book outside the U.S.A. or in non-English languages are
administered by Gospel Light Worldwide, an international not-for-profit ministry.
For additional information, please visit www.glww.org, email info@glww.org, or write to
Gospel Light Worldwide, 1957 Eastman Avenue, Ventura, CA 93003, U.S.A.

To order copies of this book and other Regal products in bulk quantities,
please contact us at 1-800-446-7735.

Contents

Part 2

QUESTIONS ABOUT HEAVEN

How to Read This Book

Like our companion volume, *I Believe in Healing*, Twila Belk and I have arranged this book into two parts. Part 1 contains true accounts of individuals. We have accepted only stories that, in our opinion, have credibility to them. They are mostly first-person stories and are presented without explanation.

Part 1 focuses on four types of stories that point toward heaven. The first type are mostly first-person near-death experiences. The estimate from various sources is that as many as 11 million people have had near-death experiences.

The second type (though there are fewer of them) are stories of individuals who claim they died, went to heaven—literally—and God sent them back. The most obvious example is the apostle Paul, as recounted in the New Testament.

Don Piper's story is also here. As far as we can tell, the publication of *90 Minutes in Heaven* in 2004 piqued the interest of readers and started the trend toward heavenly experiences. Over the course of Don Piper's travel and through other sources, we have found a number of accounts similar to that of Don and Paul.

The third type are stories of individuals who saw or sensed some spiritual presence near the times of their death. Obviously, these stories come from friends and family members who witnessed the experience.

The fourth type (and these are the most unusual) are stories of visions by various individuals. These visions, though prominent in the Bible, aren't part of the experience of most believers today. We've recorded a few that came from reliable, trustworthy sources.

Each story tells of the dying person seeing angels, Jesus or some special person in their lives, who came to escort them to heaven. These experiences have provided immense peace for those who were at the scene.

Part 2 is what we call the "theological section" or apologia—that is, a defense of our title *I Believe in Heaven*. You could also call it the "reference section." Here we bring up the most common questions about heaven and try to provide answers.

Among many of these issues, Christians are divided; so, in an effort to be fair, I've avoided making definitive statements on areas where there are differences. Instead, I've tried to be as faithful as possible in presenting the various positions on questions, such as:

- Where do we go when we die?
- Is there an intermediate state between death and the resurrection?
- Will we see our pets in heaven?
- Is hell a reality?

When I believe I can give a biblical response to the question with integrity, I do so. However, no matter how strongly some people feel about other issues, many of the common questions have no definitive answers from God's sacred answer book— the Bible.

Ultimately, I remind myself and readers of the words of Moses:

> The LORD our God has secrets known to no one. We are not accountable for them, but we and our children are accountable forever for all that [God] has revealed to us, so that we may obey all the terms of these instructions (Deut. 29:29).

I *Believe* IN HEAVEN

REAL STORIES FROM THE BIBLE, HISTORY AND TODAY

INTRODUCTION

What Is *Heaven*?
CECIL MURPHEY

Heaven is where God dwells.

Heaven refers to the perfect place where we will live in the presence of God throughout eternity. It is a place of absolute happiness and God wipes away all memories of our past imperfections.

Christianity defines our future in heaven as being in the presence of God, with dwelling places prepared for the faithful by Jesus, where we'll live in eternal bliss beyond anything we can grasp in this life (see John 14:1-4).

Those allowed into heaven receive new or glorified bodies that don't decay. Death will be gone.

PART 1

STORIES
AND TESTIMONIES OF
Heaven

"Not on Our Guest List"

(Marie C. Senter)

"Leukemia?" My fiancé glared at his doctor. "I'm getting married in six weeks and leukemia is not on the guest list."

I reached for Elliott's hand and our eyes locked in disbelief. We hadn't anticipated that wedding present.

The doctor busied himself flipping chart pages as though another look-through would change the information.

Elliott finally said, "All right, give us your best guess—straight from the shoulder."

"I'll talk to you like I would my own father," the doctor said as he looked up in obvious relief at a chance to be forthright and honest. "Your white blood cell numbers are high, and the cells look sick. You're in for a tough fight."

Elliott nodded. "Is that all?"

"Right now, I want to draw more blood and set you up for a biopsy of whatever that spot is on your lungs."

"We're going to fight this leukemia," Elliott said, "and fight to beat it. I trust you, doctor, to tell me how the fight is going. I'm not afraid. I believe in the God I've preached for 52 years. Either way, this is a no-lose fight."

The look on the doctor's face showed admiration and a hint of tears. "Let's start the fight right now."

Elliott left the exam room to get his blood drawn. The doctor signaled me to sit. As soon as Elliott was gone, the doctor said, "You're a nurse. You know what's coming. Don't waste your time getting married. I give him six weeks—three months max—to live."

"Elliott is God's answer to my prayers," I said. "We will be married, and I'll treasure every moment granted me as his wife. *We will fight.*"

A week later, Elliott died on the surgery table during the biopsy procedure, but he was revived. He had transfusions going full blast and monitors beeping energetically when they transferred him to the surgical intensive care unit (SICU). I was granted permission to be at his bedside until he lived—or died again.

When Elliott opened his eyes, I was there to see the reflection of incredible beauty and peace. Smiling through my tears, I told him he was in SICU and I asked him not to fight the tube down his throat or the machine pushing air into his lungs.

He smiled when I assured him he'd be able to tell me why he was so radiant and peaceful, but for now he needed to sleep.

Someone apparently told Elliott that the SICU was two stories below street level. Two days later, he told the doctor that it wasn't right for a living man to be 60 feet underground without monitors and breathing machines. Hours later, Elliott was resting in a regular hospital room four stories above ground. That's when he told me his story.

Elliott described floating above the surgical room as he watched the excitement of nurses and doctors dealing with someone in trouble. Then he realized he was the one being resuscitated. A brilliant light filled the room, and a radiant being in the light distracted him. Peace and joy filled his heart.

My soon-to-be-husband, who was never at a loss for words, could only smile and glow for several minutes before he told me the rest. "He said it wasn't my time." Elliott spoke with disappointment, yet joy, in knowing he had time to accomplish more here on earth. But he also had received the promise that he would return one day to that incredible place.

A week after Elliott was discharged from the hospital, we were married in a small church. God provided strength each day, even though leukemia became a member of our marriage.

The three months his doctor predicted became productive months with incidental breaks for a transfusion or a chemo shot. Elliott volunteered to be one of the human guinea pigs in a leukemia drug trial. The response was so dramatic that the drug later became the first choice for adult leukemia patients.

We fought the good fight for almost two years until Elliott went into the hospital with a persistent cough and low-grade fever. At the end of my nursing shift, I went to his bedside.

Almost immediately, the doctor came in with a chart and an odd look on his face. "Well, Elliott, you made me promise to tell you. Your body says you've had enough. Do you want to go home or into a nursing home?"

My beloved husband looked at me with a pleading expression and asked, "Can I come home?"

Through my tears, I laughed and nodded.

At home, his recliner became a throne. Friends came for blessedly short visits. Mostly we were comfortably and quietly together.

One day, Elliott started looking toward the corner of the living room. Gradually his face glowed. That happened a number of times.

Just once I asked, "Angels? Friends who wait?"

Without looking away, he nodded, pointed and spoke his mother's name.

I was sitting at his side, holding his hand when he whispered, "Thank you, dear heart." He took one breath and was gone.

Elliott had put up a good fight.

To Marie C. Senter, writing comes as naturally as reading. She is an inpatient hospice nurse, choir member, chaplain and artist (sentered@sbcglobal.net).

Priceless Memories
(STAN COTTRELL)

For 67 years, my great-grandfather, known as an old-time gospel preacher, was legendary in the backwoods of Kentucky. According to my mother, during his three-weeklong nightly church meetings, which they called revivals, people from as far away as a mile claimed to hear their shouting and singing.

Through the years, God honored all the praising and shouting, and today a Christian radio station sits in the spot of my great-grandfather's church. Around the world, people hear daily broadcasts. When I visit Kentucky and have visitors in the car with me, I tell them about my great-grandfather and turn on that station.

Their responses always seem the same. They say, "There's something different about this station. It gets hold of you in a special way."

I think I know part of the reason. When Grandpa was about to die, a crowd of relatives and old friends surrounded him. They had gathered to say an earthly farewell to a man they loved. Until the very end, Grandpa had a sharp mind and was alert, lucid and in good spirits. He spoke to each of his visitors individually and expressed his love for them. He urged them to follow Jesus.

He lay in bed barely breathing, and everyone was sure he was leaving this world. Then, all of a sudden, Grandpa sat up and stared at the foot of the bed. "Just one more minute, Jesus, please," he said. He talked to his family about how they should live after he was gone.

Some thought he was hallucinating.

"What's the matter with all of you?" Grandpa asked. "Jesus is right here." He pointed. "Can't you see Him standing there?"

He spoke a few more words to the faithful around him and smiled. Grandpa then reached out his hand to Jesus. "I'm ready," he said.

Just then, his body slumped, and he fell back in bed.

He was gone.

His funeral was different from anything people in those parts had ever attended. Instead of mournful tears, people applauded, laughed and sang. The sound was the same as it had been many times in Grandpa's church.

The hymn they sang was called "It's Shouting Time in Heaven."

Stan Cottrell is an ultra-marathon runner. He has run approximately 200,000 miles in 38 countries. Stan is also a businessman, world adventurer, speaker, visionary, author and entrepreneur. Raised in the backwoods of rural Kentucky, his early years were steeped in riveting stories of rich, spiritual heritage. See www.friendshipsports.org.

A Suicide: The Story of Tamara Laroux

Fifteen-year-old Tamara Laroux's troubles grew until she didn't think she could take any more. Her parents' divorce when she was six had made her feel an overpowering sense of rejection. She felt as if she were a burden. She was alone, depressed and afraid. She was convinced that she would never be happy and that her only answer was to end her life.

Unable to cope, Tamara went to her mother's bedroom and pulled a .38 police special from her drawer. As she slid her finger to the trigger and placed the barrel against her head, a small internal voice persuaded her to aim at her heart instead. That way, she surely wouldn't miss, and it would take her out of this world forever.

"Forgive me, God," Tamara cried as she pulled the trigger.

Death gripped her body, and her departed soul sped downward. A sulfuric acid type of fire overwhelmed her—the terrible pain and searing burn were indescribable. Deep, deep darkness enveloped her. She was in a place of torment and death. Tamara was aware she was dead.

Countless chambers and a sea of formless people, hideously screaming their never-ending cries of agony and terror, surrounded her. She was unable to communicate with them, yet when she looked at them individually she had full knowledge about their lives—all they had done wrong, their thoughts, their emotions, their wills, everything. She had full wisdom, but the only thing that mattered to her was that she had not surrendered her life to Jesus Christ. Regret engulfed her. She wanted to return to earth and warn people.

From her place in hell, Tamara looked across an expanse and saw heaven. She knew it was a place of joy, peace, love and wholeness. She fervently wished that no one else would join her in the eternal pit of doom, torment and fear. That was the mutual desire of the others in that place.

In an instant that can't be understood in the human mind, Tamara watched the giant-sized hand of God reach downward across time and space. She knew it had come for her. The hand scooped her up and carried her over the vast expanse.

She entered God's presence, a great contrast to where she had been. Instead of the death, torment and darkness of hell, love, light, grace, mercy, joy and peace overwhelmed her.

Once there, Tamara stared in awe at God's magnificent kingdom—the glory there too exquisite for words. She saw the beauty of the stones, radiant lights and brilliant colors. The sights rejuvenated her, and she was filled with knowledge and wisdom. Even though she didn't know how to communicate, she was fully aware of what was happening around her.

As quickly as her out-of-body journey began, it ended. She returned to her physical body. When Tamara became conscious, she realized she needed to straighten out her life with God. If she did that, she would be all right with everything she had to face.

Tamara had no idea how long she'd been in her mother's room, and no one knew she had gone there or what she had planned to do. After she opened her eyes, she saw her mother, who had heard her cry. As soon as her mother realized what had happened, she reached for the telephone to call an ambulance.

After the emergency medical technicians arrived, Tamara's gray pallor made them question whether they should even bother to transport her to the emergency room. She appeared to be dying. They didn't realize she was just then returning to life.

As Tamara learned later, the bullet missed her heart by less than one-quarter of an inch. With the caliber of gun she used, her heart should have shattered completely. That it hadn't surprised the medical staff. Instead of dying, Tamara experienced a miraculous physical recovery.

She no longer felt hopeless. Tamara's emotional freedom and faith came gradually through a process of applying God's promises in the Bible to her mind and emotions. The truths and lessons she learned through her experience and the process afterward have given others hope, encouragement and an awareness of God's love.[1]

Fear TO FREEDOM:
The Rosemary Trible Story

In 1975, Rosemary Trible hosted *Rosemary's Guestbook*, her own daily television talk show on WTVR in Richmond, Virginia. She focused on topics relevant to women's lives. Once a week, however, she spotlighted what she called more serious issues.

About three weeks before Christmas, Rosemary aired a groundbreaking show about sexual assault. In those years, the subject was rarely discussed on TV, but she wanted to help women who had been traumatized by abuse or were fearful of being violated.

Her guests for that special telecast included two rape survivors (whose faces were shadowed to protect their identities), a police officer and a district attorney. Afterward, the station received an abundance of calls and letters. Rosemary said that she hurt for the many women whose lives had been destroyed because of sexual assault.

A week after the show, Rosemary planned to tape extra programs so she could take time off for the holidays. Rather than drive back and forth to her home, an hour each way, she stayed at the hotel across the street from the station. As the evening wore on, she grew tired of working on show scripts and decided to go to the restaurant downstairs for coffee.

After Rosemary returned to her room, she settled back into her work. Just then, she heard a rustling noise, and the curtains parted. Before she had time to react, a man grabbed her from behind. The cold steel of his gun pressed against her temple. With his gloved hand wrapped around her neck, he leaned close to her ear. "Okay, miss cute talk show host, what do you do with a gun to your head?"

Rosemary tried to fight him off, but he overpowered her. So she did the only thing she could: she prayed. As he raped her, she talked to him about God—anything she could do to keep from going into shock. The gun never left his hand.

Before the man left, he threatened to kill her if she told anyone about what had happened, and he reminded her that he knew where she lived. He backed away and climbed out the window that opened directly onto the parking garage roof.

Because the man was wearing a ski mask, Rosemary could later say only that her assailant was tall, muscular, strong and black. Even though she reported the crime, the police never found her assailant. She was left with an overwhelming terror that choked her joy and kept her suspicious of every black man she didn't know. After several months of living in fear, Rosemary canceled her TV program. Shortly after that, her house was burglarized, which further traumatized her.

Eventually, her desperation caused her to reach a decisive moment in her life. She cried out to God, "I can't handle this fear anymore. I need Your help." She promised God that if He would take away her pain and fear, she would follow Him. God gave her peace and assurance that He was with her.

Years later, Ruth attended an event with inner-city pastors from the Washington, DC, area. There she was introduced to a large man, who reminded her of her rapist. She became nervous.

When she learned that the man was an ex-con who had spent five years in prison at Alcatraz, she panicked. However, her fears lessened when the man spoke that night and told them his life story.

The man said his life had changed after a pastor told him about Jesus and that God would forgive him. He learned that even though his crimes were immense, no crime was beyond God's love. The man confessed his wrongful ways and realized he could be forgiven—that he *was* forgiven—and that knowledge transformed him. After serving his time in prison, he moved to Washington, DC, to help the pastor work with inner-city kids.

After listening to the words of the former convict, Rosemary realized that she wouldn't be completely healed until she forgave the man who had attacked her. She went into the restroom and prayed. After Rosemary forgave her rapist, she asked God to bring someone into his path who would tell him about Jesus. "I want to spend eternity with him," she said. She continued to pray for him in the days ahead.

In February 1996, God answered Rosemary's prayer. On the way to a friend's home for a weekend retreat with a group of college students—two of whom had been raped—a snowstorm struck the area. As Rosemary was driving on the interstate, her SUV spun out of control and slammed into the railing. She continued driving but discovered that the accident had affected her more than she thought. Confused and disoriented, she pulled over to the side of the road to pray. Then she blacked out.

An ambulance took Rosemary to the hospital, where she spent three days in a coma. During that time, a beautiful, diffused light surrounded and comforted her. She said it was like a warm blanket of love, and she knew she was in heaven. She saw what appeared to be a field of wheat fluttering under a bright, blue sky. A small group of friends who had died approached to welcome her to the field. They seemed to be the same age as when she had last seen them. Each one beamed with peace and happiness.

Then, from behind her friends, a large figure moved toward her. At first Rosemary didn't recognize him, but then she understood: she was face-to-face with what she later said was one of the greatest gifts of her life.

"I'm the man who raped you," he told her. "I wouldn't be here if you hadn't forgiven me and prayed that someone would tell me about Jesus."

When Rosemary awoke from her coma, she was a changed woman. She no longer feared death, and she felt assured that she would spend eternity with her rapist—a shocking thought to some, but a joyful thought for her.[2]

Hospice Deepened My Faith

(MICHAEL W. ELMORE)

As a hospice chaplain, I've been present as hundreds of people have transitioned from their final moments of life. Not all transitions are remarkable. Some are peaceful; everyone's passage is different. However, as I have accompanied people through their final journey, certain individuals have left me with an indelible belief that heaven is a real place.

For example, Rose was a prim and genteel woman with a sense of pleasure for the finer things in life. I was surprised when I first met her, because she had brought many of her cherished belongings and transformed her austere hospice room into the familiar surroundings of home.

During one of my visits, Rose glanced at the corner of her room repeatedly. She seemed to be looking at something, and she asked me to look as well. "Do you see him?" she asked.

"See whom?"

"The angel who watches over me."

I stared but saw nothing.

Each time I visited, Rose talked about the sense of peace she felt because of the angelic visitations.

Many patients in hospice experience surges of anxiety, but not Rose. I believe the day Rose slipped from this life into something more she was borne on an angel's wings, peacefully and comfortably. Rose's sense of serenity left a lasting impression that deepened my belief in heaven.

Louise had a slow-growing form of cancer. Her final days were pitiful, as she lay in bed unable to move, eat or swallow. She could whisper a few words. Her only view was the ceiling tiles above her bed. I spent many quiet times with Louise as she clung to life. She couldn't turn her head to look at me, but we talked quietly nevertheless.

I couldn't understand why Louise gazed so intently at her ceiling. Out of curiosity, one day I asked her what she saw. With a halting, whispery voice, Louise replied, "I see Jesus. Every night when I go to sleep and every morning when I wake up, Jesus is there. I feel such peace when I look up at Him that I never want to look away."

"What does Jesus look like?"

"He's smiling. His face is so gentle, His eyes are kind and, most of all, His arms are stretched out toward me like He's waiting for me."

Each day when I visited Louise, it was the same. She gazed at her ceiling and saw something that no other human could ever perceive.

Louise's death didn't come quickly, but it finally came. She slipped from the confines of her hospice room into the outstretched arms of Jesus. Once again, my encounters with Louise deepened my belief in heaven.

Marc came to hospice in the final stage of cancer. He brought along his yellow Labrador named Jake, whom the vet also diagnosed with cancer.

Marc insisted that Jake share his bed so the longtime friends could spend their last days together. When I asked Marc about his final wishes, he shared two things with me. First, he wanted to have a few photos taken with Jake as a keepsake for his family. Second, he wished that Jake would die before him so that his dog wouldn't have to bear the weight of separation from his master.

After I shared Marc's final wishes with our social worker, she took several snapshots of Jake resting on Marc's lap in "their" hospice bed. The next day, Jake died. Marc said good-bye to his friend of many years, sad but relieved that his Lab had passed away. Comforted by Jake's passing, Marc relaxed and let go of his own ebbing life. Before the photos could be developed, Marc was gone as well.

A few days later, Marc's pictures came back from the photo lab. When we gathered round and opened the envelope, someone gasped. I looked over the shoulder of one of the nurses and saw a most unusual thing. Around Marc's bed appeared a luminescent circle of tall angelic beings surrounding him and Jake. It was obvious that these photos were not some developer's careless mistake. They were the angelic forms present at Marc's bedside, fulfilling their watchful duty of waiting for the time of Jake's and Marc's passings. A sense of awe spread over me as I realized afresh that I believe in heaven.

I'm convinced that heaven is a real place. My patients' experiences have proven it to me. As I've said, not everyone has such ethereal encounters—some pass from this life quiet and sedated, while others pass with terrible fear. But Rose, Marc and Louise deepened my belief in heaven.

Some may think it strange that a chaplain would need his be-lief in heaven reaffirmed, but we are also human. We live with the realization that one day we also will make the final journey. How-ever, moments with these folks have calmed any inner anxieties. Because of my relationship with them, I understand deeper than ever before why I believe in heaven.

Michael Elmore holds degrees from Life Pacific College and Ashland Theo-logical Seminary. He has served as a pastor and hospital and hospice chaplain for more than two decades. Michael has been published in academic journals and edited several college textbooks.

The Coma of Marietta Davis

Marietta Davis, a 25-year-old Baptist woman, lived in Berlin, New York. She went into a coma for nine days, and doctors could do nothing to arouse her. Then, suddenly, she awoke and related to her family and her minister a detailed dream about what awaits everyone in the next world.

Her experiences were recorded in a book titled *Scenes Beyond the Grave*, published in 1859. Marietta wasn't a professing Chris-tian when she went into heaven and later into hell. Her mother, Nancy Davis, and her two sisters, Susan and Sarah Ann Davis, wrote the book.[3]

Her mother said that Marietta wasn't openly religious, but during the winter of 1847–1848, her mind was "religiously ex-ercised." Months later, Marietta fell into the nine-day coma. Af-ter awakening, Marietta told the family she had been in heaven, had seen many now-dead friends and relatives, and had also seen Jesus.

After that, Marietta Davis believed and spoke of the time when she would go to heaven forever. She told her family that she would soon return there.

She predicted her own death in August 1848 and died the following March, exactly as she told the family she would.

Death BEFORE
Life After Life

Greg Taylor tells the story of Private George Ritchie, who lay close to death in a Texas military hospital in December 1943.[4]

Ritchie finished basic training and was supposed to transfer to Richmond, Virginia. But he came down with a dangerously high fever of 106 degrees. He recounted that he heard a click and then a whirl inside his head that went on and on. Confused and wondering what time it was, he jumped out of bed and turned around. Someone was lying in his bed.

He rushed out of the room and into the corridor, but he couldn't get anyone's attention. Suddenly he flew through the air and, to his amazement, arrived in Richmond. He still wore his army-issue hospital pajamas. He tried to talk to a civilian, but the man didn't see him. He attempted to tap the man's shoulder, but his hand passed straight through the man's body.

That's when Ritchie knew he was dead. Just then he remembered seeing the body in his bed in Texas and wondered if it was his. He hardly finished the thought before he was back in the army hospital. He searched ward after ward for his physical body. He finally came across a body—covered with a sheet—and it was his.

Just then the room grew extremely bright, and a "being of light"—whom he assumed was Jesus—appeared to him. Ritchie then experienced what many call a life review—he became aware of everything that had happened to him, and yet he didn't feel judged by any of his actions. The being asked him what he had done with his life.

The being took him to tour the realms of both heaven and earth, and then "gave him orders to return to the human realm." The doctor had already signed the death certificate, but just then, as he prepared the corpse for the morgue, an orderly noticed some bodily movement. The orderly called a doctor who injected a shot of adrenaline into Ritchie's heart. The soldier returned to life "with a crushing, burning feeling in his throat." He had been out of his body for nine minutes.

There's more to the story. George Ritchie became a psychiatrist. In 1965, his description of the realm of death greatly impressed one of his students. A decade later, that student, Dr. Raymond Moody, published *Life After Life*. That book documented many accounts of those who reported near-death experiences. After the publication of Moody's book, the term "near-death experience" became part of the English language.[5]

꘠━◈━꘠

Taylor records the personal account of an unnamed woman who was dying after a heart attack. The woman said she floated until she saw a brilliant light. After that, a group of people came between her and the light. One of them was her deceased brother, who gestured delightedly as she approached. Then "my mother became detached from the group. She shook her head and waved her hand . . . and I stopped."

Just then, the doctor said, "She's coming around." The woman awoke in her bed. Her first words to the doctor were, "Why did you bring me back?"[6]

꘠━◈━꘠

Taylor also gives Michael Tymm's account of a near-death experience that occurred in 1889 to Dr. A. S. Wiltse. Wiltse provided a more graphic picture than most people who tell of the immediate effects of dying. He said that life slowly left his body, beginning with his feet and moving upward. He went on to say that he floated "up and down and laterally like a soap bubble."[7]

꘠━◈━꘠

Another story concerns Admiral Francis Beaufort, who in childhood fell off an anchored ship. He didn't know how to swim and spent time submerged before being rescued.

Beaufort said that he finally gave up, and just then he felt a sense of perfect tranquility. He spoke of a "panoramic review," which is often part of the modern descriptions of that phase of a near-death experience. Along with it is usually a sense of right and wrong.[8]

❖

Taylor tells of research by Albert Heim, a geology professor in Zurich, who, in 1892, presented research collected during a period of 25 years from experiences of people "who survived acute life-threatening situations—notably, climbers who fell during their ascents."[9] Heim said that "95 percent of his subjects reported a certain, consistent experience." Consistently, they reported no anxiety or pain, "but rather, calm seriousness . . . and their probable outcomes were overviewed with objective clarity. No confusion entered at all."[10]

❖

Another well-known story about Admiral Richard E. Byrd was recorded in *Alone: The Classic Polar Adventure*. In this book, Byrd recounts how he stayed alone in Antarctica in 1934 during his second Antarctic expedition, which took place four years after his historic flight over Antarctica.

Byrd decided to spend six months alone gathering weather data. It also provided him an opportunity to be away from people. It didn't work as he planned; Byrd began suffering inexplicable symptoms of mental and physical illness. By the time he discovered that carbon monoxide from a defective stovepipe was poisoning him, he had already gone through a near-death experience.

Byrd states, "I saw my whole life pass in review . . . [I] realized how wrong my sense of value had been and how I had failed to see that the simple . . . unpretentious things of life are the most important."[11]

Seven Days of Death

Although Emanuel Tuwagirairmana was a Christian, he admitted he wasn't faithful in living the way he knew he should. In 1994, he was wounded in the Rwanda Genocide, when a Hutu-led mass slaughter of the Tutsi minority took place during a period of four months. The Human Rights Watch estimated that the death toll decimated about 20 percent of the country's population.[12]

Emanuel was seriously wounded in his left arm. To save their own lives, Emanuel and 10 other Tutsis hid inside Kabwai School in Gitarama, which was less than 25 miles from Kigali, the capital.

While there, Emanuel's wounds worsened, and he died. His friends couldn't bury him, because it was too dangerous to move outside the school. So they wrapped his body in a bed cover, laid him in a corner, and he stayed that way for seven days. His body stank, but his friends could do nothing about it.

As soon as Emanuel died, he went to heaven, although he didn't know how he left his body. In his next aware moment, Emanuel was at heaven's gate and met a man who claimed to be an angel.

As Emanuel stood there, his body changed, and he became a heavenly body—something more beautiful than his earthly form. After the change, he was escorted through a beautiful flower garden. Emanuel met Jesus, who first presented Himself in human form with the scars from His crucifixion, and then in a perfect body.

Emanuel's next memory was that Jesus took him back to the school building where his dead body lay. Although his friends were still there, they were unable to see him as he viewed his own body.

Jesus took Emanuel back to heaven and showed him a beautiful city beside a lake. On the other side stood friends who had died during the genocide. Emanuel stared at the brilliant light across the lake and wanted to go there. But Jesus told Emanuel he couldn't cross the lake and go to God's throne yet, because it wasn't his time to leave the earth.

From there, Jesus took Emanuel to hell, where the people were made to work like slaves. After that, Jesus gave him food that tasted like chocolate. After he ate it, Jesus told him that he had "eaten" the Bible. When he returned to earth, the Lord said Emanuel would be able to memorize all the verses of the holy book and keep them inside his head. He was also to tell others what he had seen and urge them to turn from their evil ways. A friend of his testified that this is true, saying, "The man has all scriptures in his head."[13]

Seven days after Emanuel's death, it was time to return to his body. He wanted to refuse to go back, but Jesus touched him with His fingertip. Immediately, Emanuel entered his maggot-filled body.

Emanuel said once he was alive again, he used his hand to wipe the maggots out of his mouth. His decaying body began shaking. Most of the others in the school were quite ill, but after they saw what happened to him, they became afraid. They crawled or ran from the building, shouting that they had seen a ghost. Emanuel cried out to them to come back inside.

Emanuel's only residual effect was a badly infected arm, and his friends were sure he would lose it. Someone took him to a hospital in Kigali. God spoke to Emanuel and told him not to worry about his arm. He also wasn't to worry that the doctors planned to amputate it.

Unknown to Emanuel, God spoke to a doctor who was then living in Australia and told him about the African's condition. The doctor flew to Rwanda, located Emanuel, and operated on his body. Once again, the African was healthy. Since then, Emanuel has travelled all over the African continent, telling people of his visit to heaven.[14]

"I See Jesus"
(DR. EMMANUEL RUDATSIKIRA)

Many years ago, one of my patients in Bujumbura, Burundi, was dying. I was on call that night. I sat beside his bed to be there with his family, who silently waited for the inevitable.

The man opened his eyes, smiled and said in Kirundi, *"Mbonye Yesu. Mbonye Yesu. Imana ishimwe,"* which means, "I see Jesus. I see Jesus. Praise God." Then he breathed his last.

I've never forgotten what I saw that night. It gave me a different perspective on death and a new meaning to Proverbs 14:32: "The wicked are crushed by disaster, but the godly have a refuge when they die."

Dr. Emmanuel Rudatsikira is dean of the School of Health Professions at Andrews University in Berrien Springs, Michigan. He has conducted research in more than 30 countries and has published 80 articles in peer-refereed journals. A native of Rwanda, he came to the United States in 1994.

Maureen's Meeting with Jesus
(DON BUXCEY)

My wife, Maureen Margaret, spent her life trying to be good. Raised as a Christian in Canada, she determined to bring up her daughter and son in a Christian home. After the death of her second husband, she struggled on her own for 20 years. Then she met me, and we were married.

My wife went to prayer workshops, dream seminars, played music for her church, and attended many Bible studies.

Because her children were grown, we moved into a creative community, where she was surrounded by wonderful writers who encouraged her to describe her life in a book. But she developed cancer in her bones and liver, just when writing had become the focus of her life.

Four days after moving to the quiet town of Minden, Ontario, Maureen collapsed. She spent the next three weeks in the hospital.

The following three months gave me the opportunity to become Maureen's nurse at home. I learned to make a bed with someone in it, among many duties that kept me close to her side. This closeness brought us together more than any other calling could have done.

Sharing every thought and movement, I heard Maureen's prayers. All her life she wanted to be close to Jesus, and she expected it to happen in some mystical way. Our priest came to administer Communion, and we sang old hymns together, with our lay pastoral assistant leading us in song.

The quiet times became longer, and my dear, dying wife shared her deepest insights of the life of Jesus Christ with me. Talking to the risen Christ was a new experience for me. The presence of the Holy Spirit gave us peace.

We didn't ask for Maureen to be restored to physical health. As the cancer ravaged her body, the Lord blessed us with grateful hearts and the gift of love, which we had not felt before.

As the pain in her frail frame worsened, the doctor applied morphine patches, which I changed as prescribed. The patches gave Maureen respite enough to enjoy food, music and prayer to a greater degree.

With a deeper awe of the healing power of Jesus' presence, we reverently awaited His activity. The wonderful effect of Maureen's attitude became evident when her children, sister and brothers came to visit.

Maureen's smiles, which shone through her pain, greeted the doctors and nurses. By that time, she couldn't sit up to read because of her deteriorated pelvis and collarbones. I read stories and Bible chapters to her and played choral music on the tape player.

When I had to go into town to shop, our cell phone made it possible for her to call me at any time. Maureen had a terrible fear of falling when nobody was near, along with being afraid the house would catch fire while I was out. Another terror that haunted Maggie was choking to death.

The hospital bed in the living room took up so much room that I couldn't stay with her. I slept in the bedroom. Maureen had visions at night and called me several times on the baby monitor. Each time I responded, she described Jesus as she saw Him during her conversations with Him. She said Jesus stood at her bedside and laid His hand on her arm as He told her to come with Him.

Maureen had been a good housekeeper and didn't want to leave things undone. To comfort her, I made sure the cats were inside and fed. I watered the plants and washed the dishes. She listened to me run the vacuum over the floor until satisfied that it was clean.

Two days before she died, Maureen asked me to clean her eyes. I gently bathed her face and used a little swab to remove the film on her eyes. At this point her face lit up and she smiled the loveliest smile I'd ever seen. She rolled over onto her good side and raised her arm. "He wants me to go home."

She stretched out her hand as if in a handshake. Strength flowed through her body and she sat up. The impossibility of such movement by her body racked by so much pain from the broken pelvis and collarbones made me want to caution her.

"Yes, Lord, I'm ready," she said, and then lay back, her face shining. She felt no more pain.

Maureen did not eat anything after that. I moistened her tongue with a swab dipped in lemon juice and dabbed her eyes with water, but she never spoke again.

At 1 AM as I sat with her, her breathing stopped and she went home with Jesus. I could say only, "Thank You, Great Physician, for healing my wife."

Don Buxcey, who has been retired for 10 years, says, "I dedicate my work to God. The Bible and people prompt me to forbear and forgive with joy in my heart."

Louis TUCKER,
a Catholic Priest

Louis Tucker, a Catholic priest, described his near-death experience in his 1943 memoir, *Clerical Errors*. The event had taken place in 1909, when he suffered from the life-threatening effects of food poisoning. The family doctor was there when Tucker lost consciousness and pronounced him dead.[15]

Tucker said the unconsciousness didn't last long, and he passed through what felt like a short tunnel on a train. After that, he was in a place filled with light, where friends met him. He saw his father, who looked exactly as he had before he died. And it didn't feel strange to see him.

Tucker realized that he and his father weren't talking but thinking to each other. He thought of a question and received the answer without either of them saying a word aloud. Tucker also admits that he didn't want to return, and he no longer had the will to live.

He was thrust into blackness again and became upset because he couldn't stay. Then he opened his eyes, and his doctor was bending over him saying that he would live.

Dr. Robert Crookall, before Raymond Moody's *Life After Life*, wrote about instances of what he called "pseudo-death." He noted many of the elements Moody later brought to the attention of the world.

In his reports of what many refer to as the "life review," Crookall wrote of one individual, "Like everyone who passes over, he had been through the whole of his past life, re-living his past actions in every detail. All the pain he had given to people he experienced himself and all the pleasures he had given, he received again."[16]

We point this out because most modern-day near-death experience stories make no reference to remorse, other than to say things such as their "whole life" passed before them.

Angelic Trio

(DAVID MICHAEL SMITH)

"Don't you see them? They're right there, in the corner."

My father, Bob Smith, was dying from lung cancer that had spread throughout most of his failing, aged body. The ravaging cancer cells had left him paralyzed from the waist down and imprisoned by a lonely hospice bed in his home. My mother, Phyllis, assisted the hospice nurses the best she could, but mostly she just loved on Dad and listened to him.

"Where? I don't see anything," she replied, looking into the corner of the room where Dad's eyes seemed to focus.

"They're there, smiling at me. Three immaculately dressed men . . . angels," he whispered in awe. Mom looked again, but she saw nothing.

Dad started smoking at the age of 12 in Knoxville, Tennessee, his hometown, mostly because all of his friends smoked. He grew up in tobacco country, where it was commonplace and accepted. His smoking grew into an adulthood addiction he couldn't defeat until at the age of 53, for no explainable reason, he went cold turkey.

Like many others who quit, he replaced one habit with another to satisfy his cravings—Life Savers candy. Dad went through one to two packs of Life Savers daily, usually Wild Cherry or Wint-O-Green flavored. He gained some weight and looked healthier than ever.

Twenty years later, the effect of years of inhaling nicotine and carcinogens snuck up on him, and he battled for his life. With his lungs shot, he could barely breathe even with an oxygen respirator.

I visited the day after his heavenly vision and sat at his bedside to talk. Soft Christmas carols played in the background. It was November, and we played the carols because we knew it was unlikely Dad would survive to experience the holiday season.

"Mom says you saw three angels yesterday, Dad," I said.

"It wasn't the first time," he said. "They've visited several times, three well-dressed men, perfect, pressed suits, always smiling. I know they're angels and they're assigned to take me home."

"I've heard people see loved ones, angels, all kinds of things when the end is near," I answered, not sure what to say. "Do they ever talk to you?"

"Your mother doesn't see or hear them. I guess it's one of those unexplainable, death things, but, yes, they talk."

I waited for him to tell me more.

"They tell me it's going to be okay, that I don't have much more time, and that great joy and love are waiting for me," he said with wet, foggy eyes. "I've never known such peace as when they're around. Perfect peace, son, perfect peace . . ."

Several days later, the family gathered around Dad's bed and prayed. We said our tearful good-byes, kissed his forehead and held his hands. He was unconscious, barely holding on. We told him it was all right for him to leave us and to go with his three angels heavenward. It was a poignant moment to watch a dear loved one about to die in our presence. Memories of my father began to roll across the movie screen of my mind, and I shed unashamed tears.

Dad exhaled his final gasp of earthly breath, and then he was gone. That afternoon the family made funeral plans, called relatives and church members, and began phase one of adjusting to life without Bob Smith in the world . . . our world.

I hugged my mother and left to join my wife and young daughter at home.

As the sun was preparing to set that night, I went out to walk my dog, Buddy Bear, and prayed for a sign—any sign—that Dad was indeed with his Savior and Creator. I was hurting inside, pretending to be strong, but really struggling. I needed something—anything—from above.

Seconds after I prayed, I looked up. Out of a cloudless November blue sky, three birds appeared on the horizon and flew directly toward me. They descended at a rapid rate and zipped over me with flapping wings. I actually ducked a bit, afraid they might graze the top of my head.

Just then, I noticed a fourth bird behind them—a little smaller—and it joined the trio. As I spun around to watch, they ascended, in beautiful aerodynamic formation, higher and higher until they were out of sight. Everything was quiet again.

For me, that was an answer to prayer. Others may not see it that way, and that's all right. I know God gave me the sign I asked for: the four birds. Dad and his three escorting angels.

David Michael Smith is currently studying to be a deacon in the Anglican Church of North America. (davidandgeri@hotmail.com)

A Christian Soldier's Near-death Experience

Roland Dell (US Army, retired), on his twentieth year in the military, returned to Fort Bragg, North Carolina, on February 6, 2005. Around that time, Dell was ordained as a Christian minister and prayed to be effective for God.

He participated in battle-group training in water survival, something he had done for 20 years. After he finished, he felt he had a terrible case of heartburn and asked for permission to lie down.

Dell lay down and apparently blacked out from heart failure. Within minutes paramedics arrived. On his right side, he felt a "being lying shoulder to shoulder with me."

The paramedics resuscitated him. On his way to the hospital, the ambulance encountered traffic. Just then, Dell was able to look down the highway and see everything as the vehicle raced along with headlights on and strobes flashing.

Dell felt good and said it was the best feeling he had ever experienced. His mind was clear. His next memory was being stabilized for an airlift to Washington Hospital Center, where he awakened in the intensive care unit. His lungs had filled with fluid, and he wasn't expected to survive the night. But he did.

Two days later, when Dell told his family about the ambulance trip and being able to see everything, his mother asked how that was possible in his condition. Dell realized he had been strapped down, facing the front of the ambulance, and there were no windows.

During his second week in the hospital, Dell experienced another heart attack. A nurse said to him, "Mr. Dell, the enemy knows who you are, but it will not stop what the Lord has planned for you."

Three weeks later, Dell was able to return to church. He shocked people because the pastor had told the congregation that Dell wasn't expected to live. The sermon that Sunday was the Good Shepherd lying down with the lambs. Dell thought about the being who had lain down next to him after his initial heart attack. He realized that had been his *own* body.[17]

Dell said, "It is because many times on this side of my existence, I have continually known Him. Death is only a continuation of the spiritual life that I already possess."

THE *Strange Case* OF
George de Benneville

According to Ken Vincent and John Morgan, since ancient times there have been reports of near-death experiences. Even though they're convinced of them, they also say that there weren't many records kept before the emergence of modern resuscitation techniques.[18]

The authors cite Carol Zaleski, who stated that we can't simply peel off the literary wrapper and put our hand on an unembellished event because, even when a vision occurred, it was likely to have been told, retold and modified many times before being recorded. Zaleski also said that the leaders of the Church wouldn't have wanted to record accounts that contradicted Church-defined doctrine.

Until the latter part of the nineteenth century, there seemed little value in reporting objectively, and they hold that this applies to near-death experiences as well. That's when the British Society for Psychical Research studied such stories.

Vincent and Morgan recount the story of a physician and lay minister named George de Benneville (1703–1793), who, in 1741, wrote of his own near-death experience, which took place when he was 36 years old. In his first-person account, de Benneville died slowly, and at midnight he was separated from his body. He was able to see people washing his body, which was the custom in those days.

George wanted to get away from his dead body, and immediately he was drawn up in a cloud. He saw such wonders that he felt were impossible to write or talk about. He came to an extensive level plain—so vast he couldn't see the limits.

The land was filled with beautiful, fragrant, fruit-filled trees. He then realized he had two guardians, one on either side of him. Both had wings and resembled angels, with their shining bodies and white garments. The guardians were so beautiful he couldn't describe them but said their love penetrated through his whole being.

The guardian on his right told de Benneville about eternal things God would do. Because of de Benneville's love and friendship for his neighbors, including shedding many compassionate tears over them, God would reward him and turn all his grief into gladness.

The guardian on his left promised to strengthen him, but first he had to pass through seven habitations of the damned. Just then they were lifted into the air, and de Benneville arrived at a dark place where he saw and heard only weeping and gnashing of teeth—the repository of souls damned because of their sins. De Benneville described many of those he saw, and he felt great pity for them. He recognized one man whom he had known on earth.

De Benneville was taken from there, and a messenger brought water to refresh him and his guardians. De Benneville stared at the messenger, who wore a robe that was whiter than snow. Then he saw and heard a multitude of the heavenly host, and they were singing praises to the Lord.

The messenger told the two guardians to take de Benneville into five celestial mansions, where the Lord's elect live. He saw what he could describe only as many wonders of brightness and glory.

De Benneville returned to his body, which was in a coffin. He recognized his brother and others. They told him he had been "dead" 42 hours, although to de Benneville it seemed like many years.

The Hinge Point

(LONNIE HONEYCUTT WITH VICKI H. MOSS)

In 2003, I visited my doctor, complaining of a swollen lymph node. He prescribed a round of steroids and antibiotics. Within a few months, however, I was back in the doctor's office, where I was diagnosed with cancer.

Some of my tumors were larger than a golf ball, although more elongated. Aggressive treatment began on November 14, 2007, with 40 radiation treatments concurrent with chemotherapies. A rash developed that ran from the top of my head to my feet. Pustules covered my body. The skin on my head was so brittle that when vomiting, my scalp poured blood through broken skin. Along with the loss of my beard, photoaging (dermatoheliosis) caused my skin to wrinkle on my face and neck. My voice was gone from loss of saliva, and I was left with no taste buds.

One night, I fell asleep in my son's bed. When my wife, Dawn, checked on me the next morning, my body was blue with only a faint pulse.

Dawn called 911. After the paramedics arrived, she asked, "Is he going to make it?"

"It doesn't look good for him," they said.

At the hospital, friends gathered outside my room to pray. The attending physician told Dawn, "Your husband's brain is hypoxicanoxic." He explained there was no flow of oxygen to my brain. "He's brain dead."

I died.

My memories of heaven began with being carried along a road of transparent gold, flanked by three angels—one on either side and behind me. I estimated the angels were between six-and-a-half and seven-feet tall. All four of us wore flowing white robes. One angel was black—like onyx or ebony. The other two were more olive complexioned.

Along with clean and fresh air, the sky was an amazing array of blue and white. I initially assumed the clouds caused the white;

however, as we got closer I realized I was watching a myriad of angels. Countless angelic legions flew back and forth as my escort angels and I walked onward. Their ranks stretched in all directions as far as my eyes could see. My vision was superior to what it had been on earth. I longed to reach the city I could see in the distance.

A massive number of people had gathered at the entrance of the city awaiting my arrival. People stood at arched windows similar to those in Spanish-style homes. There were spires, bridges, walkways and gardens with beautiful flowers and trees located where people strolled along pathways.

Words fail to describe the events I saw taking place. It was like looking through a thin, pale membrane or veil. I knew what people were doing and could see my wife and others on earth praying for me. I could also hear prayers.

As I walked with my escort of angels, I turned to look behind them and then downward toward our feet. There were no shadows—none under us, behind us, in front of us, or around the trees or flowers that lined the sides of the road.

I also experienced peace—far beyond human comprehension. I saw people I knew—those on earth who'd guided me along my spiritual journey.

I recognized one woman as my wife's mother—although we'd never met on earth. She wore a puffy-sleeved blue dress. She hugged me and gave me a personal message for Dawn.

The most unforgettable and remarkable thing from my trip to heaven was the way I felt about the people who waited for me to cross the threshold into the city. They were giddy—excited about the fact I was coming to join them and that I would be spending the rest of eternity with them and Christ.

Someone—and I don't know if it was Jesus or the Holy Spirit—asked if I wanted to stay or return. I thought of Dawn in the hospital room and said, "I want to return to earth."

After I returned, I described the woman who gave me a message and told Dawn what she said. My wife knew I had truly been to heaven because I hadn't known her mother, June, who died at age 35. Dawn showed me a faded photo, which I don't recall ever having seen before.

Thea, Dawn's cousin, heard about my meeting June. After hearing the details of the blue dress with puffy sleeves, Thea said, "That was Aunt June. I know that dress. Aunt June was thin, and I told her that because of the puffy sleeves, the blue dress looked too big on her."

Only my wife understood her mother's personal message, and I've chosen not to disclose the contents.

Vicki H. Moss is editor-at-large for *Southern Writers Magazine*, pundit for *American Daily Herald*, and author of *How to Write for Kids' Magazines* and *Writing with Voice*. Vicki is also a motivational speaker and travels to teach workshops at writing conferences. See www.livingwaterfiction.com (Twitter: vickimoss). Pastor Lonnie Honeycutt lives in Mobile, Alabama, pastors 99 for 1 Ministries, is a stage IV cancer survivor and has authored two books: *Death, Heaven and Back* and *Living Jesus Out Loud*. See www.99for1Ministries.com or www.LivingJesus OutLoud.com.

The Resurrection of Pastor Daniel Ekechukwu

Daniel Ekechukwu was the pastor of a church in Nigeria. He died November 30, 2001, and remained dead for at least 42 hours. He visited heaven and hell during the time of his physical death and was raised back to life on December 2.

On the day before his death, Daniel and his wife, Nneka, had an argument, and she slapped him. Throughout the day of November 30, he felt anger toward her.

That evening while driving home, the brakes failed as he was going down a steep hill, and his car crashed into a concrete pillar. Because Daniel wasn't wearing a seat belt, his chest hit the steering wheel, damaging his internal organs. He vomited blood, had trouble breathing, and was unable to get out of the car by himself.

Spectators pulled him out and someone drove him to St. Charles Borromeo Hospital. Once there, doctors administered emergency treatment, but Daniel didn't respond. He knew he was dying and asked God to forgive him.

After Nneka arrived at the hospital, she saw Daniel, who was in critical condition. She cried and begged him not to leave her. Convinced there was nothing he could do at that hospital to save Daniel, the doctor had him transferred by ambulance to Umezu-ruike Hospital at Owerri.

On the way to the hospital, Daniel died. In the ambulance, he saw two angels who were so large he wondered how they could fit inside. Daniel tried to speak, but one held his finger to his lips, motioning for silence. The angels lifted him, and Daniel saw his own body below him.

After the ambulance arrived at the hospital, an examining doctor told Nneka that her husband was dead. She drove his body to the Eunice Clinic, and there Daniel was confirmed dead. Next, they took Daniel's body to his father's home. Daniel's father told them to take Daniel's body to Ikeduru General Hospital Mortuary, and they arrived Saturday morning. The resident mortician, Barlington Manu, injected embalming chemicals between Daniel's fingers and into his feet. The full embalming would be done later. With the help of a staff member, he laid Daniel's body on a mortuary slab between two other corpses.

The next morning, when the mortician attempted to cut Daniel's inner thigh to insert a tube to inject more embalming fluid, an unseen force pushed him away from the corpse. The mortician tried a second time. (Daniel later said that people could smell the embalming chemicals coming out of his body for two weeks after his resurrection. They would hug him and hold their noses.)

About two o'clock on Saturday morning, the mortician, who lived next door to the mortuary, heard worship songs coming from inside the building. The music stopped as soon as he approached the door. As the mortician walked inside to find the source of the music, he saw light coming from the face of Daniel's corpse. That sight so unnerved him that he contacted Daniel's father and asked him to remove the corpse.

Just before the mortician heard the music, Daniel's wife dreamed she saw the face of her husband. Daniel asked why they had left him in the mortuary. He said he wasn't dead and wanted Nneka to take him to Onitsha, where a German evangelist named Reinhard Bonnke was preaching.

Even though the family thought Nneka was crazy, she decided to do as instructed in the dream. By the time she made the arrangements, Daniel had been dead for 24 hours. The family purchased a casket and brought funeral clothing for the mortician to dress Daniel. The mortician had to cut the garments to clothe Daniel, because his body was stiff.

The ambulance carrying Daniel's body in the casket went to Grace of God Mission, in Onitsha, about 90 minutes' drive away. Reinhard Bonnke was preaching at an afternoon church dedication service.

Because of threats by Muslims against the evangelist, security guards wouldn't let the family bring the casket onto the church grounds, thinking it might contain explosives. Daniel's wife pleaded with them, and she opened the casket to show them her dead husband. They jeered at her persistence.

Nneka caused such a disturbance that the senior pastor let them bring Daniel's body into the church, without the casket. For two days Daniel hadn't breathed, nor had his heart beat. He had been carted around for hours in an airless, narrow coffin, before his body was placed in a Sunday School classroom, where believers gathered around to pray. After a time, they noticed the corpse twitch and heard irregular breathing. Because his body was stiff and cold, they massaged his neck, arms and legs.

Then, on Sunday afternoon, Daniel sneezed and arose with a jump. Over the next few hours, he became fully coherent. He should have had severe brain damage, but he suffered no ill effects.

As amazing as the story of his death and resurrection is, what Pastor Daniel experienced following his death is even more amazing. After he was lifted from his body by the two angels in the ambulance, he was momentarily alone before a different angel joined him.

Daniel stated that when he was confused about anything he saw or experienced, or if he had a question, the new angel immediately answered him. The angel told him that they were going to Paradise, and instantly they were there.

Daniel watched a multitude of worshiping people dressed in sparkling white garments. He thought they were angels, but the escorting angel told him that they were human beings who, while alive on earth, had believed in Jesus Christ and served God.

Daniel said the people were ageless and without race—none appeared young or old or had ethnic distinctions. They all worshiped in perfect union. Only one man among them looked elderly. The angel said he was Father Abraham.

Daniel wanted to join the worshipers, but the angel said there were other things Daniel needed to see—especially the mansion Jesus prepared for His followers. Immediately they were at the mansion.

Daniel was unable to describe what he saw. The mansion had no apparent end to its height or width. It continually moved, and each room revolved in some way. It was constructed of transparent-like glass, and the floors were made of light.

He didn't see anybody in the great mansion, but he heard beautiful singing. He wondered from where the music was coming, and the angel pointed him to the many flowers around the mansion. When Daniel looked at them more closely, he saw they were moving, swaying and singing praises to God. The angel said that the mansion was ready but the saints were not. Jesus was delaying because Christians weren't yet ready.

The angel took Daniel to hell, and they stood at the gate. Daniel heard awful screams and wailing. Everything in hell was blackness. The angel showed Daniel his own record of failure and said he could also end up in hell. He reminded the pastor that if he didn't forgive others, God wouldn't forgive him.

Pastor Daniel knew he was guilty for being angry with his wife. The angel told Daniel that the prayers he had prayed as he was dying in the hospital were of no effect, because he refused to forgive his wife even when she attempted to reconcile on the morning of his fatal accident.

Daniel wept. The angel told him not to cry, because God was going to send him back to earth. He said Daniel's resurrection would serve as a sign and be the last warning for this generation.

Daniel was then taken to the top of a mountain, where he found a large hole full of darkness. The angel handed Daniel to a man—the evangelist Reinhard Bonnke. The angel told Daniel that this man would help him spread the gospel of salvation. Both Daniel and Reverend Bonnke fell into the hole.

The next moment, Daniel jumped up from the table where he lay at the Grace of God mission. He was back in his body after having been dead for at least 42 hours.

Since then, Daniel emphasizes the need to forgive those who have wronged us, so that no one would suffer as he did.[19]

Listen to the Thunder
(BARBIE PORTER)

As I lay in the hospital bed holding my precious Melissa Rose, I gently touched her 10 little fingers and 10 tiny toes while softly singing "Jesus Loves Me." Tears of joy trickled down my cheeks. My little Rose was the fulfillment of a word God gave me more than 13 months earlier.

On the final night of a revival, the words I heard were those recorded in Joel 2:25, where the Lord spoke to the prophet Joel and promised, "I will give you back what you lost to the swarming locusts." Those words brought encouragement at a time when my heart was shrouded with sadness from a recent miscarriage.

My fourth pregnancy had gone relatively well, but giving birth had been rough. Since problems had plagued each pregnancy, my physician strongly recommended a tubal ligation.

Although it broke my heart, I agreed. Content with my beautiful, healthy baby girl, I was looking forward to going home so our newly expanded family could get acquainted.

At first, I ignored the tightness in my chest and shortness of breath that started shortly after the surgery. The nurse called in the doctor. My blood pressure was good, and my heart was fine. My symptoms worsened.

After strong antacids and another round of pain medications, they took the baby back to the nursery so I could rest. About that time my friend Becky visited. While we chatted, my chest again felt extremely tight, and I couldn't get any air.

She rang for the nurse, who hurried to my bedside. As the nurse examined me, she asked questions. I gasped for breath.

"Is there anything else that doesn't feel right?"

"My tongue feels thick."

The nurse hurried from the room, and I faintly remember her returning with a shot.

I awakened to the sound of thunder. As I looked around, a soft, bright, off-white cloudiness circled my feet. The thunder continued.

I moved toward it as if the thunder were calling me. My feet felt as if they were climbing upward. The closer I drew to the thunder, the more aware I was of a unique sound.

"That's not thunder!" It was the sound of praise.

As I continued my slow ascent, distinct praises continued on either side of me, one right after the other . . .

"Glory to God in the highest!"

"Praise be to the Great I Am!"

"Holy, holy, holy!"

"Blessed be the Lord God Almighty!"

"Hallelujah!"

"Praise be to God!"

"Blessed be the Alpha and Omega, the Beginning and the End."

They continued on and on, blending together like a melody. Peace flowed through me—a peace like I had never known before. I strongly felt I was loved.

Just as I came close, the praises stopped.

"Come on now, come back to us!" someone yelled in my ear.

"Barbie, are you all right?" Someone rubbed my arm.

I looked around. Worried looks were on the faces of nurses, family and friends. I was confused. How could I be here when I was just there?

Later, a nurse told me that I had experienced a severe reaction to codeine and had given them quite a scare. They thought they had lost me.

When the nurses were convinced I was going to be okay, they left the room. At that point, I shared my experience with Becky. She teared up and said, "It sounds like you were almost in heaven. I hope you're not mad at me for praying for you to live, but you've got a precious new baby and two darling little girls to take care of. They need their mommy."

I believe Becky's prayers touched heaven on behalf of my family.

Today all of my daughters are grown with lives of their own, and I've been blessed with precious grandbabies.

Although that happened more than 20 years ago, whenever I hear thunder, I remember that almost-home journey. My heart longs for the day when I get to pass through the praises and meet my Savior face-to-face, so I, too, may praise Him personally for His amazing grace.

Barbie Porter is an award-winning journalist, the author of *The Legend of the Christmas Kiss*, co-coordinator for the Secret Pavilion Women's Conference, Faculty Chair for Kentucky Christian Writers Conference, and a missionary. She is currently compiling her book *This Little Church*.

Close to Death:
The Story of Carl G. Jung

Carl Jung, one of Sigmund Freud's leading pupils, had a series of near-death experiences after suffering a heart attack in 1944. In his autobiography, he gives a large number of details about the events. He says the images were "so tremendous that I myself concluded that I was close to death."[20]

During one episode, he was high in space, above the earth and "bathed in a gloriously blue light." After giving a lengthy description of the universe from outer space, he said everything fell away "or was stripped from me—an extremely painful process," and that he "carried along with me everything I had ever experienced or done . . . I consisted of my own history and I felt with great certainty: this is what I am. 'I am this bundle of what has been and what has been accomplished.' "[21]

Jung said he had a feeling of extreme poverty, but "at the same time of great fullness. There was no longer anything I wanted or desired . . . I was what I had been and lived . . . there was no longer any regret that something had dropped away or been taken away . . . I had everything that I was and that was everything."[22]

He writes that later he "felt violent resistance to my doctor because he had brought me back to life."[23]

While still in the hospital, Jung felt weak and depressed during the day. At night he had wonderful visions—somewhat like his near-death experience. " 'This is eternal bliss,' I thought. 'This cannot be described; it is far too wonderful!' "[24]

In a BBC interview in the 1970s, the host asked Jung if he believed in God. "I don't believe, I know."[25]

"He Won't Make It Through the Night"
(TERRY LEININGER WITH DONNA FRISINGER)

On Christmas Eve of 1995, the only light in my hospital room radiated from a miniature Christmas tree at the foot of my bed. Sherry, my wife, had put it there to brighten an otherwise gloomy Christmas. Next to the tree was a gray, plastic, football-sized elephant that, when turned on, spluttered effervescent bubbles from a gold-trimmed green circus drum.

When our grandkids sat around the bed to visit that evening, they were enthralled with the toy's nonstop play-action. However, in the quietness of the night, the monotonous repetition grated against my nerves, mixed as it was with the ebb-and-flow of excruciating pain that racked my emaciated body in its death grip.

I'd lost 60 pounds in my continued struggle with ulcerative colitis during the last two years, an existence that revolved around constantly knowing the location of the nearest bathroom countless times a day. Now, after having surgery to remove my large intestine, my left arm bloated to the size of a real elephant's leg from the mismanagement of a defective stint they had to put in my shoulder. Even the morphine the nurses administered didn't help.

Oh, Lord, please take me home.

Just then, a warmth enveloped my entire body in an ink-black cocoon of nothingness. Moments before, I'd struggled to pull up the covers to keep from shivering. Now I felt myself swaddled—beyond all physical need—in what I can only describe as pure love. It was an all-encompassing affection and longing so intense that I knew I was in the presence of God Almighty.

The next minute, I was in the hospital corridor. The walls glowed with a soft green as I floated above the floor's speckled tiles toward the nurses' station, some 60 feet away. Two figures in starched white uniforms leaned toward each other. As I drew nearer, I recognized one of them as my nurse, Sharon.

"Poor Mr. Leininger. He won't make it through the night," she said to the dark-haired night supervisor.

Why is she saying that right in front of me?

The supervisor adjusted her glasses and took a sip of coffee. "Are you sure?"

Sharon nodded. "I've never seen a case like this. His blood pressure just keeps dropping. His arm is so swollen, and the doctor won't let me take out the stint."

As I listened, I realized I'd survived major surgery only to be taken out by a faulty stint in my arm. Anger overwhelmed me. Wasn't it enough that the doctor who'd performed my ileostomy last week had suddenly felt compelled to burst my last bubble of hope just seconds before putting me under?

I could still see his masked face hovering mere inches from my nose as he dropped the bombshell: "It's my duty to inform you, Mr. Leininger, that if we don't find at least three inches of healthy tissue at the end of your large intestine, we'll have to let you go."

Why in the world is he telling me this now?

After suffering through countless ineffective medications, that new procedure had represented my last chance at life. Intestinal waste is collected in an external pouching system stuck to the skin. The pouch would be a nuisance, but I'd be alive and be able to see my grandchildren grow up. But now, tonight, my nurse was saying I wasn't going to live.

Oh, but I will live. I'll show her.

Immediately, I was back in my room. The holy presence still cradled me, and I knew the God of all creation was giving me a choice: I could go to heaven right then or I could stay. I thought of my wife and my family as well as my friends and church family. The elfin faces of my grandchildren swam in front of me. I opened my eyes.

The motorized elephant still chug-a-lugged its repetitive seesaw, but now that *clickety-clack* brought to mind the spirit of one plucky train: the Little Engine That Could. As incredible as it seemed, I heard that elephant repeat, "I think I can, I think I can, I think I can."

I dozed after that. At 5:00 that morning, my nurse entered my room. "You really upset me last night," I said.

"What are you talking about?" she asked.

"I heard you talking to the night supervisor when you said I'd never make it through the night."

"You couldn't have heard me!"

"Oh, but I did."

"How could you? The nurses' station is so far down the hall—"

"Believe me, I heard. You need to be more careful before pronouncing such a death sentence."

As she tried to absorb the information that I had actually heard her, I described the night supervisor (whom I'd never met) and mentioned the cup of coffee in her right hand and the exact words both had spoken.

"It's okay," I said. "I believe God allowed me to hear you, to make me mad enough to want to live again."

My wife still drags out that elephant at Christmastime. The oohs and aahs of grandchildren have been replaced by the giggle of a new great-granddaughter.

Has it been a struggle? Sure. But I've refused to live a woe-is-me existence. Jesus came one other Christmas, 2,000 years ago, to offer *abundant* life to all who would believe. As a result, I've lived long enough to see marriages saved and people's lives restored—all because the Lord allowed me to eavesdrop on a private conversation one special night . . . a night I'll never forget.

Terry Leininger serves as an elder at Faith Outreach Center in Rochester, Indiana, which he helped birth. Formerly employed by Bayer Corporation, it's been 13 years since his brush with death. Donna Frisinger is the author of *Bink and Slinky's Ark Adventure.* Her award-winning poetry and stories are published in *Clubhouse, Mature Living* and *Today's Christian Woman.* See http://donnafrisinger.com/.

Only Kidney Stones: The Story of Dean Braxton

On the morning of May 4, 2006, Dean Braxton woke up with severe pain in his right side. He assumed it was only kidney stones and went to work thinking they would pass sometime during the day.

Instead, the pain increased, and he went home. Eventually the pain became so severe he drove himself to the emergency room at St. Francis Hospital in Federal Way, Washington.

When he arrived, there were no other patients in the ER, and the medical personnel gave him immediate attention. They detected an infection that had built up around the kidney stones, so they started antibiotics.

They called his wife, Marilyn, and kept him overnight. They planned to treat the kidney stones the next morning.

By then, Dean's temperature had reached 104 degrees. Doctors chose to perform surgery despite the fever and infection. They used a routine procedure called lithotripsy, which uses shockwaves to blast the stones and break them up so they can pass easily.

After the surgery, however, Dean's condition worsened. The infection spread throughout his other organs, causing multiple organ failures. His breathing became shallow and his blood pressure dropped.

Then his heart stopped. His wife prayed while the medical team worked fervently to revive him.

The instant Dean's heart stopped, he left his body. His first memory was traveling at faster-than-a-blink speed. As he moved, he "saw" people's prayers passing him by as if he were standing still—prayers for him and for others. He knew that Marilyn was praying he would come back and that God would heal him.

Dean arrived in heaven and almost immediately saw Jesus, who was brighter than the noonday sun, and His presence radiated love. When Jesus looked at him, Dean felt as if Jesus' love had been created just for him.

Just then he stared at Jesus' feet, and the nail prints were still there. Everything within Dean praised Jesus, and he couldn't stop praising.

Then he noticed someone else. Dean's grandmother Mary was standing on the other side of Jesus. She stepped forward and greeted him. Other relatives were with her and joined in welcoming him. Some of them he recognized, and others he didn't. Many generations of family members greeted him, as if it were a big family reunion.

"Earth is not your home; you're just passing through," his grandmother said. "Bring back as many family members with you as possible when you return."

Heaven was an atmosphere of powerful worship and praise. Everyone worshiped God in his or her own way, yet Dean could understand each person individually. Everything in heaven appeared bright, and every being was vibrantly alive.

Happy and fully content, Dean wanted to stay there, but God told him he couldn't.

Clinically dead for one hour and 45 minutes, Dean came back with a weak-but-steady heart rate. The bacteria in his system had caused severe damage, so doctors started dialysis treatment.

Dean's doctors didn't expect him to survive, but if he did, they reasoned his prolonged ordeal would leave him in a vegetative state.

Meanwhile, Marilyn continued in prayer and trusted God for Dean's healing.

Medical records and transcripts show that Dean had 29 serious medical conditions during his 13 days in the hospital, yet he surprised the doctors with a full recovery. The medical staff at St. Francis Hospital named him the "miracle man."

Dean is fully aware that God healed him because he has a special job to do. Jesus made it clear that He needs him on earth right now. Despite that, Dean longs to return to his heavenly home.

He often says, "I'm on my way."[26]

A Soldier Named Er

Plato wrote the story of a soldier named Er who died, and his body lay next to his dead comrades for 10 days. When people came to collect the bodies, they were amazed that Er's body hadn't decayed like the others.

Er's relatives took him home to bury him. On his own funeral pyre, the soldier stood up and told others what he had seen on the other side. He instructed them how to live more fulfilling lives. (History leaves in doubt whether the story of Er was created by Plato or was a true report.)[27]

Traditional Accounts OF Heaven

We include the following stories because they make claims consistent with other near-death accounts, even though we question their authenticity. Like many ancient accounts, these visions may have been told and retold with changes and additions until they reached their present form.

✤ The Vision of St. Paul the Apostle ✤

The Vision of St. Paul, a popular book with versions in almost every European language, was reported widely as having been discovered in a lead box in AD 388 under the house of the late apostle. The box contained the story of Paul being taken up bodily into heaven, as he had written in 2 Corinthians 12. The claim is that the book contained material the apostle hadn't included in his famous letter. Supposedly, the account presents a picture of the judgment of individual souls at their death. It is also supposed to be the first record of such judgment.[28]

In the story, the sun, moon, stars, sea, waters and earth all asked God to let them destroy the inhabitants of the earth because of their sinful behavior. The Holy Spirit took Paul to the Place of the Righteous, where Michael the Archangel showed him what happens to both good and evil when they depart from their bodies.

He then took Paul to hell, where he witnessed the death of a man and the struggle to take the soul from the body, the judgment of the soul, and finally its condemnation to hell.

In his vision of hell, Paul saw a wide array of sinners as well as unworthy priests, bishops and deacons. The punishments in hell included immersion in a river of fire and worms and dragons devouring the sinners. He witnessed horrible pits into which the victims were thrown. Through the pleading of Paul, Michael and other angels, God decreed one day without torment. Michael then took Paul to heaven and finally returned him to earth.

✤ The Vision of the Blessed Ezra ✤

This account is supposed to have taken place sometime between the fourth and seventh centuries AD. Ezra prayed for a vision about the judgment of sins, and seven angels led him to the "other world." One angel acted as a guide and showed him the pains of hell where sinners were being punished by hanging or burning in flames—all according to their personal sins. Each time as the angels led him into the lower portions of hell, Ezra cried out, "Lord, have mercy on the sinners!"

Finally, the archangels Michael and Gabriel urged Ezra to go to heaven with them. He refused until after he had seen everything in hell. He reached the fourteenth level and then was lifted up into heaven, where he came to a multitude of angels who told him to pray for the sinners. Ezra pleaded with the Lord for mercy.

God replied that He had created humans in His own image and commanded them not to sin. But they sinned anyway. That's why they were in torment. God's people went into eternal rest because of their acts of confession, penitence and almsgiving.[29]

✣ The Vision of Barontus ✣

This story, dated AD 678 or 679, tells of a trip to heaven and hell. Barontus, a monk in the monastery of St. Peter at Longoreto, repented of his past life and joined a monastery. He became ill, and his fellow monks stayed with his body after he died. However, Barontus recovered. He said devils came to him trying to take him to hell, but the angel Raphael protected him. Raphael took him to heaven so he could be judged before the devils took him.

Barontus and Raphael visited four levels of heaven, and Barontus repeatedly met individuals he had known, especially monks from his monastery, while the devils kept up a constant tug-of-war for him.

Raphael sent another angel to bring St. Peter to them. After Peter arrived, he demanded to know the charges against Barontus's soul. They insisted the man had three wives. Barontus acknowledged his sin, but the devils became so annoying that Peter struck them with his keys and sent them away. Peter sent Barontus back to earth via hell so that Barontus would think about reforming his life. In hell, Barontus observed suffering sinners of every kind.

An individual named Frannoaldo became his guide after Barontus promised to take care of Frannoaldo's tomb, located near the door of their church. They left heaven, and Barontus was told to give a certain sum to the poor and to protect himself with praises to God.

Finally, Barontus returned to his monk's cell where he spoke with his fellow monks. The story closed with a statement by Barontus, who insisted on the truthfulness of his vision.[30]

✤ The Vision of Bonellus ✤

In an account written by Saint Valerius del Bierzo Bonellus, a Spanish monk of the seventh century, he said that an angel took him to heaven and showed him a dwelling built with precious gems. The angel promised Bonellus a place there after death.

Next, Bonellus went to hell, where devils led him from precipice to precipice. While there he met a young boy whom he had known, and the child interceded with the devils.

Bonellus saw the devil, the pit of hell and three giants (called bad angels). At a lake of fire, archers shot arrows at him until he made the sign of the cross and was rescued.[31]

✤ The Vision of Charles the Fat ✤

This story was known by the Latin title *Visio Karoli Crassi* or *Visio Karoli Grossi* and was often transcribed from the ninth to fifteenth centuries. The vision apparently occurred around AD 900.

In the story, Charles I, King of Swabia and Holy Roman Emperor, was resting on his bed when a "guide" came to him and held a bright ball of thread made of light. The guide tied it around Charles's finger, and it became light for the journey. It also protected Charles from devils and enabled the guide to lead Charles along.

In the other world to which the guide took him, Charles met people whom he knew such as bishops, vassals, princes, and counselors of his father and uncles, as well as his own father, uncle and cousin. All were being punished for either encouraging or participating in war. The experience was supposedly a warning of the imminent downfall of his family, the Carolingians.[32]

Some scholars believe this account may have influenced Dante Alighieri's *Divine Comedy* because of the similarity of punishments described.

The Account of Hung Hsiu-ch'uan

Another account is that of Hung Hsiu-ch'uan, a peasant farmer's son, who in 1837 failed to pass the official state examination in Canton, China, for the third time. Apparently depressed, he fell into a prolonged delirium, and for 40 days he was near death.

Hsiu-ch'uan had a vision in his comatose state, and he revived. He and an "elder brother," directed by God, killed thousands of demons.

Six years later, he read a pamphlet written by a Christian missionary. What he read confirmed what he had seen in his vision. He then said Jesus was the elder brother he had seen. He was ready to overthrow the evil forces of the Manchus and Confucianism.

Hsiu-ch'uan established the God Worshippers Society, a puritanical group that "swelled to the ranks of a revolutionary army."

Beyond Human Imagination

In 1932, Arthur E. Yensen decided to take time off from his job to research his weekly cartoon strip, *Adventurous Willie Wispo*. His main character was a hobo, so Yensen became a hobo for a time and lived among the estimated 16 million unemployed. He hitched rides from place to place.

While on his way to Winnipeg, Canada, one day, a young man picked him up. The man drove too fast for the road conditions, and the car hit a ridge of oiled gravel and flipped into a series of somersaults. Both men were thrown out of the car before the vehicle smashed into a ditch.

Although the driver wasn't hurt, Yensen was injured and lost consciousness just as two female spectators rushed to his aid.

Yensen said scenes of earth faded, and he saw a beautiful world that was beyond human imagination. For a short time he saw both earth and heaven, and then the earth disappeared from view.

Everything was beautiful, and he described what he saw. About 20 people of various ages, gloriously clothed, were singing and dancing. One of them told Yensen he was in the land of the dead and that all of them had lived on earth until they came there.

That's when Yensen understood that heaven was eternal. He didn't want to leave, but he was told he had important work to do and had to go back to earth. He was also told that one day he would return to stay.

One of the things that makes Yensen's story significant is that he had been taught about God, but he had rebelled. Yet after his experience, he became an educator and public speaker, was active in politics, became an authority on organic gardening and nutrition, and was one of Idaho's "Most Distinguished Citizens."

Yensen spoke out against the incarceration of Japanese-Americans during World War II. He openly spoke about his near-death experience until he died in 1992.[33]

Pope GREGORY AND
Last Things

Dr. Carol Zaleski says Pope Gregory the Great (AD 540–604) was writing about the "last things" when he wrote book four of his *Dialogues*. The book's purpose was to prove the immortality of the soul by relating deathbed visions, spiritual apparitions and eyewitness accounts of the world beyond death.[34]

Zaleski reports three of the accounts from *Dialogues*.

First, a hermit, revived from death, testified that he had been to hell, where he saw several men dangling in fire. While he was being dragged into the flames, an angel in shining clothes rescued him, sent him back to life, and admonished him to be careful how he lived. After his return to life, the hermit talked to others about the terrors of hell.

Second, a man named Stephen, who was a prominent businessman, died on a trip to Constantinople. He said he hadn't believed the stories about hell and punishment until a brief visit there changed his mind. In the account, Stephen saw a judge who said he had ordered a blacksmith named Stephen to be brought to hell, not Stephen the businessman. The businessman revived immediately.

After Stephen's return to life, he learned that a blacksmith with the same name had died at the same time. Apparently such stories of mistaken identity were common and not an error, but as Pope Gregory insisted, they were warnings.[35]

Third, a soldier died and was resuscitated. His experience brought additional light to the account of Stephen the businessman. Three years earlier, the blacksmith Stephen had died in a plague that devastated Rome. The soldier also died from the plague. He said there was a bridge under which ran a black gloomy river with terrible smells. Along the riverbank were also houses, contaminated by the river's stinking odor.

Across the bridge, however, the soldier saw a meadow filled with green grass and sweet-smelling flowers. People in white congregated there. On the meadow were houses made with golden bricks, and each building was filled with magnificent light. He said he didn't know for whom the houses had been built. The awful smells from the houses along the riverbank didn't affect those in the meadow.

After individuals started across the bridge toward the beautiful meadow, the unjust slipped, fell and sank into the dark, smelly river. The righteous walked across unhindered to the beautiful meadow.

The soldier spotted someone named Peter, who had died four months previously, lying in the slime under the bridge. A heavy iron chain held him there. Peter confessed to the soldier that he had been ordered only to punish others; instead, he beat them cruelly, even though no one else was aware of his cruelty.

Then a priest crossed the bridge without trouble. Later, Stephen the businessman tried to cross. His foot slipped, and he dangled from the bridge. Ugly men came from the river, grabbed Stephen, and tried to pull him downward. At the same time, a man dressed in white grabbed Stephen's arms and pulled him back.

At this point the soldier returned to his body and revived. In his commentary, Pope Gregory said that Stephen did good things but with evil motives, hence the fighting between the good and the evil for the man. Zaleski writes, "The heyday of such narratives was the twelfth-century Dante, who was familiar with the tradition and used it as raw material for his masterpiece the *Divine Comedy*."[36]

Zaleski contrasted ancient accounts with the modern and observes there are remarkable return-from-death narratives and contemporary accounts of near-death experiences. She says a model for a near-death experience story would run like this. The visionary:

- leaves his body and looks back at it with the disinterested glance of a spectator;
- is met by a luminous being who serves as his guide;
- witnesses a visual replay of his past deeds, weighing them against an inner standard of right and wrong;
- is escorted to heavenly realms and receives a brief taste of the supernal delights that are the rewards for the blessed or holy;
- calls the experience indescribable—yet attempts to describe it in detail with such terms as "immersion in light and love," "ecstatic joy" and "intuitive knowledge";
- longs to remain caught up in the heavenly state, but is sent back to life;
- returns to life and is permanently transformed; and
- is initially reticent, but is finally persuaded to tell his or her story to help others.

Zaleski states, "The story is told and retold and reshaped in the retelling, in sermons and chronicles, in scholarly treatises and across backyard fences."[37]

She also points out the differences between the ancient stories and the modern ones. Of the modern stories, she says the most striking are:

- the absence of postmortem punishment;
- no hell or purgatory;[38]
- no chastening torments or telltale agonies at the moment of death; and
- the life review, when it occurs, is a reassuring experience contrasted with previous negative tales, modeled on contemporary methods of education and psychotherapy.

She adds, "The guide figure is often a family member or a generic spiritual presence and is always friendly and comforting. In the medieval accounts, the guide is usually a guardian angel or patron saint, who for the sake of the visionary's eventual salvation is not above dangling his charge over the pit of hell. The possibility of loss is genuine in the medieval accounts—if one botches the second chance, eternal damnation is the likely result. Today it seems that there is scarcely any possibility for loss. Life and afterlife flow together as an unending stream of fresh opportunities for personal growth."[39]

Movie Star Near-death Experiences

Many famous people, such as Elizabeth Taylor, Sharon Stone, Ernest Hemingway and Larry Hagman, have reported having near-death experiences. In spite of these experiences, no written evidence shows any remarkable changes in their behavior. However, here is one man whose life changed radically.

Gary Busey, once Hollywood's bad boy, was nominated for an Oscar for the movie *The Buddy Holly Story*. Busey fought addiction with drugs and alcohol for several years. He had supernatural encounters in which he nearly died three times from a drug overdose, cancer and a motorcycle accident west of Albuquerque, New Mexico, in 1988.

The motorcycle accident was the most tragic and changed his life. Gary was driving between 40 to 50 miles an hour when he crashed. He wasn't wearing a helmet and was thrown over the top of his cycle, head first into the curb, which cracked his skull.

While dying on the operating table after brain surgery, Busey had a near-death experience in which he saw angels surrounding him. They didn't appear in the form that people see on Christmas cards; the angels he saw were large balls of light that floated and carried nothing but warmth and unconditional love.

After Busey had his near-death experience, he dedicated his life to Jesus. He has since been a prominent speaker at many Christian Promise Keeper rallies. He is no longer the "bad boy" of Hollywood.[40]

Mom's Final Gift
(ANN VAN DE WATER)

My mother had been a teacher for English as a second language. She became aware she had a problem when students pointed out that she gave the same tests a second time to her classes, never remembering that she had given it only the day before.

That experience was difficult for her to accept, but a second experience made her realize something was seriously wrong.

One day Mom shopped, loaded her groceries into the trunk and headed home. By the time she got to the house, she had forgotten that she'd been to the supermarket. In fact, she settled into her after-school routine and made dinner with what she found inside the refrigerator.

She decided that she needed to go to the store and restock. Before school the next day, she made a list of groceries. She drove to school and put in her normal eight hours. As she got into her car, she thought she had better pick up the items she needed for dinner. She had no recollection of her time at the supermarket the day before.

After filling her cart with groceries, Mom walked out to the car and opened the trunk. There she saw the groceries from the day before. "How could I have forgotten so easily?" she asked herself.

Worse than a memory slip, Mom felt devastated because she knew the signs immediately. She was no stranger to dementia. It had slowly eaten away at her own mother's life, and now she faced the same diagnosis.

She went to her doctor, and after extensive tests, my 56-year-old mother was diagnosed with Alzheimer's disease. After that she learned everything she could about Alzheimer's. It must have been terrifying for her to watch her basic life skills being slowly stripped from her grasp. It was hard for me to realize that such an intelligent and inspiring woman could become a victim of such a devastating disease.

At first, she was high functioning, often berating herself and saying, "That darn Alzheimer's," anytime she forgot something or couldn't find the right word.

Over time, she lost her basic skills. That's when she sat in a wheelchair for hours—bewildered and confused. In time, Mom had trouble putting sentences together, but she kept trying. Eventually she lost the ability to speak. The last few years, she couldn't feed or take care of herself.

We watched helplessly as our beloved mom slipped away.

When my sons hit their teenage years, I made no more phone calls to Mom to say, "I need your advice." There were no more chances to glean from a loving mom the fine points of mothering and the wise counsel of someone who understood the fragility of family relationships.

During my visits, I used to sit next to her bed and softly sing hymns. One time Mom's garbled voice joined me. She was a devout Episcopalian and knew many hymns by heart. As a younger woman, she had played piano at church.

I'm not sure why, but I asked her a question—which I didn't expect her to answer—but it concerned me. After years of not hearing her speak, I asked, "Mom, do you love Jesus?"

"You bet I do!" she said.

I stared at her, and there was more lucidity in her eyes than I had seen in a long, long time. I hugged her and my tears flowed. I pulled back and stared into her eyes again. She had retreated into her foggy world.

About a week before she died, we were having another one-sided conversation in her private room where she lay peacefully dozing. Her eyes flew open, and she stared at something. I looked to where her gaze was riveted. She was staring straight up into the corner of her ceiling. I couldn't see anything unusual.

The only explanation for her unwavering focus on that spot was a glimpse of heaven. She looked as if she were holding her breath with awesome anticipation. In that moment, there wasn't the slightest doubt in my mind that she saw heavenly beings.

Mom's mind deteriorated slowly until there was no one behind those dark brown eyes. We mourned her passing after the 20 years she had suffered from the disease. It was a long and devastating journey that ripped our family apart.

However, I have no doubt that Mom is smiling down from the heavenly realms now as each of her grandchildren accomplishes something new and wonderful, overcomes an obstacle, marries their chosen beloved, or welcomes a new little one (who would be her great-grandchild) into the world.

I can picture her rejoicing with each proud moment, lamenting every falling tear, comforting us all from afar. Her spirit lives on through the generations in each little kindness, every caring word, every courtesy given and every hand extended in warm welcome.

God promises that in heaven there will be no more tears, and I cling to that. I imagine Mom: radiant, beautiful, happy and free of the chains of Alzheimer's, still teaching me how to live and to love my family—reminding me that being a mom is a privilege and something she loved.

Loving her family was her legacy to us, and a glimpse of heaven was her final gift to me.

Ann Van De Water is a musician, painter and author of a humorous memoir about motherhood. She and her husband of 33 years live outside Buffalo, New York.

Near-death EXPERIENCES
from the Past

The following accounts show general near-death experiences in the past. Many of them reflect the cultural and theological understanding of the time period.

❖ The Vision of the Monk of Bernicia ❖

The Vision of the Monk of Bernicia (c. AD 704–709) tells of a vision by a sinner who sees the place reserved for his punishment after death. As a monk, he led a drunken life and didn't participate in church services. The Church kept him on at the monastery because they needed his blacksmith skills.

In most of the visions from the *Dialogues* of Gregory the Great, repentance follows the vision. This monk, however, did not repent with the knowledge obtained from his vision. He immediately despaired and died.

❖ The Vision of Drythelm ❖

This account comes from the work of the Venerable Bede (AD 672–735), an English monk and scholar known for his *Ecclesiastical History of the English People*.[41]

Drythelm, a religious man, died after a severe illness. The next day, however, he frightened his mourners by sitting up in his deathbed and talking about what he had experienced in the other world. He urged his wife not to be afraid and said he had been allowed to live again. From then on, he promised to live differently.

A monk repeated the story to Bede. Although unlike other near-death experience accounts by Bede, Drythelm's gives a fuller account of his experiences. According to him, he first saw misshapen souls who were tossed to and fro between fire and ice.

Drythelm's guide called it a place of temporary torments reserved for deathbed penitents who could be released from their punishments by masses, prayers, alms and fasts performed on their behalf.

To reach the mouth of hell, Drythelm traveled through a land of darkness, and he described hell as a bottomless, stinking pit with fire heaped on top of damned souls. He watched demons drag the unhappy souls of a priest, a layman, and a woman into the abyss. Although the spirits threatened Drythelm, his guide protected him.

They followed a wall of light until they reached the top. On the other side, happy people were in a flower-filled meadow. Drythelm assumed he was in heaven. He was wrong; it was an antechamber for the not-quite perfect.

As the guide took Drythelm forward, he heard beautiful singing and smelled a wonderfully sweet fragrance. Although he wanted to stay, he was sent back to his body. The guide promised Drythelm that if he remained diligent, he would eventually have a place among blissful spirits.

Bede recorded that after his experience, Drythelm gave away his property, lived in a Benedictine monastery and became a devoted Christian.

Zaleski wrote, "The most impressive part of Drythelm's story to Bede was that he said it was a greater miracle to convert a sinner than to raise up a dead man. It was even a greater miracle if the tale of a once-dead man's spiritual transformation changed his hearers."[42]

❖ Sent Back to the World ❖

In his book *Phantom World,* Augustine Calmet wrote about a story that St. Augustine of Hippo (AD 354–430) told of a Roman politician named Curma who became quite ill. For several days the man showed no signs of life other than that he breathed just enough to prevent their burying him.

Then, after several days, he opened his eyes and asked about a blacksmith who was also named Curma. He learned that the other man had died at the very moment he himself was resuscitated from his deep slumber. Curma stated that this was an instance of the wrong man facing death. It was not him, the politician, who should have been facing death, but the blacksmith of the same name.

Curma went on to tell what he had seen during his near-death experience. He had recognized several of his deceased acquaintances and ecclesiastics (who were still alive), and they had advised him to go to Hippoma to be baptized by the bishop, Augustine. According to their advice, he received baptism in his vision, after which he went to paradise.

However, after he had been there but a short while, he was told that if he wished to stay in paradise, he would have to be baptized. Curma insisted he had been, but they said it had occurred only in a vision—he had to receive the sacrament in reality. So, after recovering from his illness, he went to Hippoma and, along with other catechumen, received the rite of baptism from St. Augustine.

Augustine, for his part, didn't know of Curma's experience until two years later. After he heard, he sent for the man and asked him to recount his adventure.

Calmet tells a similar story from Plutarch's *Book on the Soul* about Enarchus. This man, being dead, came to life again and related that the demons who had taken away his soul had been severely reprimanded by their chief. They had made a mistake—it was Nicander and not Enarchus they were supposed to have brought.

Their leader sent the demons for Nicander, who was immediately afflicted with a fever and died that day. Plutarch heard the story from Enarchus himself, who was told, "You will get well certainly, and that very soon, of the illness which has attacked you." He fully recovered.

+≻═❧❀❧═≺+

In another account, a severe plague ravaged the city of Rome during the time of Narses (AD 478–573), who was the governor of Italy. Livonian, a godly shepherd, was taken ill with the plague in the house of his master, a lawyer named Valerian.

Just as it looked as if he were dead, Livonian awakened and told them that he had gone to heaven. While there, he learned the names of those in Valerian's household who would die of the plague, but he said Valerian would survive.

As proof of his experience, as the story goes, Livonian, who knew only Italian, "had acquired by infusion the knowledge of several different languages."[43] He spoke with Valarian in Greek, and he spoke with those who knew other languages in their vernacular.

After two days Livonian died, followed by the deaths of those whom he had named. As Livonian had predicted, Valarian did not die from the plague.

+≻═❧❀❧═≺+

Men and women who fall into trances remain sometimes for several days without food, respiration or pulsation of the heart, as if they were dead. Thauler, a famous contemplative philosopher, maintained that a person might remain entranced a week, a month or even a year.

He claims to have seen an abbess, who when in a trance lost the use of her natural functions and passed 30 days in that state without taking any nourishment.

Instances of such trances were frequent among the saints, although they're not all of the same kind or last the same length of time.

Women in hysterical fits remained that way many days as if dead—speechless, inert and with no pulse. Galen mentioned a woman who stayed that way for six days. Some who seemed dead and motionless later said their sense of hearing remained strong and they heard everything said about them. They made the effort to speak and reveal that they were not dead, but they were unable to show any signs of life.

The Throne Room

(Susan M. Watkins)

Several years of excruciating pain and two failed surgeries brought me no closer to relief. My second surgeon was amazed at my body's interior condition. There was little he could correct. Given the placement of rogue endometrium on vital organs, he wisely opted for pharmaceutical therapy.

Eight months later, I reached my breaking point. Every effort to restore my reproductive system failed, yet the pain increased, stripping me of mobility. Determined, I went to meet with God at church.

During the worship service, I left my body. Two angels whisked me away, and I traveled through the earth's atmosphere as if riding an escalator at breakneck speed. The three of us appeared encapsulated in something invisible, although our hair and clothes blew gently from an unknown source.

The atmosphere darkened. Slowly, the earth's reflective light dimmed and the sky's blue changed to indigo, and then to black. Stars were only visible for moments before the angels holding each elbow increased our speed. Celestial objects rushed past me as enormous stars became streaks of light against the black velvet sky. Our speed increased again, and the blur of starlight became specks until they disappeared altogether.

I felt no fear; I was completely safe, supported only by both angels' touch under each elbow. Looking around, I saw the universe hidden from earth's gaze. Nothing above or beneath—just suspended in space.

We slowed and burst into indescribable white light. There were no walls, floor or ceiling, yet I was inside a massive room. We flew toward the center of the light.

My escorts suddenly moved backward and directed me to advance toward the center. I walked, but my feet didn't touch anything solid. The floor resembled gossamer-like clouds.

The heavenly music grew louder, and I saw God's throne. The sweet aroma of incense filled the atmosphere and small bursts of light continually dotted the area. God's throne was elevated on a platform with smooth white stone steps leading up to it. The incense swirled about Him, creating a halo. Varied angels fluttered about the room while smaller ones flew in and out of the incense curtain and brought something to Him. I realized these were the prayers of His covenant children.

Praises were offered to God continuously, sung to ethereal music filling the room. The music was alive with heavenly voices.

I was about three-quarters into the room. The light emanating from God was blinding white—so white I couldn't distinguish His face, only His massive form sitting on His throne. Angels continued collecting prayers, disturbing the smoke from the incense momentarily.

I studied all I saw, heard and smelled to imprint that rare experience. With God's increased brightness, electrified light arced in every direction from His being except where I stood. Vast and loud arcs of power resembling smooth bolts of lightning went upward, arched and disappeared into the misty floor. Their multiple routes spanned 50 to 100 feet from point to point. The entire room shimmered with His glory, making the charged atmosphere even brighter.

Overwhelmed by His magnificence, I pleaded to stay. Despite having young children at home, I couldn't bear to leave. We communicated without speaking a word, but He told me about my unfinished earthly assignments and promised I would be healed. He also revealed His plans for my yet-to-be-born son.

I knew, still without words, that no one but I could complete what I was born to do. I knew I must return.

My escorts moved into place just behind me, touched each elbow, and we were instantly gone.

The next moment I was back in my body at church, singing along to a different song. Although I had been gone about 30 minutes, no one knew I'd left. Two weeks later, my scarred and barren womb was healed. One year later, I cradled my promised son.

Twenty-three years later, I remain homesick for heaven, although still committed to my ordained assignments.

> Susan M. Watkins is an award-winning author who formerly wrote for CBN and the *700 Club*. She's featured in *The One Year Life Verse Devotional, Heartfelt Inspirations, Praying from the Heart, America Remembered, Life Lessons from Dads* and in Max Lucado's projects. She is a three-time winner in *Writer's Digest* competitions.

"I Get to Go Home Today"

In 1958, evangelist F. F. Bosworth told his family that God had assured him he had finished his course and would die soon. His granddaughter said Bosworth was deeply disappointed to awaken the next morning and realize he was still alive. Although he had not been diagnosed with any condition that would cause death, he persisted in saying he would be going to heaven soon.

Word spread among ministers and friends, who visited him to say good-bye. When evangelist T. L. Osborn came to see him, Bosworth cried out, "This is the greatest day of my life! God has told me I get to go home to be with Him today."

Loved ones gathered around Bosworth's bedside, and he lay there with his eyes open and focused toward heaven.

Those present in the room listened as he said hello to the departed family and friends he was seeing in heaven. He described the glories of heaven he was witnessing and then, a few hours later, he passed away. He was 81 years of age and had no sickness or disease. He simply went to sleep in the Lord.[44]

HE *Died* THREE TIMES:
The Kenneth Hagin Story

Kenneth Hagin (1917–2003) was a world-famous evangelist, pastor, author of many books and publisher of *Word of Faith* magazine. Because of two serious, unknown congenital heart conditions, Kenneth had a near-death experience when he was 15 years old.

In his book *I Believe in Visions,* Kenneth said his body became partially paralyzed, and his condition remained that way for three weeks. He was bedridden, and his mother and his grandmother cared for him.

On April 22, 1933, his heart stopped beating. According to Kenneth, "Then the inner man rushed out of my body and left my body lying dead."[45] Kenneth started going downward. "The farther down I went, the blacker it became until it was all blackness."[46]

He finally saw the lights on the walls of the caverns of the damned, which were caused by the fires of hell. He didn't want to continue on, but he was pulled forward. When he was about a yard from the entrance, he knew that if he continued forward, he "would be gone forever and could not come out of that horrible place!"[47]

A creature grabbed his arm to force him to move forward. Just then, an unrecognized voice spoke from the darkness in a language Kenneth didn't understand. The creature released his grip, and Kenneth began to ascend. He saw the lights of earth, then his grandparents' home, and then he went through the wall back to his bedroom. Kenneth states, "It was just as real to me as it was any time I had entered the door."[48]

Once inside his body, he spoke with his grandmother. She said, "Son, I thought you were dead."[49]

Minutes later, Kenneth sensed he was dying once again. His mother was on the porch, and he could hear her praying loudly. He felt himself slipping, and his heart stopped for the second time. Again he descended into the darkness and was grabbed by the creature, but once again the unknown voice spoke and Kenneth returned.

Kenneth's heart stopped beating, and he died yet a third time. "I could feel the circulation as it cut off again," he states, "and I leaped out of my body and began to descend."[50] As he was going down, he cried out to God that he belonged to the Church and had been baptized. God didn't answer him. Kenneth reached the bottom of the pit, but this time he was determined to fight the creature.

According to Kenneth, the third time he heard the voice, it was "as if there was a suction to my back parts, it pulled me back, away from the entrance of hell."[51] He prayed for forgiveness.

After he was back inside his body again, Kenneth continued to pray. He asked God to forgive his sins. He writes, "We didn't have all the automobiles in 1933 that we have today—that was in the Depression. But they tell me that between me and Momma praying so loud, traffic was lined up for two blocks on either side of our house!"[52]

Kenneth Hagin points to this time as the moment when he was born again. "I felt wonderful," he said. "It was just like a two-ton weight had been rolled off my chest."[53]

He adds that even though the doctors told the family that Kenneth would die, and that his mother's pastor and others still expected him to die, Kenneth was no longer afraid of death. One day, he read Mark 11:24 and held onto that promise spoken by Jesus to an anxious father: "I tell you, you can pray for anything and if you believe that you've received it, it will be yours."

That promise wasn't fulfilled immediately. Several months passed before Kenneth was healed.

The three-fold near-death experience changed Kenneth Hagin's life. He no longer relied on his baptism or church membership. After that, he relied only on his faith in Jesus Christ. For the rest of his life, Kenneth exemplified that change.

In 1949, he began his career as a Bible teacher, an evangelist and later a pastor. He founded Faith Library Publications, with 65 million book copies in circulation. He regularly delivered messages on radio, TV and the Internet. Because he saw the need, he started the Rhema Correspondence Bible School and later the Rhema Bible Training Center near Tulsa, Oklahoma.

"I Am with You"

(Susan Avery)

At 8:00 in the morning, I was in pre-op awaiting my scheduled 8:30 surgery. The nurse had already set up my IV, so I was ready. "Routine surgery," my doctor had said, telling me he had performed the operation hundreds of times. "Nothing major. You can go home in the afternoon."

By 9:30, I began to feel oddly cold and shaky. When the nurse came into the room, she was startled to see a pool of blood under my bed. She said I was deathly pale. The nurse who put in my IV had left the cap off, and blood was running out and onto the floor.

As the nurse quickly capped the line, she mumbled that the doctor had been called to do an emergency tracheotomy from a car accident. I fell asleep, probably from blood loss.

Because of the delay, they had given me no medication. At 10:00, I awakened as I was being wheeled into surgery. My doctor was there, and I asked about the blood but drifted off to sleep without absorbing his answer.

I awakened to a flash of bright light, unlike any light I'd ever seen before. I sat up and realized that I was in the surgical unit. My doctor stood at my right side, and two nurses stood on my left. One nurse was telling the doctor that there was a problem with my heart. The arrhythmia had gotten worse, and my heart had slowed almost to a stop.

How can the doctor be operating on me while I'm sitting up? I asked him this question, but instead of answering, he yelled for the anesthesiologist to lower the anesthesia.

I saw my hands—both my arms were tied to my side, and yet I could hold them up in front of me. *How could that be?*

The nurse called out that my heart had slowed even more.

My doctor stopped working and joined the anesthesiologist in trying to save me. I couldn't fathom what was happening, except that I was witnessing the whole thing.

I might be dying.

Fear gripped me as I watched everything taking place around me.

There was another flash of light, and a voice said, "Relax. Everything is going to be all right." I knew it was Jesus talking to me, and I felt at peace.

"Am I dying?" I asked.

"It's not your time yet."

"What's happening to me?"

"I have it all under My control. Don't worry."

Then, as if a hand had been gently placed on my chest, He said, "Lie back and relax. I am with you." I lay back.

I looked around, and my arms were once again bound. He placed a warm hand in my right hand and squeezed. "It's all right. You are going to be okay. Relax now and know that I will never leave you, no matter what you will face in the future." He squeezed my hand once more, and peace washed over me.

I awakened in the recovery room. Two nurses stood to the left once again. One of them said to the other that the arrhythmia was still there, but it was much improved. I fell back asleep, confident that the Lord was with me.

They kept me for overnight observation. That night when the doctor came to my room, I asked him what had happened during my operation. Before he could answer, I told him that I had seen it all.

He laughed it off, but blanched when I asked about the arrhythmia.

"Do you have a history of arrhythmia?"

"I don't even know what it is."

He asked me to describe what I saw. I told him everything, and he said that was exactly correct—with the exception of my sitting up. I was under anesthesia the entire time and never woke up. He couldn't explain, but he said that I had developed a sudden problem with my heart, and it may have been caused by the blood loss before surgery. I asked him if he, or anyone else in the operating room, had held my hand. He said no, because they had been concentrating on getting me through the operation.

The doctor had no answers, but he kept asking me about my story. I knew who had held my hand and who had comforted me. I knew who had control of the situation in that operating room.

I went home the next day, having survived a near-death experience that reassured me there is more to dying than just going to sleep. The Lord had been present for me and I was still alive, even though I had been unconscious and was being worked on while I watched.

Even now, I often feel the imprint of His hand in my right hand. Whenever I face a serious problem, I can feel the pressure of His hand as if He is still holding it.

And He really is holding it, isn't He?

Susan D. Avery, a freelance writer and published author, is working toward a future in curriculum development in religious education. She writes short stories, articles for magazines and is a ghostwriter. She and her husband, Bill, founded Bluesun Ministries See www.bluesunministries.com/Susan-Avery.html.

Swimming in the Crystal River
(BARBARA WELLS)

The summer I turned 16, I attended a youth camp located near Louisville, Kentucky. Something wonderful happened to me at camp: I was voted Youth Camp Queen, which was exciting.

Lots of singing, the youth orchestra played, and then the youth camp director spoke and invited us to kneel for prayer at the front of the auditorium. As I prayed, I had a vision—something startling to me.

I stood at the edge of a river and stepped into the water. I drifted out to the middle of the wide river. I wasn't afraid. I floated in the clear, clear body of water. No matter how deep the water became, I didn't sink or become scared.

I looked down and saw nothing but clear water. I didn't see a bottom, as if the river had none.

I'm not drowning, and I'm not dreaming—this is really happening.

I floated upstream, all the way to heaven and the throne of God. I saw Jesus with people around one side of the throne. They were singing, "Hosanna! God, You are holy. Alleluia." They sang the words repeatedly. It sounded like the roar of a waterfall.

I bowed before Jesus. "Thank You, thank You, God, for letting me be here." The light around everyone was intensely bright. I couldn't look up, but stayed kneeling at Jesus' feet. I felt peaceful and loved. I was in awe of His holy presence.

I don't remember leaving—I became aware of the other young people still on their knees in prayer in the youth camp auditorium.

I was just a typical American girl, but that night in our dorm room, I was quiet and still. The youth counselor asked each of us about our events that day. When I didn't say anything, she said, "Barbara, you haven't shared."

"Something happened, and I can't talk about it just yet," I said. "But tomorrow I'll be ready to tell you about it."

The next day, I shared what I had seen and heard. The counselor told me I had received a vision—an experience totally new to me. I didn't even know what one was. It wasn't a dream, because I had been awake, kneeling at an altar, praying.

She suggested I read Revelation, the last book of the Bible. As I read, I realized I had seen what John describes in Revelation 22:1—and other verses I hadn't known before—"Then the angel showed me the river of the water of life, as clear as crystal, flowing from the throne of God and of the Lamb" (*NIV*).

As I write about this experience, I can still see it and feel the awesome happiness that enveloped my whole being while I was there—and that still does. The vision of my trip to heaven forever changed my life. In high school and college, peer pressure wasn't an issue. My choices in life—career, spouse, purpose and plan— were easy to decide, because I knew there really was a heaven where Jesus lives.

I know there is a real heaven. Until I live there someday, I will continue to serve humanity and gladly share the love of Jesus. I can honestly say the vision of the crystal river and heaven has been a strong anchor that has increased my faith. It truly has helped me see a dimension of living that far exceeds this earthly life.

Barbara Wells is a speaker, writer and published author of *Cameos*. She also serves as coordinator for the Kentucky Christian Writers Conference in Elizabethtown, Kentucky. See www.barbarawells.webs.com.

The Life BEYOND DEATH:
The Story of Arthur Ford

Critically ill, Arthur Ford (1896–1971) lay in a hospital in Coral Gables, Florida. His doctors told him he wouldn't survive, but they continued to give him the best possible care. His friends had been told that Arthur wouldn't live through the night.

He overheard a doctor say to a nurse, "Give him the needle; he might as well be comfortable."[54] Hearing those words, Arthur sensed they expected him to die at any moment. He wasn't afraid and wondered how long it would take to die.

Apparently, he received the injection, because the next moment he floated in the air above his bed. He saw his body but had no interest in it. He felt peace and floated effortlessly through space "without any sense that I possessed a body, as I had known my body. Yet I was I *myself*."[55]

Arthur reached a green valley illuminated by a brilliant light. People came forward to greet him—individuals he had known when they were alive. Many of them he hadn't thought about for years. The recognition was more by personality than by physical qualities. They were different ages—some who had died elderly were young, and those who had died in childhood had matured.

Arthur compared his time in heaven with traveling in foreign countries. In the same way as on earth, his friends greeted him enthusiastically and showed him the places they thought he should see. He wrote that his memory of those places remained as clear in his mind as any of the places he had visited on earth.

He experienced one surprise: He didn't see people he would have expected to be present. Arthur asked about them, and when he did, "a thin transparent film seemed to fall over my eyes. The light grew dimmer, and colors lost their brilliance. I could no longer see those to whom I had been speaking."[56]

Then, through a haze, he was able to see those about whom he had asked. They were real, but as he stared at them his body became heavy, and he felt he was in what he called a "lower sphere." Arthur called to them but received no answer. Someone urged him not to worry about them, because they would be able to come there "if they desire it more than anything else."[57]

Arthur goes on to say that everyone was busy and happy. Another difference between Arthur's story and other reports was that several people with whom he had once been close weren't particularly interested in him; however, others he had known only slightly became his companions. He writes insightfully, "I understood that this was right and natural. The law of affinity determined our relationships." By law of affinity, he probably refers to the fact that two substances or people have a disposition to combine or form a deeper relationship.

Arthur, like many others, said that he had no awareness of time while he was there. At some point, he entered a dazzling white building and was told he had to wait in an enormous room until a disposition had been made of his case. While there, Arthur glimpsed two people sitting at long tables in the other room talking about him. He referred to his feelings of guilt as he inventoried his life, and he said it didn't make a favorable picture.

In another insightful comment, Arthur stated that those who were sitting at the tables didn't have much interest in the things that bothered him. They barely mentioned what he called "the conventional sins of childhood"; instead, they focused on issues such as his selfishness and egotism. They repeated the word "dissipation" several times to mean a waste of his energies, gifts and opportunities.

At the tables, they also referred to his good and kindly deeds, "such as we all do from time to time without thinking them of much consequence."[58] In their review of his life, they were trying to figure out the trend of his actions. As he listened, he heard them say he had failed to accomplish things he knew he had to finish. They implied that he had a purpose in his life that he hadn't fulfilled. "There was a plan for my life and I had misread the blueprint."[59]

Arthur thought they would send him back, and he didn't like it. Finally, they made a decision and told him he had to return to his body. At that moment, Arthur stood in front of a door, and he knew that if he went through it, he would be back in that hospital bed. He fought going through.

Without warning, he felt as if he were being hurtled through space. He opened his eyes. A nurse stared back at him. Later, he learned that he had been in a coma for more than two weeks.

After his return, Arthur referred to the "beta body," or what the apostle Paul refers to as a heavenly body in 1 Corinthians 15:40. He conjectured that we live with the misconception that our five senses are the only way of knowing what's available to us. "If we could only stop to think . . . we have many more senses than these. Nobody has ever seen a person. We see the physical body . . . but the *person* is invisible."[60]

Arthur concluded that we can prepare our beta bodies now. For example, he says our character isn't developed by dying but by living. "One cannot convince another of the truth of immortality by intellectual arguments or external evidence. It must be known by that inward awareness which is part of every human psyche."[61]

Daddy Talked?
(SUSAN DOLLYHIGH)

I couldn't imagine being anywhere but home on Christmas Eve. With the excitement of a small child, I anticipated gathering with my five siblings and our families at Mama and Daddy's house, the home where we grew up.

Like the snow on our jackets, the years melted away as we walked into Mama's warm kitchen, filled with the aroma of her delicious cooking. Her outstretched arms met us with soft hugs.

My parents were in their mid-fifties, so I hadn't imagined our Christmas celebrations ever changing. On December 10, 1991, however, Daddy went into respiratory failure and was rushed to the ER. He was resuscitated and placed on a ventilator. A few days later he suffered a stroke, and his condition deteriorated.

On Christmas Eve, instead of going home, I visited Dad at the hospital. As I walked down the corridor, I dreaded gathering with my family in the intensive care unit. I reluctantly entered the cold, sterile, hospital room. Mama's outstretched arms still met me with a soft hug, but she was sobbing.

The doctor was also there and repeated what he had already told Mama. "I'm sorry. His EEG is flat, and he's not responding to any stimuli." He shone a light into Daddy's eyes. "You can see his pupils are non-responsive." He touched Daddy's eye with a cotton swab. "He doesn't blink." He tested Daddy's gag reflex by touching his throat with a cotton swab. Daddy failed that test too.

I was beginning to feel that the doctor had become a lawyer and was presenting his case to us, the jury.

"All of this means your daddy is brain dead; there's no hope for recovery." He looked down before continuing. "The ventilator is the only thing keeping him alive. You have a decision to make. Are you ready for us to turn off the machines?"

We were in shock, and none of us knew what to say.

"I leave in the morning; I'm going to my folks for Christmas. I'll need a decision tonight."

I was angry—angry that instead of celebrating the holiday, we were watching our daddy die; angry that the doctor was going home for Christmas; angry even with God. *How can you let this happen? Daddy is only 55. And on Christmas Eve?* My anger was irrational, but it was the only way I knew how to cope with the shock and the loss.

My family returned to the ICU waiting room, knowing we had to make a decision. We knew Daddy didn't want to be kept alive by machines if there wasn't any hope for recovery, but our emotions didn't follow rational or logical paths.

After agonizing for less than an hour, we made the decision that wasn't really a decision. They'd told us that Daddy was already dead. We needed to turn off the machines and let go of his body.

The doctor returned to the waiting room, and we told him our decision.

"We want to give you time to tell your dad good-bye," he said. "Go in as a group or individually. Take all the time you need."

We went individually, and when my turn came, I walked calmly into his cubicle. As I stared at him, a dam of tears broke my resolve to be steady. "Daddy, I love you," I said. "I'm going to miss you so much."

Random thoughts and memories poured from the depths of my soul. "Thank you for hitchhiking your way home from the army base to see me the day I was born," I said. I thanked him for many other acts of love and kindness. Finally, exhausted of emotion and words, I gazed at my daddy's chest rising and falling in time with the ventilator, kissed his still-warm forehead, and walked out of the room.

"It won't be long," the doctor told us.

After waiting for what seemed like an eternity, my brother, Frank, walked back to the ICU. He returned to the waiting room a few minutes later and said, "He's talking. I just spoke to him." We all stared back at Frank in disbelief as our minds tried to comprehend his words.

There's no way that is possible.

The doctor finally returned to talk with the family. "Your dad is hanging on. He's a real fighter."

"Yeah, he just talked to me," Frank said.

The doctor smiled sympathetically. I could tell he'd dismissed Frank's words. "I'm going to move your dad to a regular room so you can all be with him. We'll keep him on oxygen and keep him comfortable."

Okay, what's going on?

When they told us that he had been moved, we went to Daddy's new room.

His eyes were open as they had been in the ICU, but something was different. As Daddy gasped for breath, he turned his head, stared at us and tried to talk. I moved to Daddy's side, put my ear down close to his mouth and strained to make out his low, raspy words.

"I love you, Susie." Daddy continued to talk. I couldn't decipher all of his words, and he couldn't say many at a time, as the effort exhausted him.

My sister dashed out to the nurses' station to report the miraculous change in Daddy's condition. "Would you please ask his doctor to come and re-evaluate him?"

"The doctor is already gone. He won't return until after the holidays," the nurse said. "But I'll check on him."

When the nurse walked into Daddy's room, he had returned to staring straight ahead, and he made no attempt to respond to her. She looked at us much the same way we had looked at Frank when he'd told us Daddy had talked.

"I'll be back to check on him later," she said.

Once she was gone from the room, Daddy began talking again, and he talked most of that Christmas Eve night. We didn't understand why he hadn't responded to her—and we didn't care. He was talking to us, and that's all that mattered.

On Christmas morning, a single red poinsettia on the window ledge was our only decoration. Soon the family members who'd gone home for a few hours of rest returned, and our family was again gathered together.

Daddy began to speak of heaven and tried to describe its beauty to us.

"There's Daddy," he said, speaking of our grandpa. He spoke of angels and told us Jesus was in the room with us. On that Christmas day, we were each given what we would later come to realize was the most special Christmas gift of our lifetime—a glimpse of heaven through our daddy's eyes.

Daddy lived four days after the doctor turned off the ventilator. The doctor was amazed that he survived that long, but it was obvious he didn't believe Daddy had talked with us. However, a family friend, who is a doctor on staff at the same hospital, stopped by to visit and also talked with Daddy.

Later, when we asked her to explain medically how that could have happened, she simply said, "Some things in medicine cannot be explained because they are of God."

Susan Dollyhigh is a freelance writer, speaker and a contributing author to *Spirit and Heart: A Devotional Journey; Faith and Finances: In God We Trust;* and *The Ultimate Christian Living.* Susan's articles have appeared in *Connection* magazine, *Exemplify* magazine, Mustard Seed Ministry, *P31 Woman* magazine, *The Upper Room* and *The Secret Place.*

Holding Her Hand
(MARILYN WALLBERG)

Evelyn Christenson wrote *What Happens When Women Pray.* She also traveled throughout the world and taught prayer internationally until she was into her eighties.

When she was nine years old, Evelyn prayed, "Lord, I want to teach the world to pray," and she did. Even in her declining years, as her body became frail, her spirit continued to roar like a lion. I was on Evelyn's prayer board and listened month after month as she taught us from the Bible and what the Lord was teaching her.

Toward the end of her life, Evelyn came to our board meetings in a wheelchair and on oxygen, but she taught. She continued to share her teaching and faith by phone worldwide. Evelyn is the only person I know who led a worldwide prayer ministry from assisted living.

In her waning days, we spent many hours together. My mother lived in the same facility, so I was in and out of Evelyn's apartment often.

One Tuesday night, Evelyn and I sat together on her couch enjoying each other's company. We talked about the trips we had taken together that included Europe and Asia. We reflected on God's hand in her ministry and in our ministry together—our adventures, the blessings and the many funny things that happened along the way.

That night we seemed more like two girls remembering and then giving thanks as we laughed and prayed together. We talked, as we so often did, of her anticipation of going to be with the Lord. We prayed for her family members by name as well as for the United Prayer Ministry, which she had founded many years before.

I reached for her hand again and said, "Lord, one more thing. When the time comes and You take Evelyn home, please may her children be with her and may they know that she sees Jesus."

Later that night, Evelyn broke her hip. The surgery went well, and her spirits were high. Despite that, Evelyn said, "I know I am going soon."

Evelyn died on Saturday. At her funeral, one of her family members came to me and said, "Her passing was beautiful. One daughter was with her, and her son arrived within 10 minutes. As they sat and talked quietly, Jan asked her mom, 'Do you see purple?' " That was Evelyn's favorite color.

"Oh, yes! It's beautiful," her mother said. "I see so much purple."

A little time passed before Evelyn said, "Jesus is holding my hand." Then, on November 1, 2011, she left with Him.

Her children knew she had seen Jesus.

Marilyn Wallberg is an international conference speaker and a retreat and special events speaker. She is a retired flight attendant; an executive board member of United Prayer Ministry; a member of America's National Prayer Committee; a national board member of Mission America Coalition; and is affiliated with Fellowship of Christian Airline Personnel.

Vision of the Heavenly Choir
(KAREN WHITING)

My husband, Jim, battled breast cancer for more than a year and a half as it moved into the tissue surrounding his spine. Constant back pain caused sleepless nights. He spent those nights in prayer while lying on our couch.

Early one morning after hours of prayer, Jim saw a vision. He reflected on the vision for three months before sharing with me his description of what God had shown him and told him. Here is what Jim dictated:

> I looked up from the couch and saw the Holy Spirit like an amoeba—all white and floating. He cleaned my heart, soul and mind. I looked past the Holy Spirit and saw Jesus smile. He had pearly white teeth and a big smile.
>
> He said, "Come, let Me share your burdens."
>
> I got closer and touched Him and felt the load of the world leave. Nothing else needed to be lifted.
>
> Like in photos with only one set of prints, Jesus carried me on His shoulders and helped me. Then I looked up to heaven and saw brilliant light around the Father. I thought it should have been burning, but it wasn't. It was like a white heat fire burning, but nothing was consumed.
>
> God said, "You'll be with Me soon. Try to prepare those around you, but don't alarm them. Tell them that you'll be with Me all the days of the rest of your life."
>
> Then I gazed beyond and saw pure blue sky. I looked up and saw white clouds and heard heavenly hosts singing melodies of praise to God. One of the beings touched me and said, "Please join us." It was so wonderful to be with people whose only purpose was to praise God.
>
> Jesus said, "It's not quite your time yet, but you will join us soon and be part of the heavenly choir and sing praises to God forever."

We prayed about how to use the time left. We encouraged our children to visit and planned a final trip in July to Florida, where most of the children and grandchildren lived. For the next few months, four of our children spent time with Jim.

In July, we drove to Florida. Jim enjoyed one granddaughter's fifth birthday party, saw his siblings, visited friends who had prayed for him for two years, smiled for photos with grandchildren, and spent time talking to loved ones.

We returned to Maryland, and Jim's health continued to deteriorate. All five children took turns visiting again. Our oldest son stayed for the final weeks.

After Jim's death, I shared the vision with all of them. It brought great peace to know God chose the timing but allowed him so much time with loved ones, as well as time for more photos with grandchildren. Jim sang in military and church choirs in several states, where many heard his rich baritone voice that is now part of the heavenly choir.

Karen H. Whiting is the author of 16 books. She writes nonfiction for busy women, military families and children, including the popular inspirational craft book series *God's Girls*. She and Jim enjoyed 38 great years of marriage. See www.karenwhiting.com.

A *Descent* INTO HELL:
The Story of Howard Storm

Kenneth Storm was a 38-year-old art professor at Northern Kentucky University, and he was also an atheist. While he was visiting Paris on a European tour with a group of students in 1985, he was stricken with an attack of peritonitis. He collapsed in his hotel room with a perforated duodenum. Unable to find a surgeon immediately, he spent hours in agony, knowing he was going to die.

At one point he fell unconscious. Suddenly pain free, he stood next to his bed. He tried to talk with his wife, but she didn't respond. He thought she was ignoring him. Then he saw someone lying in the bed—a dead person—and the body strongly resembled his.

From outside the room, voices called out telling him it was time to go. They also said, "We know all about you. We've been waiting for you."

Howard assumed they were from the hospital. But once he walked into the corridor and was led forward, the hallway grew increasingly darker until he stood in complete darkness. He says he went into a hallway and had a clear sense "that the 'portal' back into the room was . . . closed. I could never go back. The people led me away, and the hallway subtly became darker and darker and darker over a long period of time."[62]

Howard realized that he was in complete darkness, encircled by a crowd of people. Fear overcame him, and he said to them, "I want to go back." Ignoring his words, they pushed and pulled at him. They bit, scratched and tore at him while they screamed. The more he fought, the better they liked it.

He became aware that those fighting him were people—like him—individuals who had rejected God and lived selfish lives. He said they were like rats in a cage and lived in a place with no light, hope or love.[63]

Finally, he was so beaten up and defeated that he could do nothing. He was in great physical pain, but the emotional pain was worse. As he lay on the ground, a voice said, "Pray to God."

"I don't pray. I don't believe in God," he said.

Two more times the voice said, "Pray to God."

Howard tried to think of a prayer and mumbled a few words. Each time he mentioned God, the people around him became angry and screamed, "There is no God," and, "Nobody can hear you."

His words angered them so much they retreated, because the mention of God was unbearable to them.

Seeing their responses, Howard mumbled other jumbled half-remembered phrases: "Glory, glory hallelujah; God bless America; our Father who art in heaven . . ."[64]

After that, he was alone in the darkness. As he reflected on his life, Howard felt he deserved to be where he was. "I felt that there was some kind of justice in the universe and that if you lead a miserable life you go down the sewer pipe of the universe into the septic tank. And that's where I was. Yet I knew I hadn't been flushed down into the deeper part, just yet."[65]

In that state of hopelessness, he remembered being a child in Sunday School and singing "Jesus Loves Me." He also had a vivid feeling of being a child and feeling that "there was a wonderful God-man named Jesus who was my friend and who loved me."[66]

Howard cried out for Jesus to save him. Just then, a small light appeared in the darkness and came down over him. Out of that light came two hands, and they reached down and touched him. All the gore and filth of his life fell away.

Jesus picked him up and held him, and they moved straight upward, faster and faster, toward light. Howard thought they had made a terrible mistake and that he didn't deserve this. He called himself garbage.

The upward movement stopped, and for the first time Jesus spoke to him. "We don't make mistakes. You do belong here." The words weren't audible but inside his mind.

Angels came and took him through what's often called a "life review"—everything that he had done in his life flashed before him. Howard was so ashamed of who he was and what he had done that he begged to go back to the pit so he could hide in the darkness. Remembering the times he had scoffed and cursed at godly things, he felt unworthy and didn't want to go any farther into the light.

Eventually, the angels told Howard that he wasn't ready for heaven and would have to go back to earth. Although upset, he accepted their words. Instantly he was back in his body in a Paris hospital, being prepared for surgery.

After that experience, Howard's life changed. He said his friends ridiculed and scorned him, but he found new friends in Bible study groups. Eventually, Howard became ordained as a minister in the United Church of Christ.[67]

"Go Back and Be Happy": The Story of Julie Papievis

On the evening of May 10, 1993, Julie Papievis, a successful executive with Estee Lauder in Chicago, went to the mall to purchase a bottle of tanning lotion. As she pulled out from the mall on her way home, a teenager in an Oldsmobile Cutlass ran a red light. His vehicle slammed into the driver's side of her Mazda sports car at an estimated 50 miles per hour.

The impact of the collision jarred Julie's head and neck, leaving her with a severely injured brain stem. Even though paramedics and firefighters attempted to revive her, she remained unresponsive.

After examining her, they tested her using the Glasgow Coma Neurological Scale—a reliable and widely used system for determining the conscious state of a person. The results score a person's level of consciousness in a range between 3 and 15. Those with a score between 3 and 8 are usually in a coma. Julie scored a 3, the lowest rating, which meant she had a minimal chance of recovery.

Firefighters had to use the Jaws of Life to remove Julie from her car, after which an ambulance rushed her to Loyola University Medical Center, a level-one trauma center.

Shortly after she arrived, she started agonal breathing—a labored pattern of abnormal breathing characterized by gasping and strange vocalizations. This indicated that her bodily functions were shutting down.

Julie's neurosurgeon, Dr. John Shea, gave her family little hope for her survival. If she lived, he said that she would most likely be in a "persistent vegetative state." After several weeks in the hospital, the medical staff urged her parents to release her to a nursing home.

Julie went to the nursing home and, despite the prognosis, her parents refused to stop asking God for a miracle. Along with their church family, they continued to pray even though days passed without a change in her condition.

While Julie's body lay in a comatose state, her spirit was drawn to a bright, pure light, which led to a place of perfect peace—a place without concerns or worries. To her it felt like home, and she knew she belonged there.

Julie was aware she was in that beautiful place because she was dead, but that didn't bother her. She was happy; and instead of being afraid, she yearned to stay.

Julie saw both her grandmothers and recognized them as the elderly women she had seen before they died. Now they were healthy and full of joy. She wanted to stay with them.

"You can't stay," one grandmother said. "You have to go back."

"But I can't. I'm not physically okay."

"Your body will heal."

As if a warm blanket had been wrapped around her, Julie sensed that she was in heaven. With the assurance that God was there and that her grandmother's message was from Him, she listened.

"Go back and be happy."

Abruptly, Julie awakened after a month in a coma. As she would learn, she was in the brain-injury wing of a rehab hospital. The left side of her body was paralyzed, and she drooled and couldn't swallow. A gastrostomy tube inserted in her abdomen fed her. She wore diapers. She was unable to open her left eye or hear out of her left ear.

Before the accident, Julie had been an athlete. Now she faced the reality of physical limitations. "God, why did You bring me back to a body that doesn't work?" she asked. "Why didn't You let me stay with You?"

While she struggled emotionally because of her physical disabilities, she also clung to the message of hope her grandmothers gave her. "Your body will heal."

After two months of extensive physical therapy, her body slowly healed. Feeling and movement returned to her left side. Dr. Shea was amazed and delighted at her progress. He called it a miracle.

With a lot of exhausting effort over a long period, Julie learned to sit up, feed herself, stand and eventually to walk again. She overcame her paralysis and won the battle over severe depression.

There was more good news ahead.

In 1999, she participated in a 5K race.

In 2007, she competed in a triathlon, which many consider the most demanding physical competition. As the name implies, a triathlon features three endurance events that are continuous and sequential. Although the forms vary, most of them revolve around swimming, cycling and running.

Living with disabilities from a brain-stem injury is still some-times stressful for Julie, but she is fully aware that God has a pur-pose for her life. Today she is an advocate for other survivors who need hope and guidance.

Julie's heaven experience, and the felt presence of God in her life afterward, changed her. She's now less concerned about what people think, more grateful, has deeper relationships and lives without fear.

Her grandmother said, "Go back and be happy." That's what she's learned to do.[68]

The Face of Forever
(KRISTI M. BUTLER)

I'll never forget his face.

After being nearly comatose, my grandfather looked up to the corner of the room. With glistening eyes, he smiled before he whis-pered, "Jesus."

I like to think of my gregarious grandfather as grabbing Jesus' hand and saying, "Barbee's the name." In my mind, I hear Jesus say, "Oh yes. I know you, M. A. Barbee. Well done, good and faith-ful servant!"

My grandfather, whom I called "Grandy," was a genuine encour-ager, compassionate friend, and a truly joy-filled man.

Grandy fell while hanging out with some of his best buddies at "the store," an old-gas-station-turned-repair-shop. He broke his pelvis, which wasn't the worst of the diagnosis. At the hospital, CT scans showed aggressive cancer in his lungs and bones.

Grandy lived those last four months in much the way he'd lived his life—loving others, patting them with his calloused hands, giv-ing them smooshy wet kisses on their foreheads, and telling them how "purty" they looked.

He no longer worked hard, but instead he acted as primary care-giver for his "little sweetie"; his wife of 70 years, who was feeble and diagnosed with dementia.

Grandy loved to watch the Gaithers sing on TV, and he would pat his hands to the beat of the music. He also loved his small, country church and was a committed member.

During his last days, we played Christian music for him on his little CD player, and sang hymns to him. As he listened, he often smiled, nodded his head and raised his hands in worship.

There was one odd thing, however. Grandy often glanced up at the corner of the room during those moments, smiling and reaching heavenward. That happened again on his last day, and he whispered, "Jesus."

Peace came over his body. His breathing, previously raspy and labored, stilled. The beat of his heart stopped. Granddaddy slipped away.

I'll never forget the way his face looked as he gazed on the face of forever.

Kristi Butler is a public speaker whose audience spans the generations, from preschool classrooms to assisted living facilities. An author of two children's books, her keyboard now taps adventurously toward a book for grownups. See www.kristibutler.blogspot.com.

Seven Minutes

(Jenny Farrell)

During an angiogram, my heart stopped for seven minutes. I don't remember the details, only that I knew I was in God's presence. Afterward, although I had a husband and two teenaged children whom I adored, somehow it no longer seemed like I belonged. It took a long time for me to truly reconnect with my life.

The first time I was in church again after my angiogram, I heard what seemed like hundreds of the most beautiful voices, even though there were only about 20 people in the building. For a few minutes, once again I felt I was in God's presence and a bittersweet longing filled me that was almost unbearable, yet beautiful at the same time.

One thing reminds me that I had been with Jesus in an amazing way. Several times near the anniversary of my death, I've been struck with heart-wrenching grief. Each time I sob because I miss my heavenly Father so much.

More than seven years have passed since my heart stopped, and I'm completely healed.

Jenny Farrell is a writer and speaker, specializing in women's events and retreats. She is also a pastor's wife and full-time nurse manager at a local pregnancy center. She enjoys writing and creating jewelry. See www.jennyafarrell.com.

Proof OF HEAVEN:
The Story of Eben Alexander

As a scientist with an analytical mind, academic neurosurgeon Eben Alexander was skeptical of spiritual things. He didn't believe in everlasting life or life beyond death of the body and brain.

He had a "casual belief in God and prayer" until the year 2000, when a devastating personal experience derailed his life and caused a crisis of faith. He lost his sense of worth and could no longer grasp that there was a loving God or that prayer mattered.

He wanted to believe the way others did, but his more than 20 years in neurosurgery, along with his research, made him understand that consciousness depended on the brain. He had heard many stories about near-death experiences and always assumed they were hallucinations or dreams with a brain-based explanation. That was the only logical answer to him.

But on the morning of November 10, 2008, a chain of events transformed his way of thinking. Eben awoke in the predawn hours with severe back pain that worsened with time. He also had a searing headache.

His wife realized that he was having a seizure, so she called 911. Paramedics rushed him to the same hospital where he practiced as a neurosurgeon. The doctors discovered that an extremely rare and virulent meningitis of unknown cause was eating away at his brain. It plunged him into a coma.

While he was still in the emergency room, doctors gave him, at best, a 10 percent chance of survival. In the days that followed, those chances diminished to about 2 percent with no possibility of recovery—which is virtually no chance. They predicted that he would spend about three months in the hospital and receive chronic care in a nursing home for the rest of his life. Even if he lived, he would never communicate again.

The meningitis wiped out his neocortex, the part of the brain that produces consciousness. He lost all memory, emotion and language as well as visual and auditory functions. While the medical team treated Eben and tried to revive him, he was on an astounding odyssey in another realm.

His journey took him first to a hideous, murky place underground, and then a beautiful, bright, spinning white light rescued him. The light moved slowly toward him. It had many fine filaments coming out of it, and it came with an incredibly delightful melody. The light expanded and became a portal to another dimension, one with a vivid verdant valley rising steeply into a bright light. Its beauty was beyond earthly words—it was a place of pure joy and bliss.

A lovely woman appeared and escorted him on his journey. They flew on the wings of a giant butterfly, surrounded by millions of butterflies, and soared over flowing rivers and lush greenery. As they passed by, trees blossomed and flowers bloomed.

Eben didn't know his companion, but she looked at him with an endearing smile and gave him an important, comforting message. She didn't use words; the concepts went straight to his mind. *You are loved deeply. You are cherished forever. There is nothing you have to fear.*

Overhead, billowing clouds with indescribable colors made a gorgeous setting in a blue-black sky.

Later, in a TV interview, he said, "It was so much more real—it makes sitting here in this studio seem dreamlike in comparison. It was so sharp and crisp . . . all around and above us were these billowing clouds that had beautiful colors in them against this blue-black sky, and there were these arcs of shimmering beings—these orbs of light that were shooting through the sky leaving these trails. The music they were putting out was indescribably beautiful—it would crescendo after crescendo after crescendo higher and higher in response to any kind of questioning in my mind about what was going on."[69]

During his experience, Eben saw God—a divine, all-loving, omniscient, infinitely powerful, indescribably awesome presence who appeared as a brilliant orb of light more brilliant than a million suns. Because he wasn't restricted by physical limitations, Eben looked at and communicated with his Creator. The loving divine presence was everywhere.

After seven days in a coma, Eben miraculously awakened. Although his recollection of earthly life and relationships had vanished, the vivid memory of his rich heavenly adventure remained. During the next few weeks, he regained his language and his memories of family. Then memories of neuroscience and neurosurgery returned.

He had moments when he doubted his own story, but when he tried to write a neuroscientific report of all that occurred, he couldn't reconcile his former beliefs with his reality. He knew he had had a transcendental spiritual experience that happened despite his nonexistent brain function.

An event that occurred four months after he awakened from his coma convinced him that heaven is real and there is life after death.

Eben had been adopted in childhood and had a sister, Betsy, whom he had never met (she had died in 1988). He received a picture of Betsy from his family of origin, and when he looked at it, he recognized her as the woman who had accompanied him on his journey into heaven. That realization was the most shocking and eye-opening moment of his life.

He had to rethink everything he had previously believed about existence, consciousness, God and the reason we're here. He believed he had proof of heaven and God, and he was transformed with a sense of faith, wonder and purpose.

Eben's life is now more meaningful, and his newfound knowledge has become a beautiful gift for his family—knowing God, knowing God is real, and knowing prayer works.[70]

Eben Alexander insists his experience proved that consciousness is independent of the brain . . . and that "an eternity of perfect splendor awaits us beyond the grave."[71] He adds, "I intend to spend the rest of my life investigating the true nature of consciousness and making the fact that we are more, much more, than our physical brains as clear as I can, both to my fellow scientists and to people at large."[72]

Freddy Vest's Amazing Trip

Cowboy Freddy Vest was doing what he loved on July 28, 2008—performing in a calf-roping competition in Texas. A championship roper, by one o'clock that afternoon he had already made three successful runs.

He was mounted on his horse and ready for his fourth run, when, without warning, his heart stopped and he fell to the ground.

Out of the corner of his eye, a friend named Dennis saw the awkward fall. He jumped the fence and ran to Freddy. Dennis cradled his friend's head and immediately started praying for him.

Two firefighters who were present rushed over to give Freddy CPR. They worked on Freddy for 45 minutes until the ambulance arrived. While they tried to revive him, Dennis told the crowd what happened and asked them to pray.

Paramedics defibrillated Freddy's heart twice while en route to the local hospital. Once there, doctors were able to get an irregular heartbeat. Freddy was airlifted to Harris Methodist Hospital in Fort Worth, where he could receive better care. His heart flatlined two more times during the flight.

Freddy was rushed to surgery. Loved ones gathered in the waiting room and prayed. After the procedure, the surgeon reported that they were able to repair his heart, but he couldn't predict a long-term outcome. He expressed concern that because of the amount of time without blood flow, Freddy might have brain damage.

The instant Freddy's heart stopped during the rodeo, he was present in another realm—a place that expressed more love than he could imagine. It was also a place of perfect peace and safety. There was no sense of time or pressure to get things done.

Without using words, Freddy had conversations with God. Communication came from within and was understood without the need to be spoken verbally.

God "showed" him the prayers being sent up on his behalf. They came in as bolts of light. The more that came in the brighter the light, and finally so many came in that the bolts exploded into an unexplainable ultra-bright light. That's when God told Freddy he couldn't stay—he had more to do on earth—and sent him back.

When Freddy opened his eyes, he was lying in a hospital bed on life support with tubes and IVs attached to him. He struggled to get up, but the nurse stopped him.

"Mr. Vest, you're okay," she said.

"No, I'm not," he said. "This doesn't compare to okay. You don't know where I've been."

Freddy recovered from his heart-stopping ordeal, but his trip to heaven left him with questions. He knew he had returned to earth for a purpose, and he wanted to make something happen but didn't know what he was supposed to do. For several months he asked God for direction and clarity.

One morning he read Jeremiah 1:7-8 in the Bible where God said to the prophet, "You must go wherever I send you and say whatever I tell you. And don't be afraid of the people, for I will be with you."

Freddy understood that was God's message to him and that He would provide opportunities for him. His job was to make the most of those opportunities, but he didn't have to force things to happen on his own.

Heaven is on Freddy's mind a lot these days, and he looks forward to returning to the place he calls home.[73]

My Desperate Prayer
(LOO-GEN SEAH-MCCREA)

My father, a retired naval officer, was losing his battle with cancer. His foray into alternative and traditional medicine was at an end. Doctors said to take Papa home, as they could do nothing more for him.

The hospice doctors showed us how to care for Papa's needs. They didn't know how long he would live, so we were to make him comfortable.

My relatives in Malaysia and Singapore answered Papa's request for a visit. They came, young and old, sensing the urgency and finality of his request.

But other things lay heavy on my heart. My mother and I were the only Christians in our family. I wanted Papa to be with me in heaven, so I asked the Lord for my father's soul.

Papa was raised in Singapore in the faith of his ancestors—Buddhism mixed with Taoist Chinese ancestor worship. He later came across the writings of Charles Darwin. He was contented with a pluralistic approach to religion because he wasn't sure that God existed.

One day, I came home from college and told Papa that I had become a Christian. He was upset. He didn't think I should go to church because "churches only want money." He also told me that faith healers were tricksters and that preachers brainwashed their listeners.

When my father became terminally ill, those things weighed heavily on my heart, and I dreaded talking to him again about Jesus Christ. It was clear, however, that it would be my last chance. So I approached Papa one afternoon and asked him if he had changed his mind about God.

To my surprise, he closed his eyes and nodded. I grew braver and asked him why he hated Christianity so much. I sensed there was more than what he'd told me. He said that years before, a Christian had hurt him. I was strangely relieved and told him that he should not reject salvation just because of the way one Christian behaved. People sometimes fail us, but God doesn't.

My father fell silent. I didn't know what else to say, so I left tracts for him to read. Over the next few days, people were always around, so I couldn't talk privately with Papa again. Despite being given tranquilizers, Papa was restless and wanted to be walked around indoors. A few days later, he grew weaker and he could only lie in bed.

On September 22, 2000, Papa was unusually cheerful when the doctor visited him. He even joked with her that he wouldn't be needing her services after that day. That same evening, Papa fell into a deep sleep. My mother, a retired nurse, said that he was in a coma.

After dinner, we gathered around Papa's hospital bed in the family room. We were exhausted. I curled up on the couch under the staircase while my siblings slept on the other couch. Mom was keeping vigil.

When I woke up around midnight, Mom told me that Papa's pulse was getting weaker, which was a bad sign. I felt sad but fell asleep again, still praying that my father would turn to God. *Lord, it says in the Bible that You will not fail those whose hope is in You, so please don't let me down. I know You love me and my family, so please keep Your promise.*

At 2:40, I was awakened by what I can describe only as the fierce bite of a mosquito attacking my neck. Just then, I heard my mother calling to me from across the living room. "Come quickly, Loo-Gen, he's going!"

I rushed past my still-sleeping siblings to my father's bedside. My heart was overwhelmed with a strange peace and great love for my father. Papa, with his eyes still closed, silently stretched his arms toward the ceiling as if he were embracing someone from above. He smiled and curled his arms toward his chest.

He didn't say a word, so I cradled his bald head, saying, "Papa, we love you. Jesus loves you. I'll see you again soon, in just a little while." As he drew his last breath, I saw my father's peaceful and radiant face. He was still smiling.

A week after Papa's funeral, I received a telephone call from my Chinese-speaking aunt. She was a Buddhist who had never read the Bible. She excitedly told me that she had had a dream about my father. In her dream she met my father in an enormous mansion, and my father was showing off dozens of rooms to her. Furthermore, she described a big feast in the mansion attended by people from all over the world.

I believe in my heart that my father saw the Lord Jesus, who had come to take him to heaven. This was further confirmed by my aunt's dream, which reflected the Lord's words in John 14:2: "My Father's house has many rooms; if that were not so, would I have told you I am going there to prepare a place for you?" (*NIV*).

I was at peace.

Loo-Gen Seah-McCrea (Genii McCrea) is a UK-trained attorney who left Malaysia to marry a Michigan scientist. She is now a full-time mother, part-time writer, and shares her husband's ministry of distributing free Christian media to the poor around Detroit (geniimccrea.wordpress.com).

What HE SAW:
The Story of Marvin Besteman

In April 2006, Marvin Besteman awakened to horrible pain after his surgery to remove a pancreatic tumor at the University of Michigan Medical Center. Days earlier, he had been diagnosed at Spectrum Health Butterword Hospital in Grand Rapids with insulinoma, a rare disease that is the opposite of diabetes. His blood sugar level had dropped to 31, dangerously low. To get to the tumor, the doctors had to move his internal organs out of the way. During surgery his nerve endings were severed, which was the reason he was having such intense pain.

The operation proved successful in getting his blood levels to a normal rate, but the resulting fiery pain was unbearable. For several hours that evening, nurses tried to manage his pain; however,

Marvin was restless, and he wanted only a little sleep and escape from the misery.

He forgot his discomfort when two angels lifted him and carried him upward. Marvin had no fear, only a deep sensation of peace. They flew through a brilliant blue sky and arrived in another realm—a place where he saw, felt, and heard things he couldn't imagine. The angels left him in front of a monumental gate.

Glorious colors and radiant light, both beyond description, surrounded him. Incomparable music—a choir of what sounded like a million voices with thousands of instruments—filled his ears with lush, pure and beautiful sounds. He knew where he was and what things were without being told. A love like nothing he'd ever felt warmed his heart.

Marvin stood at the gate with people from all over the world. They were dressed in their typical clothing. Everyone smiled, and their faces expressed contentment and joy. His 71-year-old body felt strong and fully alive. All the aches, pains and limitations of age were gone.

The apostle Peter welcomed Marvin at the gate. He wore ancient robes and sandals and had bushy hair and a beard.

Inside the doorway was an open area with deluxe green grass and a magnificent blue lake. An inner, glass-like gate rose upward and disappeared into a mist. Although Marvin couldn't get through the invisible barrier of the inner gate, he witnessed incredible things taking place on the other side.

Countless babies in all stages of development—beginning with pre-born as well as children and grownups—were laughing and playing on the greenest grass he'd ever seen. They were obviously highly valued, cherished, happy and content. He watched them for a time and then noticed familiar faces.

He saw six significant people in his life: Grandma and Grandpa Besteman, his mom, Paul and Norm (his friends), and his beloved son-in-law who had passed away of a horrible disease two months earlier. They all appeared healthy, joyful and radiant. They wore clothing similar to what they had worn on earth.

From a distance, Marvin noticed the throne of God surrounded by huge white pillars and an enormous crowd of people dancing and praising. He longed to go through to the other side, but Peter told him he couldn't stay. His name wasn't in the Lamb's Book of Life for that day, and he had work on earth to finish.

Just then Marvin was back in his hospital bed, attached to tubes and in tremendous pain. Something with the monitor alerted two nurses to rush in and check on him. He was crying.

"Why are you crying?" one of the nurses asked.

"I want to go home." They didn't realize he meant his heavenly home.

He went back to his earthly home after a five-day stay in the hospital, but he couldn't stop thinking about what he had seen, heard and felt. His half-hour in heaven left a yearning in him to return and stay forever. He wrestled with negative emotions and depression, but he knew God had sent him back for a purpose and with a mission.

For several months he didn't talk about what had happened to him because he didn't think anyone would believe him. Eventually he realized that God gave him the experience so he could comfort the grieving, encourage those who were dying (and their loved ones), and plant seeds of hope in those who didn't know Jesus Christ.

Marvin had many opportunities to share his story in public. At the end of each talk, he told people that the next time he went to heaven he wouldn't come back. He also said he'd wait at the gate for each of them.

Marvin shared his story many times, and he finished the manuscript for his book. His job on earth was done.

In January 2012, Marvin returned to heaven. This time he stayed.[74]

To Heaven and Back

(ANN KNOWLES)

Holidays are always busy for pastors and their families, and Father's Day, June 17, 1984, was no different. My husband, John, preached two amazing sermons that day. The children were home early that evening, because Vacation Bible School was to begin on Monday.

We went to bed earlier than usual to re-energize everyone for the week ahead.

When I awakened Monday morning, I reached across the bed. John wasn't there. I squinted at my watch—5:30 AM—too early for him to be up. I lay there a few minutes and waited for him to come back to bed. He entered the bedroom, and when I looked up at him, I knew immediately that something was terribly wrong.

"I feel weak." He was trembling. "I've never felt like this before."

Thinking his sugar was low, I suggested he drink some orange juice to bring it up quickly. A few minutes later he was still weak and having trouble breathing.

I was getting scared, but I didn't want to alarm him. I tried to hide the fear that was taking over my thoughts as my heart beat faster. Is this how a heart attack begins?

Ten minutes later, I woke the children and told them Daddy was sick and I was going to take him to the emergency room. "Don't worry, he'll be all right," I said. I promised to call them as soon as he saw the doctor.

We headed to the ER. I flew through red lights with the flashers blazing. John spoke little, and I prayed as I'd never prayed before. His brother, at age 51, had died in April with cancer. I prayed for John, our children and myself and for John's mother. What would happen to her if she lost another son just two months after losing his brother?

What if John dies now? My mind raced faster than my heart, but I refused to let the tears fall. I had to be the brave one.

Fifteen minutes after we left home, we arrived at the hospital, and I urgently approached the entrance to the ER. Two male nurses met the car. "I think my husband is having a heart attack," I cried out. They whisked him away without giving me a chance to kiss his cheek or tell him I loved him.

Then began the interminable waiting and one of the most difficult times of my life. The only word I got was, "The doctors are doing all they can, and they will talk to you soon."

I didn't want to call the children until I spoke with the doctors. I paced the floor, crying out to God with thanksgiving for the man He had brought into my life to be my husband.

Oh, God, please don't let him die, I prayed. I don't know how many times I repeated that line. I didn't know that John was as terrified as I was. He feared leaving the children and me. He, too, was praying, "Please, God, don't let me die. What will happen to Ann and the children?"

As John prayed, he saw a bright light, and a peace came over him. His body lay on the table below him, and he was floating above the operating table. He could see that the heart monitor had flat-lined and that the doctors were working frantically to bring him back to life. He also saw a beautiful door with a jeweled doorknob. He reached toward the door and a voice said, "Don't go in there. If you go through that door, you can't come back."

He dropped his hand, and instantly he was back on the operating table. The doctors put a defibrillator on his chest in one last effort to start his heart again. The operating room was chaotic. With a jolt, his heart began to beat. There was an audible sigh as the doctors looked at each other and one said, "He's back!"

John made remarkable progress the next week. The children and I were eager to spend every possible moment with him. We had come so close to losing him, and we couldn't praise God enough. Several members of the church family were at the hospital day and night, trying to help us and show how much they loved us.

John told us about his near-death experience. He believed he was allowed to come back in order to be assured that God would take care of our family. He shared many things with his children that touched their lives and drew them closer to the Lord.

We didn't know that he was really saying his good-byes to us. The following Monday, June 25, 1984, John suffered a fatal heart attack that took him back to the door of heaven. This time, he grabbed hold of the jeweled doorknob and entered into the presence of his heavenly Father.

Today we look back and thank God for that week and the long talks we had together.

Ann Knowles, a freelance writer and editor, wants to touch lives with her words. She has been published in two compilations, numerous magazines and online. Her passion is mentoring writers as they learn the writing craft. She loves teaching at

Christian writers conferences and interacting with other Christian authors. See
http://writepathway.com.

Touched by Gabriel

(MARCIA GADDIS)

Death teaches us that what we love about a person is not his or her smile or touch, but that which comes from deep within the soul. I began to understand that as we watched Megan leave this world.

As death drew near, the light in her eyes dimmed. She looked like a breathing skeleton. Her face became expressionless and pale. Her body temperature began to cool, and her skin felt dry and rough. She became almost unrecognizable. Megan—our daughter, sister and friend—was no longer there. They diagnosed her with Creutzfeldt-Jakob disease (CJD), which is extremely rare and fatal.

On the morning of September 12, 2008, I suggested to our nurse that she put Megan's traveling clothes on her, because I thought death could come any minute. While the nurse was drying and brushing Megan's hair, I saw two tears running down Megan's cheeks.

Surprised by the tender communication, I whispered, choking back my own tears, "I think she's telling us good-bye."

That night, as we stepped away from her bedside for a few minutes, Megan's spirit flew away to God. Free at last, she took flight to new life.

My heart broke, but I remembered three words spoken by an innocent child who was a student in my daughter's kindergarten class. The story came back as a reminder, and I pondered the mystery of heaven, knowing God sent an angel to prepare us for our daughter's impending death.

His name was Gabriel. He was six years old and just beginning to learn the English language. He had captured the heart of Megan, his kindergarten teacher. When she became seriously ill, he was unrelenting in his plea. "Mama, I must pray for Miss Gaddis. I must pray for my teacher. When will she return? I must pray."

His mother contacted the school principal to see if my daughter would return. Yes, the principal said, Megan would return for a short visit to celebrate their first year of school in the United States.

The mother shared with the principal her son's fervent request, and the principal's heart was touched. He assured Gabriel and his mother that when Megan returned for her visit to the classroom, Gabriel would get his wish and he could pray for his teacher.

The day was planned, and Megan was well enough to walk. Although she didn't talk much, she was full of smiles and hugs for her kindergarten students who missed her terribly. She handed out small gifts of books and educational toys for their summer fun. The children were thrilled with their presents as well as her visit.

After refreshments, Gabriel, his mother, the principal and a few teachers joined Megan and me for Gabriel's prayer.

Megan sat with Gabriel by her side, holding her hand. He seemed wiser and older than his years, as though he had an important mission before him. With his left hand, he confidently reached up, put it on her forehead, and bowed his head. He prayed softly in Spanish.

Only Gabriel and God knew the words spoken that day. After he said amen, he raised his head, looked tearfully at his teacher, and said in English, "It is finished."

I still think often about that event, marveling at the love of a child, his angelic name, his privately offered prayer, and that last powerful sentence he spoke to Megan in English: "It is finished."

The angel Gabriel appeared in the Bible at times of great importance—Daniel's dream, as well as Joseph, Mary and Elizabeth's news of the birth of Jesus and John. Gabriel's prayer will always be a mysteriously wonderful gift to me. That he solemnly concluded with the same statement Jesus uttered before He died, "It is finished," gave me great comfort.

God sent young Gabriel to prepare us for what was to come.

I often hear stories about people being prepared for death—making that unplanned visit or phone call days or weeks before seeing someone for the last time. Gabriel, our little angel, came to us through the persistence of a willing child, obeying the nudging of his tender, loving heart. Through Gabriel, we were forewarned of our own child's death. Through Gabriel, we could know God's peace, and our hearts would heal.

Marcia Gaddis is the author of *When God Comes Near*. When her 26-year-old daughter died from the rare and fatal Creutzfeldt-Jakob disease, Marcia wrote a book of hope and healing for others. See marciagaddis.blogspot.com and www.marciagaddis.com.

A *Visit* to Hell:
The Story of Ronald Reagan

Ronald Reagan (not the former President) lived a troubled childhood. As the result of his father's unmerciful abuse, hatred and violence controlled the young man's life, and he had no respect for authority. By the age of 12, he was a runaway, in the juvenile system and was arrested several times. By 15, Ronald had been jailed for car theft and stealing. He served a jail sentence because of his involvement in an accident that killed one person and crippled others. He wondered if that's all there was to life.

His troubled childhood followed him into his adult years, and his mental state deteriorated. Along with problems holding a job, he became a drug addict. Even getting married and having a family did nothing to help him. His wife filed for divorce, and his children feared him.

In 1972, Ronald took his son to a supermarket. On the way out of the store, Ronald met a man, and an argument erupted. The angry words escalated into a fight. Ronald struck the man, knocking him into a stack of bottles. Several of the bottles shattered.

Grabbing a broken bottle as a weapon, the other man charged Ronald. In an attempt to defend himself, Ronald lifted his left arm to block the blows. The man stabbed him, and the glass severed his bicep muscle and major arteries in his upper arm. Even with that horrific blow and severe bleeding, Ronald didn't give up. He struck back repeatedly.

The fighting, noise and Ronald's son's hysterical cries caught the store manager's attention. He stopped the fight, looked at Ronald's wounds and said, "If you don't get to the hospital immediately, you'll bleed to death in a matter of minutes."

The manager drove Ronald to the emergency room. By the time they arrived, Ronald was barely conscious.

The medical attendants assessed his situation. "We're not equipped to help him here," they said. "He needs to be transported to another hospital."

Someone had called Ronald's wife, and she arrived at the emergency room before they took him to the other hospital.

"He'll probably lose his arm," a doctor said.

Ronald's wife rode in the ambulance with him. As the vehicle pulled away, a young paramedic looked down at Ronald and said, "Sir, you need Jesus Christ."

Although weak and hardly aware of his surroundings, Ronald cursed him.

The paramedic repeated his message. "Sir, you need Jesus."

Just then, to Ronald the ambulance appeared to blow up—exploding in flames and smoke. He passed through the smoke and entered a dark tunnel. A multitude of voices cried, groaned and screamed in agony.

He looked down and saw a volcano-type opening filled with fire and smoke. It was crowded with people who were burning but not being consumed. As Ronald moved toward that place, the stench of sulfur penetrated his nostrils.

He got close-up views of people and saw them writhing in pain. The heaviness of loneliness, depression and frustration permeated the atmosphere. Hope was nonexistent. He recognized many faces—people he had known who had died in burglary attempts or who had died driving drunk. He identified others who had died from drug overdoses—people with whom he had partied.

"You don't want to come here," they cried to him. "There's no way out. No escape. Go back!"

In an instant everything faded to darkness. When Ronald opened his eyes, he was in a Knoxville, Tennessee, hospital, and his wife was sitting nearby. He still had his arm, but close to a hundred stitches held it together.

Despite the safe, quiet environment of the hospital, he couldn't stop visualizing what he had just experienced.

"I've been to a terrible place," he finally told his wife. "I don't know what or where it was, and I don't understand it, but it was terrible."

"You've been here in this hospital the whole time," she said.

"No. I've been in another place. A terrible place."

After his release from the hospital, he and his wife didn't talk much about his experience, but Ronald couldn't free his mind from the terrible ordeal. Because of his lifestyle, he had experienced many terrible things. He thought nothing could frighten him, but being in the pit of torment left him terrified, and the memories haunted him. He could still hear the screams, smell the horrible odors and feel the heat.

No matter what he did to try to stop the inner turmoil, the agonized voice of one of his dead friends yelling, "Go back!" continuously replayed in his mind. He tried to erase his fears by getting drunk or stoned, but nothing worked.

One morning several months later, after trying unsuccessfully to get drunk, he walked into his house and found his wife in the bedroom, sitting in bed with an open Bible on her lap.

When she looked up, he was aware that her wrinkles caused by years of his abuse and pain were gone. She stared at Ronald and smiled, her face aglow. "Jesus saved me tonight," she said.

Ronald was only vaguely aware of what she meant, but he could see that she was different.

She leaned forward. "Will you go to church with me to learn about Jesus?"

Realizing that nothing he'd tried had helped him overcome his suffering, he decided he might as well try God.

On the morning of November 2, 1972, he went to church with his wife. At his insistence, they sat at the back, and he observed what went on. He didn't know how to act in church, and he didn't know anything about the Bible.

Minutes later, the preacher read John 1:29, where John the Baptist pointed to Jesus and cried out, "Look! The Lamb of God who takes away the sin of the world!" Those words piqued Ronald's emotions and caused him to remember something from his childhood.

When Ronald was nine, he owned a pet lamb—his only friend. His precious lamb helped him endure the abuse at home. One night in a fit of violent anger, his father plunged a tire iron through the lamb's body and killed it. That event threw Ronald's life into a downward spiral.

So now, he wanted to know more about the Lamb of God whose name was Jesus. The more he heard, the more Ronald wanted to know this Lamb—he wanted a friend and a relationship with Jesus.

He prayed, "God, if You really do exist—and Jesus, if You really are the Lamb—either kill me or cure me. I don't want to live this kind of life anymore."

In his prayer, he spilled out the things he hated about himself and asked for help. Just then, the darkness of his life vanished, and he cried for the first time since he was nine years old.

As if by magic, God healed his mind, his memory, his drug addiction and his alcoholism. Ronald believes God spared his life so he could tell others about what he had seen in hell and so he could offer hope to others.

Since then he has learned that there *is* more to life, and he now takes that message with him wherever he goes.[75]

My Mother's Heavenly Visit
(MARLENE KELLY)

The verse, "Keeping [my] eyes on Jesus, the champion who initiates and perfects [my] faith" (Heb. 12:2), enabled me to wait patiently in the stillness of a hospital waiting room for my mother to emerge from a seven-hour surgery.

My mind began to tell me something was wrong. She wasn't going to make it. And yet my faith in God gave me the strength to persevere in prayer for her recovery.

Finally, a word came from her doctor that she was in the recovery room and I could see her as soon as she regained consciousness. Those words dispelled my doubts.

When I entered Mom's room, she was smiling. Her brown, deep-set eyes sparkled as she beckoned me to her bed. I bent down near her fragile body so I could hear her whispered voice.

"I saw Jesus."

"What?"

"I saw my Savior, Jesus," she repeated. "I want you to write down what I'm telling you so I won't forget."

With tears in my eyes, I took a pen and pad from my purse, sat quietly and waited. She closed her eyes and seemed to calmly collect her thoughts. I gently called out to her, "I'm ready to write, Mother."

Through smiling lips she repeated, "I saw Jesus."

"Yes, Mother. I've written that down," I answered. "What else?"

"I died on the operating table."

Her words shocked me, but I said nothing.

"I traveled through a long, dark tunnel and I cried out, 'Jesus!' He met me at the end of the tunnel. He stood in the midst of a bright light. He stretched His hand toward me, and I felt the warmth of the light over my body." She began to cry.

I laid aside my pad and pencil and held her hand until she regained her composure. "Do you want to go on, or do you want to rest?" I asked.

"I must go on. I promised Him I would tell what I saw. It's part of the work He said I have yet to do." She smiled and added, "Jesus said I had to go back and finish the work He's given me to do."

"What happened next?" I was ready to write again.

"He promised not to leave me and that He would be with me every step on my way back through the tunnel and beyond. He said I was to trust in Him. And I will—forever. Then I let go of His hand and traveled back through the tunnel. This time the tunnel wasn't dark, and it wasn't long."

That was her story, so I said, "Thank you for sharing this with me. I will share it with others, too."

She closed her eyes once again and drifted off to sleep. My mother is still alive, and in 2013, she turned 100.

Marlene Kelly is a retired educator and a former journalist. She has taught writing at the college level and is currently working as a freelance writer, editor and ghostwriter. See www.mekelly-solidrock.blogspot.com.

Garrett's Secret

(CHRISTY JOHNSON)

"Unfortunately, Jake didn't make it," the doctor said on the phone.

Unable to say anything, sobs came from deep within me. I hung up but I could still hear those words. "Unfortunately, Jake didn't make it."

I collapsed against the kitchen counter when I heard about the accident that my two sons, Jake and Garrett, had been involved in. My fiancé, John, grabbed me. I blurted out what the doctor told me. John hugged me, grabbed my purse, and hurried me out to his truck. We rushed to the hospital.

"How can I tell him? How can I tell Garrett that Jake was pronounced dead on his way to the hospital?"

"Do you want me to talk to him?" John asked.

"I have to do this myself."

"Why don't you wait until Garrett asks about him?" John suggested.

That seemed like a good idea. Why traumatize him until he was ready?

I entered Garrett's room and was shocked at the sight of my five-year-old son. They hadn't yet cleaned him, and the blood from the wounds on his face had already turned a crusty black.

"Hi, Garrett." I forced a smile and leaned down to kiss his forehead. "Where did you get this stuffed bear? He sure is cute."

Garrett's eyes gleamed. "From the ambulance man," he struggled to say.

Garrett was fascinated by emergency professionals. His favorite TV program was *Rescue 911*. Before each show, he lined up his fire trucks, police cars and ambulances on the carpet in front of the TV. His emergency crews were ready for action. I never imagined he would be a victim in his own episode.

Just then, the curtains swung open and the doctor entered the room. "We need to check for internal injuries," he said as he walked over to my son. "Garrett's jaw is too swollen, so I'll need to insert a tube up his nose and down his throat in order to inject the dye for the X-ray."

I nodded that I understood the procedure.

"Would you like to stay in the room?"

"Of course." I said those two words while fighting back tears. I could barely watch my own blood being drawn.

Later that day, the doctor gave us the first bit of good news. "Garrett has a hairline fracture to his jaw, but the X-rays show no internal injuries."

My son's face was too swollen for him to say anything, but I knew he was trying to smile. He didn't want me to worry.

The next morning, I squirted juice into Garrett's mouth with a baby eyedropper. I was falling apart emotionally, but I didn't want him to know.

"What's wrong, Mommy?" I could hardly make out his words.

"Nothing," I lied. Despite the peace I felt, the truth was that I didn't have a clue how I was going to tell him about his two-year-old brother, Jake.

Garrett's face brightened. "Look, Mommy," he said. "Bruce brought me some more stuffed animals. *And* the Transformer I wanted—Optimus Prime."

"That's nice, honey." I scooted a chair beside his bed.

We didn't talk much. Garrett slowly recovered. By the fourth day, he still hadn't asked about Jake.

"Garrett."

"Yeah, Mommy?"

"What would you say if I told you . . . ?" Tears filled my eyes, and my voice broke. But I had to tell him, so I tried again. "It's Jake. Jake didn't make it." Tears streamed down my face.

"I already know."

"What do you mean, 'You already know'?"

"After the accident, I got to go to heaven with Jake." Garrett swooped his Optimus Prime through the air. He made gun sounds as he beat up his invisible enemies. "Jake got to go inside, but God told me it wasn't my time."

His words shocked me, and I hardly knew what to say next. "What—what was heaven like?"

"Mommy!" Garrett's eyes squinted with apparent irritation. He set his Transformer down. "I can't tell you that!"

"Why not?"

"It's a surprise!"

"I'm sure God won't mind if you tell me, Garrett. I'm your *mother*."

"No, Mommy, I *can't!*"

"Why not?"

"'Cuz. God told me it's a secret."

He went back to playing with his toys while I sat back in my chair, flabbergasted. I knew he wasn't making it up, but I couldn't absorb it. However, as I sat there, peace filled my heart.

Jake left this life, but he was with God. It was all right.

I spoke at Jake's funeral and then, in front of hundreds of people, held the microphone while Garrett told us about escorting his little brother to heaven.

In the days and weeks following his release from the hospital, I tried to squeeze details out of Garrett, but he never said anything more. His childlike trust amazed me, yet I fought skepticism. Did Garrett really take a trip to heaven, or was his story a figment of his five-year-old imagination?

Preschoolers have vivid imaginations, but if it was make-believe, it worked for him. He didn't grieve in the way the grief recovery books that well-meaning friends had given me predicted. He never had a nightmare about the accident. And even though his biological father received a deferred sentence for negligent homicide (for driving under the influence of several narcotics), Garrett held no bitterness toward his dad. Even so, I tried to get him to open up about his trip to heaven.

Garrett never told me anything else. It was his secret, shared only with God. He kept it faithfully.

Christy Johnson, a writer and speaker, is passionate about imparting hope. See www.christyjohnson.org.

Waiting RIGHT HERE: The Story of Barbara McVicker Dye

On a summer day in 1971, 18-year-old Barbara McVicker drove toward her sister's house in her '63 black Falcon station wagon, a car she had purchased six months earlier with her own money. She came to a stop on a side street and looked both ways for oncoming traffic. As she pulled out, a car crested the hill so fast she had no time to react.

Barbara panicked. *Shall I back up? No, he's too close.* Pictures of her family and her dog, Snow, popped into her mind. *I'm going to die.*

In the next instant, tranquility embraced her. She was walking on a path that led to a huge open gate. Inside the gate, she saw people walking around in white gowns, and then her friend Pam greeted her. Pam had been her best friend who had died of a brain tumor at the age of 15. They had been closer than sisters, and Barbara missed her deeply.

"Hurry, Barbara," Pam said. "We can be together again. I've missed you."

As Barbara moved closer, the gate slowly closed. A man standing to the right said, "You need to go back. Your life isn't over." He spoke in a powerful voice that possessed authority. "You have more to do."

Before the gate completely closed, Pam called out, "I'll be waiting for you right here!"

Barbara had been given just a glimpse of a beautiful-beyond-words serene place with streets of gold, and she hadn't seen enough or experienced enough and wanted to see more. But she had to go back home; she understood that. The man said she had more to do, although she didn't understand what those words meant.

She woke up, wondering where she was. Why was she lying in somebody's front yard on a hilltop? A deep cut on her forehead left her dazed and with a bad headache. She slowly sat up and steadied herself. Why was her station wagon across the street, and why did it look that way? It was smashed but parked neatly between the lines in a church parking lot. That's strange, she thought.

She finally rose on wobbly legs and scanned the area for someone to help her. She stumbled toward the neighbors, but every time she came near people, they backed away. They seemed shocked, but she didn't know why.

She approached a team of paramedics working on a man. Even they seemed startled at her appearance. One of the paramedics came to her and insisted she lie down. She did, and they loaded her into an ambulance and took her to the hospital.

Barbara had cuts and bruises over her entire body, but there were no serious issues.

"You're lucky to be alive," the emergency room doctor said. He treated her and released her.

After she returned home, her dog, Snow, stayed by her side and wouldn't let her out of sight. Barbara's mother said that at precisely three o'clock that day Snow had started howling. She cried as if she had a broken heart. The accident had happened at that time.

Once Barbara's fuzzy thinking cleared up, she realized she had died on impact and had come back to life. She remembered her visit to heaven and decided to be baptized as soon as she got well. Before that, she had been too afraid of getting up in front of a crowd, but now she wanted to tell others that she had a relationship with God.

As her faith increased, she understood more and more what that authoritative voice meant. She loved helping people, caring for people and praying for them. Maybe that's why she had to return to earth.

Barbara's life-to-death-to-life experience changed her outlook. She has no fear of death and looks forward to the day she can see her parents, relatives and friends again in heaven. She says, "After such an experience, anyone who wasn't right with God would want to be."[76]

A Glimpse of Eternity
(DIANA LEAGH MATTHEWS)

Ralph, a dedicated member of the church for decades, often served on the board of deacons and was an elder of the church. Many younger men approached him for wisdom and advice.

We were devastated when we learned he had cancer. He put up a valiant fight against this disease that ravaged his body. As the end neared, his family gathered around his bedside at home.

Ralph slipped into a coma for several days. At one point, he appeared to be looking straight up at the ceiling with such clarity that those with him had no doubt he was looking into the face of Jesus.

We were surprised when he awakened from the coma and began to talk. "I have to tell you," he said. "I saw the gates of heaven. I can't describe the beauty and majesty of everything I saw—"

"Please don't wear yourself out—"

"I have to tell you that Jesus is very real."

No matter how much his family tried to make him comfortable and told him not to wear himself out by talking, he refused to stop and waved away their objections.

"I can tell you that Jesus is very real. I saw the wounds in His hands where the nails held Him to the cross."

Tears filled the eyes of his loved ones. As they listened, they were comforted and felt assured that Ralph would be all right. He would be with Jesus when his time came to go home.

"That's not all," Ralph continued. "I also saw the gates of hell. I have to tell you that hell is just as real as heaven. I could feel the heat and was afraid of the things I saw."

No one interrupted Ralph as he told what he had seen. "I was told to come back and tell everyone about what I saw. Heaven and hell are both real places. I want to see all of my loved ones in heaven."

For the next two days, an energized and excited Ralph shared the visions he'd seen with everyone who entered his room—including the hospice nurses.

Ralph died with a smile on his face.

Diana Leagh Matthews shares her story as a vocalist, speaker, writer and genealogist. She has a Bachelor's in Music. See www.dianaleaghmatthews.com and www.alookthrutime.com.

Do Not Resuscitate
(Susan K. Stewart)

When I walked into the emergency room that evening, I wasn't prepared for the ER doctor to declare that Dad might live only another 48 hours. His heart was giving out from complications of surgery.

"Does he have an advanced directive?" the doctor asked.

Suddenly I was alone with a life-and-death decision. Just five months earlier, Dad lived in his own home, drove himself wherever he wanted to go, and prepared for hip replacement surgery. He needed an existing artificial hip replaced because he had worn it out square dancing and walking, along with his many other physical activities. Dad was an active and healthy 82-year-old man.

Since Dad's previous hip replacement surgery had gone well, we weren't prepared for the difficult recovery this time. What should have been a few weeks of limited mobility turned into months.

During that time, his heart muscle weakened, resulting in this trip to the emergency room. Just the day before he had walked to a neighbor's house; now he lay in a hospital bed barely conscious.

As his only living family, it was up to me to decide what to do, and the emergency staff was in a hurry. I could have lied, but Dad and I had talked many hours about his end-of-life wishes. How could I dishonor him?

After Mom died 12 years earlier, Dad had lived, as a friend of mine says, with one foot in heaven and the other foot here. I knew he didn't want his life prolonged. He didn't want to end his life, either. But when called to heaven, he didn't want to stay here longer than God intended.

In my mind, I agreed with him, to the point that my own living will states, "Do not resuscitate."

Now that the time had come to say those words for my father, I no longer knew what they meant. In the urgency of a busy emergency room, there wasn't time to ponder the meaning. They needed an immediate answer.

"He doesn't want to be resuscitated," I said. I hadn't expected to make an end-of-life decision now.

I made the decision. I said the words that can be so hard for many loved ones, "Do not resuscitate." "DNR." "No extraordinary measures." All such words felt like issuing a death sentence.

Three weeks after the 48-hour prediction, Dad still lingered. He slept most of the time and talked little. He rarely wanted to eat but accepted sips of juice.

I sat in my rocking chair as the questions and doubts ran through my mind again. My usual time to sit quietly reading God's Word and praying is in the early morning. *Was my motive as pure as I think? Am I forgoing medical treatment that God is providing? Did I really do what Dad wanted?*

Dad hadn't spoken in several days. I wanted to hear him tell me that I had done the right thing.

"My Lord!" Dad suddenly exclaimed in a strong voice filled with awe and wonder. His eyes were open, but he wasn't looking out the window or at anything in the room. Dad was looking beyond this world.

I witnessed what few are privileged to see—Dad was seeing his Savior. Had I decided to allow the doctors to take measures to prolong Dad's life, he might have been in a hospital rather than my home. I would have missed Dad's introduction to heaven.

Although his body remained for another 10 days, Dad—the person and soul of the man who raised me—was no longer there. He had seen heaven and had spiritually moved on. Dad's body slowly and quietly closed down. He didn't open his eyes again. He didn't take the liquid offered. He didn't speak again.

God welcomed Leo Max Luse home and relieved me of the burden I had been carrying in my mind. Was I responsible for the death I had been watching? No. It was in God's time, and He gave me the assurance never to doubt the decision again.

Susan K. Stewart is a teacher, writer and speaker. In addition to writing and editing, she teaches Introduction to e-Books, Creating e-Books and other classes online and at conferences. Susan is the author of three books, and her current work in progress is *Making an e-Book: Design to Distribution*. See www.practicalin spirations.com.

$\mathscr{J}ohn$ $\mathscr{B}unyan's$ VISION

John Bunyan (1628–1688) is best known for his allegorical book *Pilgrim's Progress*. Another of his books is called *Visions of Heaven and Hell*, in which he wrote that God sent an angel to show him heaven and hell. Although the term "near-death experience" hadn't yet been coined, in many ways the chronology reads like such an experience.[77]

Apparently discouraged and depressed, Bunyan went into the woods to kill himself. Just before he could take his own life, he heard a whispering voice warning him not to do that. "The fatal stroke you are about to give yourself will seal your own damnation."

Bunyan believed that was the voice of God, and he begged God to take away the blackness of his soul. Just then, he was surrounded with a light that was brighter than anything he had ever seen. A heavenly messenger—an angel—took Bunyan to heaven. Like many others, Bunyan wrote that he was unable to describe the music or what he saw. While there, Bunyan met the prophet Elijah, who taught him about heaven.

Before Bunyan could return, the messenger told him he must visit hell to see firsthand the reward for sin. Bunyan went there and watched and heard individuals groan in terrible torment and pain. Then the angel took him back to earth.

After Bunyan went home, his family was surprised at how his face had changed. Bunyan wrote that they told him, "Yesterday you looked so depressed that you seemed the very image of despair. But now, your face appears radiantly beautiful."

Bunyan replied that if they had seen what he had witnessed, they wouldn't have been surprised at the change. He then went into his room and tried to write down everything he had seen and heard.

I've Been There
(ED LONG JR. WITH ANNA L. RUSSELL)

I want to tell the world that I know what heaven will be like. I've been there.

On the fourth Sunday morning of December 1998, I awakened at two o'clock to get some medicine. By mistake, I went into the kitchen instead of the bathroom. My wife, June, and I were married in September and had lived there only three months.

"Ed, where are you?" I heard her say.

"I think I'm in the kitchen," I called, "and I'm dying."

Immediately June was beside me with her hand on my back.

"I'm dying," I mumbled.

She released me and picked up the phone.

I vaguely recall the ambulance arriving. Two big hands forced me to breathe. After the EMTs put me on the gurney, they pushed me into the ambulance. The voices faded, and I was alone.

The next moment of awareness, I stood in an open field, overlooking an expansive meadow filled with sweet-smelling grasses and flowers. At the far end were large ivory gates, illuminated, but not by the sunlight.

Then I sank into darkness.

"For a couple of minutes, we thought we'd lost you," a paramedic said.

The next thing I remember, I was at the hospital.

"This man's lungs are shutting down," someone in the emergency room called out. "He isn't getting enough oxygen to his brain."

In a flurry of activity, they rushed me to the operating room.

I had pneumonia, and it was so bad that they removed part of my right lung.

Four of my sisters—Lillie, Mamie, Minnie and Katie—traveled from Florida. They came during the night and stayed with me. On the second day after surgery, Johnny Johnson came to visit. Johnny and I had gardened and farmed together, and he now taught the Sunday School class I was in. As he talked with my sisters and me, that same eerie feeling swelled in me again, so I said, "Please leave the room. I want to meditate for a while." Only the attending nurse stayed.

A strange calmness filled me. I seemed to float in the air, looking down on my body. At the same time, I saw myself get out of bed and walk toward the wall. The peculiar thing is that when I got to the wall, it disappeared and I entered a long corridor filled with light.

About halfway down the glowing hall, I sat on a chair. Across from me was Jesus, but only His hands and the bottom of His robe were distinct. He talked to me, and His words gave me deep peace. However, after I got up I couldn't remember anything He had said to me, but I remembered His loving presence and His comfort.

I continued through the glowing passage. The next moment, I was standing in a field. I was close to ivory gates—almost near enough to touch them. Yet I couldn't touch the gates and walk on through. I didn't know why.

Many people moved about in the meadow beyond the gate. I recognized my mother. I saw my sister who died when she was three years old. Back then, her legs were crippled, but now she looked like a perfectly healthy child. She stood next to Mother, who looked as young as she did when I was a child.

I recognized others. They were close, and I wanted to touch them. But I couldn't—I seemed unable to move forward.

If I extend my hand a little farther, I can touch them.

Before I could move, darkness seeped over me.

I was back in the hospital bed. Just then, a defibrillator jolted my whole body as a technician activated my heart. Later I learned I had been clinically dead for 27 minutes.

"Why were you so agitated when you were coming to?" one of my sisters asked.

"Because I didn't want to come back," I said. I told them what had happened. "I wanted to stay in that beautiful place."

After I returned from heaven's gates, I became calm and tranquil. I didn't worry about life or death. Before my journey, I had been afraid of the day I would die. Since then, however, I've been at peace with God. No matter what my physical condition, I haven't worried because I saw what heaven will be like.

I know how perfect heaven is, because I've been there.

Ed Long Jr., an active leader and member of Rose Heights Church in Tyler, Texas, farmed for a number of years. Award-winning author Anna L. Russell helps people tell their stories. She is a member of East Texas Writers Guild, Write with Grace critique group, and has credits in many magazines and newspapers.

Stoning Stephen
(ANN SULLIVAN)

Grandma's was a life well spent, and it came to its end very quietly. Because she contracted rheumatic fever as a child, she had been plagued with valve problems in her later years. As she neared the end, she was in the hospital again, and my mom and sisters stood beside her bed.

Grandma was still fully alert, and although plain in appearance, she asked for a comb and a mirror, which they gave her. "After all," she said, "it's not like I'm dying."

Hours later, Grandma slipped into a coma and lay completely still throughout the evening and well into the night. The doctors said she'd most likely be "passing" very soon.

Without warning, Grandma sat up. With her eyes opened wide, she seemed to look beyond the sanitized walls and the people who stood beside her. She released a sigh of utter joy and expectancy over what she "saw."

Grandma lay back down, closed her eyes, and she was gone.

Trying to make sense of that strange event, I read the story of Stephen in the Bible. Like many persecuted Christians, Stephen spoke boldly of the Lord, and his enemies stoned him to death. As he stood before the men, the Bible says he saw the glory of God and Jesus standing at the right hand of the Father (see Acts 7:54-59).

Could that have been what my grandma saw before she breathed her last? Like Stephen, was God giving her a gift for a life well-lived?

Of course, we live by faith, and not by sight (see 2 Cor. 5:7). We're not supposed to have visions or hear voices. But don't tell Grandma.

Ann Sullivan is a freelance writer and conference speaker. She and her family live outside of Chicago.

Stories FROM A HOSPICE CHAPLAIN

(GARY ROE)

I'm a hospice chaplain, and the following are a few of the experiences I've witnessed during my two years of service.

Sally suffered from stage-four lung cancer. In the span of a year, she'd gone from her own home, to an assisted living facility, to a nursing home. She finally lost her mobility and became bed-bound. Her world had shrunk to the size of her tiny room.

During my visits, she talked almost non-stop about her family and about Jesus. "Those are my two favorite subjects," she would say.

As the cancer progressed, Sally slept more. One day, I walked into her room. She had her head back and mouth wide open, snoring. I smiled and quietly sat next to the head of the bed. I prayed silently.

After a while, Sally no longer snored. Her mouth was shut, her lips pursed. Still asleep, she had a thoughtful, questioning look on her face.

Just then she opened her eyes, raised her head and gazed at the end of the bed. She continued staring for a long minute.

Finally, she lowered her head back to the pillow. That's when she noticed me. She stared into my eyes. "Did you see Him?"

"See whom?"

She looked again toward the foot of the bed. "I don't know. He was down there." She waved her hand. "He was huge. Absolutely massive. He filled that half of the room. Who was He?"

I just smiled.

"Oh! You don't think . . . ?" she asked with awe. "For me?" She lay there for several moments, staring straight ahead.

It was something she needed to figure out for herself.

"You know, as I looked at Him, I got the feeling He's been here a long, long time. Maybe my whole life. He looked and felt so familiar." Sally gazed into my eyes. "It's getting time for me to go home, isn't it?" she asked.

"Yes, I think so."

"He was so big. He looked so strong. How did I get so lucky? No. Not lucky. Blessed. I'm so blessed." Tears ran down her cheeks.

Sally passed peacefully a week later.

Orin had been a career military man who'd fought in Korea and Vietnam. He was known around his assisted-living facility simply as "the colonel."

Orin showed up to nearly every activity at the facility. He never missed a Bible study.

One day when I led the study, we talked about forgiveness. It was an emotional lesson. As everyone shared, I noticed that the colonel was uncharacteristically quiet.

"Colonel, what do you think?" I asked.

Orin looked at me for a moment, then said, "About forgiveness? Tough stuff. Very, very tough."

He dropped his gaze and began to shake. Then the tears came. "I can't do it!" he stammered. "I've tried. What they did to me, to my buddies . . . inhuman . . . horrible."

The rest of the group sat in silence.

"I was a POW in Vietnam for two years. It was hell, absolute hell. If I could've taken my own life, I would have, but God wouldn't let me." The colonel sighed. "He didn't let me do that."

He paused and we waited.

"I made it. Others didn't. I've lived with those horrors every day since. Forgiveness? I've tried."

Orin pushed his chair back and slowly rose. "I'm sorry. I've had enough for today. Please pray for me."

The following week, I came for the next Bible study. As the group gathered, one of the members asked, "Did you hear about the colonel?"

"No. What happened?" I asked.

"He passed last night. The night nurse went to check on him about two in the morning. She found him sitting upright in his bed, staring straight in front of him. She asked him if he was okay. He told her not to interrupt. He said there was a huge soldier dressed in white at the end of his bed giving him orders for his next assignment. Then he lay back down, closed his eyes, and died. Just like that. Now, what do you think of that?"

"I think the colonel's war here is over," I answered. "He's been promoted."

"Do you think he was seeing an angel?"

"Sure sounds like it. The Bible describes them as powerful warriors. At times I believe the Lord pulls back the veil a little and gives us a glimpse of what's on the other side. Isn't it amazing to know that there are probably other beings in this room with us right now?"

Those lovely folks looked around the room in awe. Maybelle, who was 95, grinned and said, "Now, that's cool!"

We laughed and someone led us in singing, "Angels We Have Heard on High," even though it was March.

Ralph had battled ALS for several years. His body slowly ceased to function. Although his mind was fully intact, he'd spoken his last word about two weeks previously.

On what turned out to be my last visit with Ralph, the nurse stopped me outside his room.

"Honestly, chaplain, I think he's getting close," she said. "I would be surprised if he made it another week."

When I walked in, Ralph tracked me with his eyes. He could no longer move his head. As with most ALS patients, he was a prisoner in his own body.

I bent over him and laid my hand on his forehead. Gazing into his eyes, I said, "It won't be long now. It's okay to go. You know Jesus. He's got you. He's carrying you. He'll see you all the way home."

Ralph looked toward the ceiling, then back at me, then toward the ceiling again. He did that repeatedly. He was trying to tell me something.

I looked up at the ceiling, and then it hit me. "Ralph, are you seeing something up there?" I asked.

Ralph, of course, couldn't speak, nod or shake his head, but he kept looking from my face to the ceiling. Back and forth.

I assumed Ralph was seeing something—or, more likely, somebody. I prayed accordingly.

I told his nurse what had happened. She looked at me thoughtfully and said, "That explains it. About a week ago, when he could still move one finger, he kept pointing to the ceiling and trying to say something. His speech was so slurred, we couldn't make it out. Our best guess was, 'They're here.'" It suddenly struck her. "Wait. You don't think—"

I shrugged. "Ralph knows Jesus, and perhaps during his final hours he sees the Lord."

The nurse and I stood in the hallway, looking toward Ralph's room.

"Heaven is far closer than we realize. It's all around us," she said, "if only we had eyes to see."

Leroy had suffered with dementia for years. It had progressed to the point where his body was shutting down. By the time I began my hospice visits, he could no longer speak. He merely looked at me and smiled.

Leroy's family told me he was a man of strong faith. "Jesus was, and is, his best friend," his sister said. "I'm not the least bit worried about him spiritually."

During my visits with Leroy, I read the Bible, prayed and sang. When I sang, he smiled and hummed along.

One day I walked in to find Leroy staring at the far corner of the ceiling in his room. He glanced at me, smiled and pointed upward. Then he raised both hands, as if he were reaching out for something. His face beamed.

He kept staring up and didn't look at me again.

I remained silent for several minutes before I read several Scripture verses, prayed and sang. Leroy just kept gazing raptly at that corner of the ceiling, raising his hands periodically.

I wasn't surprised when I got the call that night that Leroy had passed. I had seen the signs before. I'm reminded of Jesus' words: "There is more than enough room in my father's home. If this were not so, would I have told you that I am going to prepare a place for you? When everything is ready, I will come and get you, so that you will always be with me where I am" (John 14:2-3).

Sammy had been one of those healthy people who'd hardly ever been to the doctor and had never been in a hospital. Until colon cancer struck. After that, his life changed quickly and dramatically.

Our hospice team started to visit shortly after Sammy's diagnosis. The cancer was so advanced that doctors gave him between two to three weeks to live.

"I've been ready a long time," he told me. "In fact, my philosophy has been to get ready and then stay ready."

Sammy talked often about Jesus. His father had been a pastor, and so had two of his uncles and his son. "Jesus is everywhere," he said. "Couldn't get away if I wanted to."

One Saturday morning, I received a call that Sammy was unresponsive. I headed for the hospital. When I arrived, the hallway was full of people.

His son saw me, greeted me and said, "We're here to see him home."

Sammy's son and I walked into the room together. The family became quiet. I looked at Sammy and was surprised to find him smiling, eyes open, looking around the room above everyone's heads. He was clearly joyful.

"He has that look of transition," his son said. "It won't be long now."

"What do you think he's seeing?" I asked.

"I don't know, but I have some pretty good guesses," he answered. "Whatever and whoever it is, it's wonderful."

We prayed together with the gathered relatives. Toward the end of the prayer, one family member started singing "Amazing Grace." The rest of us joined him. Sammy kept gazing above our heads, looking around like a delighted child.

"We don't have a clue what heaven will be like, do we?" the son whispered in my ear.

Actually, we did have a good idea. But whatever our concept of heaven is, we're going to be surprised. It will surely be more wonderful than we expect.

Many times in my role as a hospice chaplain, I've seen that look of transition.

Gary Roe serves as a hospice chaplain in Central Texas. A former missionary and pastor, he is the co-author (with Cecil Murphey) of *Not Quite Healed: 40 Truths for Male Survivors of Childhood Sexual Abuse* and *Saying Good-bye, Facing the Loss of a Loved One*. See www.garyroe.com.

Home
(KAREN JORDAN)

Loud wails and intense sobbing echoed as I walked up the sidewalk to Mother's door. When I stepped up to the doorstep, I recognized her voice. I pushed the door open and rushed in without knocking.

Mother sat on the edge of her rocking chair with her hands covering her face. My sister, Cathy, sat close to her on an ottoman. She frowned and shrugged as our gazes met.

"Mother, I'm home!" I embraced her.

"She's been like this all day." Cathy fought back tears while she talked. Confusion and darkness ruled Mother's thoughts. She battled a disease that was destroying her mind. As I knelt down to hug her, she melted into my arms before I asked, "Are you afraid of dying?"

"No, of living."

Mother had faced death before and survived. A few years earlier, her heart had failed during surgery. Mother had a vision in which she caught a glimpse of a dark afterlife. The vision terrified her and made her face the emptiness of her life. After that horrible experience, Mother sought answers to her questions and fear of dying. She discovered what was missing: an intimate relationship with Jesus Christ.

This time, after Mother realized the illness would be fatal, fear and doubts flooded her. I asked myself if Jesus would alleviate her fear this time. Could she trust Him to be with her as she walked through the valley of her impending death?

I couldn't save Mother from disease, but I prayed for her and reminded myself of God's promise, "Even though I walk through the darkest valley, I will fear no evil, for you are with me; your rod and your staff, they comfort me" (Ps. 23:4, *NIV*).

I sat beside my mother on her sofa one day near the end of her journey. Her gaze was fixed on the high ceiling in her townhouse living room. "What do you see?" I asked.

"Heaven."

"What does it look like?"

"Huge."

What a perfect description of heaven.

After sharing her vision of heaven with me, Mother remained silent, but I knew she was convinced it was her destination. During the next few weeks, Mother lost her ability to communicate. As the end drew near, we sang songs about heaven to her and read her passages from her Bible.

A few weeks later, in the final moment of her life, Mother whispered, "I'm home."

Karen Jordan encourages others to tell the stories that matter most to them. She is an author, speaker and writing instructor. (kj@karenjordan.net; www.karen barnesjordan.com.)

Without Words

A serious car accident the day after Christmas in 1988 left Linda Evans Shepherd's 18-month-old daughter, Laura, unconscious. A team of 24 healthcare professionals gave the family no hope for her life.

"Laura isn't in a coma, she's in a vegetative state," one doctor said. "She won't wake up."

In the months that followed, Linda and her husband, Paul, clung to hope. They prayed and trusted in God's plan for Laura, even as she lay unresponsive and connected to life support. Nearly a year after the accident, Laura awakened when her newborn baby brother was placed in her arms.

Although Laura is still paralyzed, has many disabilities and remains on life support to this day, she is whole in spirit and innocent in heart. She beams with joy and has good understanding. She's full of peace and love. She's happy, smiles at jokes and enjoys the world around her.

Laura can't speak, but she has learned to communicate through tongue signals and facial expressions. Because of conversations they've had, Linda believes her daughter spent that year after the accident with the Lord and came back transformed.

Linda had to tell Laura about a friend of hers who died in a tragic car accident. "Jessica is with Jesus," she said. Rather than being sad, Laura became excited and smiled. She understood what that meant in a different way than most people would.

Linda and Laura have had many conversations about Jesus, and Laura has made it clear on numerous occasions that she has knowledge of things beyond this world.

⊷⊰❧⊱⊶

Linda recently heard from an old college friend who told her he'd lost his faith. "What I don't get," her friend Terry said, "is that if God is God, why don't amputees grow their limbs back?"

Later, Linda mentioned Terry's question in front of Laura. To Linda's surprise, Laura laughed in a way Linda rarely saw. Great and loud guffaws filled the air, and tears ran down her cheeks.

"What's so funny?" Linda asked.

Poor Laura couldn't catch her breath, and her hoots wouldn't stop. It took a while before she was calm enough to communicate with her mother.

"Is that funny because when you were in heaven," Linda asked, "you saw people with new arms and legs?"

"Yes!" Laura told her through her tongue signals. She began to laugh again.

"Were you one of those people?"

"Yes! Yes!" she signaled again.

Linda later told Terry that her disabled daughter had responded concerning his lack of faith. He felt that God was speaking to him, and his doubts dissipated.[78]

TO *Heaven* AND BACK:
The Story of Dr. Mary C. Neal

In January 1999, orthopedic spine surgeon Mary Neal and her husband joined friends in the Los Rios region of southern Chile to kayak the Fuy River. Athletic and adventurous, the Neals had kayaked many times. Their friends were professionals who ran a raft and kayak company.

The Neals enjoyed a week of boating, and on the final day they went to a section of the river known for its waterfalls, with drops of 10 to 15 feet. Because of back problems, Mary's husband, Bill, didn't join them this time.

The kayaker in front of Mary got stuck, but Mary was already in the current, so she veered away to prevent an accident. Her slight change of course sent her toward the main drop of the waterfall, and she went over. Mary hit the bottom of the waterfall, and the front part of her boat became pinned in the rocks. She was trapped 8 to 10 feet below the river's surface.

She tried to dislodge herself, but the force of the water pressed her torso against the deck of the kayak and held her there. She realized her survival chances were slim. When it became clear she couldn't do anything more to help herself, she surrendered control to God and asked that His will be done.

She immediately felt a comforting embrace, as if she were a baby being rocked. She thought of her husband and children, yet she felt reassured that everything and everyone would be fine.

Parts of her life played out in front of her. She understood the ripple effects of different events and decisions she had made. She was aware of what was going on; though at the same time everything seemed unreal. She felt fully alive—more alive than ever—but as a doctor she knew she'd been submerged too long to still be alive. After five or six minutes, a human brain without oxygen dies. She was well beyond that mark.

She felt the water, the boat and the current pulling her body out of the boat. Her knees bent backward and broke, and her ligaments tore. But she felt no pain. There was no fear.

Her spirit then separated from her body. She rose up out of the river, and a welcoming committee of spiritual beings greeted her. They had physical forms with heads, arms and legs and wore robes. They weren't people she recognized; yet she had a special sense that they had known each other for eternity. Her greeters exuded love and joy.

Intuitively, she knew that they had come to her from God to welcome and guide her. She understood things in the core of her being without being told.

Mary traveled with them down a path to an area where she saw a giant field. She was overwhelmed with the resplendent colors and intense beauty of everything she saw. The whole atmosphere emanated feelings of love and joy such as she'd never known.

The path led to a domelike structure, shimmering and brilliant, exploding with love. She was home—a place where she truly belonged.

They arrived at a large arched entryway. Inside she saw a multitude of other beings doing a variety of things. They looked up at her and expressed great joy at her arrival.

She was ready to walk through the threshold and pushed herself forward. But she was unable to go inside. Instead, she received the news that she had to return to her body on earth. It wasn't her time, and she had more work to do.

"No, I don't want to leave; I want to stay," she said, saddened that she had to go back. She loved her husband and children, but that love didn't compare with the perfect love she felt in that place.

The beings gave her information about some of the work she yet needed to do on earth. They then took her to the river and reunited her with her body.

A number of miracles took place to get Mary Neal from that remote, inaccessible river area in Chile and return her to the United States. She felt no pain for about 10 days, despite her touch-and-go condition with multiple fractures, torn ligaments and other serious medical problems. She sensed she was living in two realms—the physical realm and the heavenly realm.

While in the intensive care unit at the hospital, she contemplated what she had experienced and why she had to come back. Twice during that time she went back to that brilliant field, beautiful beyond description, and had a conversation with Jesus. He sat on a rock and she sat at His feet, in awe of His love, patience, kindness and compassion.

He gave her insight into the serious questions of life and told her what was expected of her. Among those expectations were that she'd protect her husband's health, be the rock on which her family and community would stand after her son's death, and that she'd tell her story. Because her son wasn't sick, it shocked her to learn that he would die.

As she lay back in her hospital bed, everything seemed incredible to her. A skeptic by nature and a rational thinker, she tried to process what had happened, even to the point of asking the nurses what type of drugs they had given her. Hallucinations were ruled out when she discovered her only medicines were antibiotics.

For a long time, Mary didn't talk to anyone about her trip to heaven and her encounters with Jesus. She questioned her experiences and tried to come up with alternate explanations. After 10 years, she felt compelled to write a book. She finished what she thought was the final manuscript only hours before a car killed her oldest son while he roller-skated. Then she understood Jesus' message.

Mary has changed as a doctor and as a person. Although a highly skilled, trained surgeon, she now sees herself more as a healer. Once a woman who went to church on Sundays and didn't think much about God during the week, she now communes with Him daily. She once had faith; now she also has knowledge.[79]

You'll Never Go Alone

(GINGER GARRETT)

My father-in-law, Martin Garrett, had been in hospice for three weeks following an exhaustive battle with chronic pulmonary obstruction. In his seventies now, the disease that had been a minor inconvenience for so long suddenly turned into a life-threatening crisis.

We held out hope for his recovery, but his condition didn't improve. He was unable to speak, so he communicated with the family by simple gestures. We spent many hours just holding his hand.

Especially hard hit by his sudden deterioration was his new bride, Elaine. They had met late in life. Together, they were like young newlyweds, giggling, holding hands and stealing kisses. Elaine had waited for so long to find her Prince Charming. The thought of a life alone—of a life without Martin—seemed overwhelming.

If Martin died, how would Elaine bear the grief? Would her faith hold up if she lost her great love?

As we approached the fourth week of Martin's hospitalization, a strange event began to unfold. One afternoon, Martin saw something in the upper right corner of the blank white room. He got a far-away look in his eyes, but it wasn't the look of a dreamer. Martin focused intently on something or someone in the distance that none of us could see. After a few moments of intense staring, he relaxed and fell asleep.

It happened again when he awoke and continued throughout the week. Martin's attention would suddenly shift to the same corner, and his eyes would open wide as an air of expectation came over him.

What was he seeing? None of us knew, so we asked a hospice nurse. "We nurses see that sort of thing all the time here." She smiled and added, "We think our patients are seeing angels, but then, we don't really know, do we?"

The next day, Elaine shaved Martin's face as usual and combed his hair. He took such pride in his appearance, especially around her. But he was exhausted and fell back asleep. Later, as the evening shadows fell, he sat up and rapped his knuckles on the metal bed rail. When he had Elaine's attention, he motioned to his face. He wanted a fresh shave, and it seemed important to him that he look his best at that very moment.

This time, however, he also wanted his glasses on, as if he was ready to leave. Again she obliged, although there was nothing to see and nowhere to go. Once he was prepared, he lifted his hands toward the mysterious visitor in the corner, and waited.

A peaceful calm descended over Elaine. She felt warm and comforted, remembering the words of her own father before he passed. "You won't go alone," he had promised her. Now she was witnessing proof of that promise. Someone was waiting for Martin, and he knew it.

His arms grew tired as he held them out. After a time, he removed his glasses and set them on his chest. He rested for the night, apparently aware that he wasn't going anywhere.

This ritual replayed itself several times during the next two days. Martin was clearly ready to go. He undoubtedly wanted to breathe again, to speak once more, and to walk. Perhaps the only reason he did not was his great love for Elaine.

The mysterious visitor returned every day, and Martin repeatedly gestured that he was ready to go. Yet Elaine couldn't bear to have him leave.

So we waited—all of us, perhaps even the mysterious visitor. Elaine at last was comforted to know that Martin wouldn't go alone and that her faith, the bedrock of her life, would hold. Jesus was real and would be there for her, too, for every step of her own journey that must soon begin.

On the third day, Martin's oldest son, Mitch, sat with Elaine beside Martin's bed. Once more, Martin held out his arms. Terribly weak now, he lifted them as if to be picked up by someone much stronger and carried from the room. His eyes focused on the corner, although, as always, Mitch and Elaine saw nothing there. Holding his arms out proved too much. He let them fall back on the bed, too weak now to ask the visitor to carry him.

Then Elaine announced she had to run to the bank. She stepped out of the room, and Mitch held Martin's hands.

"Thank you," Mitch whispered, "for making me the man I am today. It's okay to go now, Dad."

Seconds later, Martin was gone.

When Elaine returned, Mitch was waiting for her. God's children never go alone into the next life, but there is also comfort for those who must remain. We don't have to go into the darkness of grief alone. We can stay close to each other, with eyes open wide, seeking glimpses of the hope that awaits.

Ginger Garrett is the author of *Chosen: The Lost Diaries of Queen Esther*; *Reign: The Chronicles of Jezebel*; and *Desired: The Untold Story of Samson and Delilah*. See www.gingergarrett.com.

A Self-made Man

(SCOTT HUTCHESON WITH PENNY SHREVE)

I was a self-made man, and felt I needed no one. Even after I married Shari and started a family, my life revolved around sex, drugs and rock 'n' roll. That lifestyle continued even after the birth of our two children.

Although I was into drugs, I was a successful used car salesman and knocked down $150,000 a year. I was living what I thought was a blessed life, but it was really a life of sin and darkness.

In 2003 and 2004, my life began to fall apart. My brother, Brady, had surgery for a brain tumor. After that, Shari went into a diabetic coma, and one of her kidneys no longer functioned. She fell one day and broke her leg, and the next day she broke the other because she was favoring the leg she had broken. Eventually she went on permanent physical disability.

I had to have an umbilical hernia repaired, and then our son, Heath, lost a finger in a motorcycle accident. It was re-attached, but they kept him in the hospital for a week.

Family health issues distracted me so much that I lost my business and had to sell our large house. We moved into a much smaller one.

A year later, I ruptured my right bicep and had to have surgery. For the first time in my adult life, I had lost all the business ventures I had started. I was out of work. Even worse, my drug use and gambling increased as I tried to make money any way I could. I tried to pay my bills by gambling, which was foolish.

Not surprisingly, the situation worsened. By November 2006, I had a disabled wife, no job and a 90 percent decrease in income from three years earlier. I was living in a dark world, but it didn't cross my mind to reach out to God.

On December 28, 2006, I took Shari to see her doctor, and afterward I talked her into driving over to a casino so I could play poker. I won $202, and we decided to stop at a restaurant on the way home.

I chose shrimp. After the meal while I was driving home, my feet and hands started itching. By the time I reached home, my eyes had swollen shut and I could hardly breathe. Our son rushed me to the ER. Immediately they went to work on me and put an oxygen monitor on me. I hadn't known I was allergic to shrimp.

Four nurses and a doctor worked on me as I struggled to breathe. They inserted an IV in both arms and shot me full of Benadryl as I went into anaphylactic shock (a life-threatening allergic reaction).

"We're losing him," one nurse said.

I knew I was dying. It was difficult to believe it was because I ate shrimp. Everything went black.

I find it impossible to explain what happened next. In front of me was a large body of water—the most beautiful water I'd ever seen, and it looked as if diamonds were sprinkled across the top of the waves. I didn't know where I was, but I loved it. "Just a Closer Walk with Thee" was playing, and it was the most beautiful rendition of the song I'd ever heard.

I stared at the shoreline. It was beautiful. People wearing white, incandescent robes were rejoicing and singing. They looked back toward me as if to say, "Come with us." The love I felt in heaven was like oxygen.

Somehow I knew I was home and that I belonged in that place. I wanted to go with them. I moved toward them, but the people turned away.

Just then I felt as if I were being thrust through a vacuum hose. I opened my eyes and I was back in the hospital.

A doctor stared at me. "Scott, are you with us?"

I said I was. I felt no pain, but tears ran down my cheeks.

Beside me sat Heath, my son. He watched me come back to life.

"I went to heaven," I said to him.

"I prayed for you. When I finished praying, your blood pressure started going back up." Even though I'd taken him to church no more than a dozen times when he was growing up, apparently something about prayer had gotten through to him.

⊹⟡⟡⊹

It took time for me to get past the allergic reaction, but I recovered fully. I also returned to the faith of my boyhood, where I first trusted the Lord. I believed in God, and I certainly believed in heaven. Everything changed in my life, and I no longer smoked a quarter-ounce of marijuana daily. I never touched cocaine again.

Years have passed since my heavenly trip, but I still can't wait to go back to heaven. I'm not depressed or afraid. I know where I'm going when I leave this life—I'll go home. Forever.

Cecil Murphey and Twila Belk

Scott Hutcheson is an ordained minister and evangelist for Seen Heaven Ministries. Contact Scott for speaking engagements at 812-568-5103 or SHMinistries777@yahoo.com. Penny Shreve has been involved in journalism since she was 15 years old and spent 35 years working in the community newspaper field. In 2012 she became the publisher of the *Wayne County Outlook*, a local news/feature magazine in Illinois.

Heaven IS FOR REAL:
The Story of Colton Burpo

Normally a vibrant and active almost-four-year-old boy, Colton Burpo lay nearly lifeless as he awaited emergency surgery for a misdiagnosed ruptured appendix. Poison had infected his body for five days, and the doctor didn't offer any hope. His father, Todd, a Wesleyan pastor, recognized the shadow of death on his little boy. He had seen it many times during visits to hospitals, nursing homes and hospice patients.

After Colton was taken to surgery, Todd went to a room by himself. As a father, and especially as a pastor, he wanted to be strong in front of everyone else. But when he was alone, he opened his heart to God.

He'd recently endured one series of bad events after another, and he was discouraged. "After all I've gone through and all I've done for You, and now You're going to take my son?" he cried out. "Is this how You treat Your pastors?" He questioned whether he wanted to continue serving God.

He paced the room and poured out his pent-up feelings for about a quarter of an hour. Then he dried his eyes and went to see his wife, Sonja, who sat in the waiting room. She had been praying, and between prayers she called friends and family members.

Todd called his secretary and asked her to activate the prayer chain. They were desperate and needed the strength of others to get them through the ordeal.

Ninety minutes passed before a nurse came to them. She said Colton was in recovery and was screaming for his dad. That news gave Todd and Sonja hope. They were allowed to see their son. Even though Colton was pale and had dark rings circling his eyes, he was alert and alive. He was glad to see his parents, and they were overjoyed to be with him.

While Sonja was away from the room filling out paperwork, Colton looked up at his dad and said, "Do you know I almost died?" Todd assumed he had heard the medical staff say that, because he and Sonja had been careful not to mention his condition in front of him.

Todd didn't pursue the conversation further until four months later on a road trip with the family. During that trip, Colton said things that caught his parents' attention.

As they passed the turnoff for the hospital where his surgery happened, Todd teased Colton that he could go back.

"Do you remember the hospital?" Sonja asked.

"Yes, Mommy, I remember. That's where the angels sang to me."

When Todd and Sonja wanted to know more, Colton said, "Jesus had the angels sing to me because I was scared. They made me feel better."

Intrigued by his mention of Jesus, Todd continued to ask questions. Colton claimed that while the angels sang, he sat on Jesus' lap.

"Where were you when you saw Jesus?"

"At the hospital."

Although his parents were unsure that Colton knew what he was talking about, he proved it by saying that while he was with Jesus, he saw his dad praying alone in a little room, and his mom was in another room talking on the phone. "How did you know what we were doing?" Todd asked.

Colton matter-of-factly said that he went out of his body and looked down on them while the doctor operated on him.

Pieces of new information surfaced in subsequent days and months—information that shocked his parents. Colton revealed things he shouldn't have known at such a young age. He said that Jesus wore white robes with a purple sash. He also mentioned that Jesus had markers.

"What do you mean by markers?" Colton's dad asked. "Where were they?"

Colton pointed to his hands at the palms and bent over and touched the tops of his feet. "They were red."

Some time later while traveling with his father, Colton asked, "Did you have a grandpa named Pop?"

Todd said he had, and Colton talked about how Todd used to play with Pop, worked on the farm with him, and shot guns with him. Pop had played a significant role in Todd's life as a child, but he had died in an automobile accident before Todd turned seven.

"He's really nice," Colton said.

"How do you know that?" his dad asked.

Colton recounted his meeting with Pop in heaven. Later, the boy was able to point to his grandfather in pictures.

Another time, while Colton's mom was busy paying bills, he came up to her and said that he had two sisters. She didn't pay attention at first, so he repeated it several times. Colton's words didn't make sense, because he had only one sister. Finally, she asked what he was talking about.

"You had a baby die in your tummy."

Sonja stared at him, amazed. She had miscarried, but Colton couldn't have known that. "She looked like Cassie [his sister]," he said and went on to describe her. "When she saw me, she came up and hugged me." Sonja tried to absorb what Colton was saying to her. Not even she had known her miscarried baby was a girl.

He told his mother that his sister was waiting for them to come to heaven.

Over time, Colton brought up many fascinating things. He talked about meeting John the Baptist—Jesus' cousin—and that Jesus had a horse. He saw many beautiful colors and angels. He also mentioned the throne room of God. He described how big God was and told of God's great love. When he talked about all the people he saw, he said, "Nobody was wearing glasses. Nobody was old."

After learning so many wonderful details about Colton's trip to heaven, Todd was eager to know something. "Did you want to come back?"

"I wanted to stay, but Jesus told me I had to go back. He said he was answering my dad's prayer."

Todd thought back to that day and that prayer—his meltdown with God—and marveled at Jesus' goodness.

Colton's experience left him with an important message to share: "Heaven is for real, and you're going to like it."[80]

Roll Call

(RUSSELL TIDD SR. WITH BARBIE PORTER)

January 1995 was the first time I heard a voice from a distance call my name. Once a week, I'd hear the same voice, in the same tone, simply call out, "Tidd?" Each week the call, which only my ears could hear, became a little louder. I didn't know what it meant or why. I only knew I couldn't stop it.

In late February of that same year I became ill, and my doctor gave me a grim diagnosis. I had cancer. The good news was it was carcinoma and completely operable at that stage. However, they also had to remove my left kidney.

March 8 was the surgery date. As I lay on the gurney ready to be wheeled into the operating room, friends and family surrounded me. We had a word of prayer, and after saying amen, I began to sing "Shall We Gather at the River?" I was so filled with peace that I was still singing as they wheeled me down the hall. The doctor and staff commented how they had never seen a patient so content before major surgery.

The next thing I remember, I was walking up steps. I climbed until I arrived at a stunning gate made of exquisite pearl. After entering, I met one who called himself Gabriel. He welcomed me and instructed that when I heard my name, I was simply to say, "Here, sir."

He began walking, and I followed. I was awestruck by the picturesque beauty that lay before me—everything glistened, colors were brilliant, and nearly everything was transparent, even me. Accidentally, I stepped on a rose. When I saw that I had crushed it, I started to cry, for it was so lovely.

"Don't worry," Gabriel said. "Just lift your foot." When I did, the rose sprung back to the way it had been.

We came to a magnificent banquet table. It was so long I couldn't see an end in either direction. Where we stopped, my gaze fell on a placard at a place setting. Its golden letters spelled out "Russell Dean Tidd."

Just then, I heard a thunderous voice. "Tidd?" It was the same voice I had heard since the beginning of January. I knew it was a roll call. I had to answer. Just then someone else spoke up, "Here, sir." Looking across the table, there stood my cousin Paul Tidd. A wide smile stretched across his face. He nodded toward me.

Gabriel motioned me on. As we continued walking, something caught my attention. It seemed so out of place. It was a large, pearlescent door, arched high at the top with a fiery red opening. Even from a great distance I felt a fierce heat and a foul stench came from it. We walked in solemn silence until we passed it.

We came to an area that shone so brightly I couldn't see ahead, and yet I knew I was standing before a throne. I bowed.

A voice like thunder said, "Well done. Continue on."

Gabriel continued to lead the way until we entered a large room. It contained only an enormous scroll. I began to read. As soon as I finished reading, he said, "Go tell the people what you have seen and heard."

"How can I remember all this? I have no pen or paper."

"The Holy Spirit will bring it to your remembrance."

Then it was time to leave.

I awakened, lying in a hospital bed hooked up to beeping and whirring machines. My wife and children were at my bedside. The surgery had gone well. They had removed all the cancer, and they told me I would fully recover.

Five days later, I went home. For the next five days I cried constantly as I shared my heavenly experience with anyone who would listen. I cried because I didn't want anyone to miss going to that special place. I cried because I didn't want anyone to go to the other place of which I had caught only a glimpse.

And I cried because I missed that place.

That was nearly 20 years ago, and I still cry when I tell about that heavenly encounter. But, now I cry mostly because, at age 75, with each passing day, I get nearer to answering, "Here, sir! This time, I'll stay.

Russell Tidd Sr. has been a minister since 1966. He has been married to his wife, Alma, for 54 years. The joy of his life is preaching, teaching and praying for others. Barbie Porter is an award-winning journalist, the author of *The Legend of the Christmas Kiss*, co-coordinator for the Secret Pavilion Women's Conference, Faculty Chair for Kentucky Christian Writers Conference, and a missionary. She is currently compiling her book *This Little Church*.

Reprise
(PHIL LEFTWICH)

Bobby, the nephew of musician George "Fuzzy" Ballard, called me and asked if I would come to the ER to say a final prayer for his uncle.

When I got there, Bobby acted as if he'd seen a ghost.

Fuzzy Ballard was sitting upright on the gurney in the last cubicle of the emergency room where the dead await the hearse. He thrashed wildly with the sheet that covered him from head to toe. Like Lazarus peeling away the wrappings of death and walking from his tomb, Fuzzy had returned from the dead.

"Sit still, Fuzzy, and let me help you," I said. I helped untangle him from the sheet covering his head.

Bobby, who was a hospital orderly, hurried to get help. I knew doctors and nurses would descend on him quickly. Scientific shock would pervade their probing. The bruises on his chest from the defibrillation paddles had already begun to turn purple.

"What happened?" I asked. Death was no stranger to me, but Fuzzy had been *dead* for more than an hour.

"Why'd you bring me back here?" he asked in a weak voice as he coughed his way back among the living.

"Do you know where you are?"

"Of course I do. I'm back in the hospital." Tears trickled through the wrinkles that lined his face, dampening his thin, gray beard. His sighs turned to moans of pain and sadness.

"I was there!"

"Where?"

"On the other side."

"The other side?"

"Heaven!"

By then a crowd surrounded us. I raised my hand in a gesture for them to wait before they began shaking their heads in disbelief.

"You went to heaven," I said. "What was it like?"

"I looked down and saw myself lying on the table," he said. "It was like I was floating in the air."

"And?"

"I went through a dark tunnel toward a bright light. I was scared. I thought I was going to hell."

I'd heard similar accounts and read of such events, but I'd never spoken with someone who made it through to the other side.

"He was right there," Fuzzy said in a voice choked with longing.

"Who was there?"

"Jesus!"

"Jesus?" I replied.

"You hard of hearing?" he said in an irritated voice I knew from the many hours we had spent together. "Why did you bring me back here?"

The medical staff pushed me aside.

I squeezed his hand and told him I'd see him later. I knew they would take awhile. They would also have to redo their paperwork and tear up the death certificate.

Fuzzy was more stubborn than they imagined. In the late afternoon, he asked for his clothes and checked himself out. "I'm through with you people," he told them. "You're not sticking me with anything else, including any more bills!"

I drove Fuzzy home, got him settled into his reclining chair, and sat across from him. I listened, and he was his normal cantankerous self.

"I'd give my right arm for a drink," he said. Fuzzy had given up the hard stuff about a year earlier when he learned he was dying of lung cancer.

The toll of booze, bars, smoky rooms and fast women had wrecked his life as a jazz musician. He had been good in his day. I'd heard the solo riffs of his baritone sax from the worn vinyl of his recordings with Tommy Dorsey, Harry James and Cincinnati Radio Orchestra. He had come home to the mountains of West Virginia to die.

"It was beyond anything I could imagine."

I smiled, remembering Fuzzy's talks about his doubts of getting to heaven. The first time we met was in the chapel of the church I served.

"I'm nuthin' much now," he had told me, "but a beat-up old sinner in need of prayer and forgiveness."

Then a quick trip to heaven granted him the certainty of God's unconditional love. "You are my beloved son," Jesus had told him. "Heaven waits for you, but not yet."

"I've got stuff left to do here," Fuzzy said, staring out the window at the twilight. "He told me so."

The "stuff" of which Jesus spoke was reconciling with his two estranged daughters, setting his business affairs in order, and making peace with himself.

A couple of weeks before he died, Fuzzy gently knocked on my office door. Badly out of breath from climbing the stairs, he handed me an oil painting titled *The White Church*. It was signed G. W. Ballard and dated 11-81. A handwritten note stuck to the back with Scotch tape read, "Painted for my good friend." That painting has hung on my study wall everywhere I've gone as a reminder that heaven is real, even for those who doubt.

When my faith is weak and God seems distant, I study Fuzzy's painting and remember him. Heaven was a fact for him, because he'd been there. Perhaps he came back to assure some of us that we could take his word for it. Maybe we were also a part of his *unfinished business*—a *reprise* of a tune only partially played before.

In the painting, I see a boat peacefully anchored on a bayou, its sails neatly folded. A coal camp occupies a spit of land to the left. In the middle stands a white church, its reflection captured timelessly in the stillness of the water. When I listen, I imagine the reedy voice of a baritone sax—raspy, deep and blue. The painting is a composite of Fuzzy's life—a life often lived in deep despair, other times loud and brassy, but now a life of abundance. Far off, a bridge merges into the golden hues of a tranquil evening sky.

Beyond lies the horizon. Sunset. Home.

Phil Leftwich is a retired minister in the Presbyterian Church (U.S.A.). He is the author of numerous articles; a collection of poetry; *Watermarks,* a novel; *Will Henry's Angels;* and he is co-author with Vii Maurice of *Conversations with Vii Aboard Papa Being's Big Waters Tour Bus: The Spiritual Journey of Recovery of a Sexually Abused Child.* See www.philleftwich.com.

It's Not Time Yet
(Marie Weaver)

I was 20 years old when my migraine headaches began. Going out to the park or to the beach on a sunny day was impossible. The sun and heat set off such an unbearable headache I'd end up in bed with my head deeply buried under my pillow.

My headaches became more frequent and debilitating. The pain moved from my back, up my neck, over my head, and down my forehead.

The only comfortable place was my dark bedroom, and light became my enemy. I couldn't leave the house without pain. I felt a constant, unbearable throbbing. The doctor explained I had what appeared to be a seizure, which sent me staring blankly into space.

What is happening to my body? I feel miserable all the time.

I lost my job. Over-the-counter medicines no longer helped. The decision to be admitted to the hospital was met with fear as well as the hope that we were finally going to figure out a way to get rid of the agony.

The doctor prescribed a strong pain medicine.

The next thing I remember, someone walked up to me and said, "Come, sit." He took my hand. His love radiated to me, causing me to feel warm, relaxed and cared for. We sat on a beautiful, dark-oak park bench. It was just the right size for two.

We sat next to each other for a few minutes. I stared ahead because the view was breathtaking.

I faced a beautiful meadow. There was a light breeze, and I could see the soft graceful wave of silver-green grass. Just beyond the meadow, a flowing brook cut through the soft earth, and a footbridge spanned the stream.

An amazing brilliance of light was right near me. I loved it all, and I sensed it was for me. People stood on the other side of the brook. I recognized several of them—loved ones who had gone on before me. They appeared to be waiting for me.

My grandmother beckoned, reaching out her hand and calling, "Come, come on."

Other family members and friends also motioned for me to join them. As they stretched their hands toward me, I longed to go to them. I tried to move, but the one beside me wouldn't let go of my hand.

"It's not time yet."

"I want to stay in this lovely place—to cross over and be with them."

"No, not yet. You have to go back."

The next conscious moment I was back in my bed. My body shook, and I began to cry. I was scared and happy at the same time. Part of me was glad to be back, and the other part wanted to re-experience that overwhelming love.

Then I realized what had happened: I'd been sitting with Jesus. We'd been together in the most beautiful place I'd ever seen. I kept saying to myself, "I met Jesus. I met Jesus face-to-face!"

It wasn't time for me to go. I had a loving husband and two wonderful children. My job wasn't complete. My eyes opened to my husband's blue eyes staring at me. The desire to live and care for my family grew stronger as I looked into his eyes.

God had given me another chance to grow in obedience toward Him. Since this experience, my migraine headaches have been better controlled. I'm grateful every day that God has made my life more fulfilling and exciting. I opened up my life to live and be guided by Him.

I look forward to the day when I'll hear His words, "Yes, come now."

Marie Weaver is a writer of Christian devotions and children's books; speaker at special events for churches and other organizations. See www.mariesdevotions.wordpress.com and www.christiandevotions.us.

THE *Little Boy* WHO WENT TO HEAVEN:
The Story of Alex Malarkey

Kevin Malarkey pulled his Honda Civic to a stop and looked both ways for oncoming traffic. He saw no cars for at least a quarter of a mile. He was on the phone with his wife, Beth, who had given birth to their fourth child two days earlier. He wanted her to know that he and their six-year-old son, Alex, were on the way home from church. The road was still unfamiliar to him because his family had recently moved to the rural town of Huntsville, Ohio.

Alex asked a question, and Kevin glanced at him before he slowly turned his car into the intersection. Kevin couldn't see the car that was approaching in a dip of the road. At 55 miles per hour, the other vehicle broadsided the passenger side and bent the door all the way into the gearshift. The impact ejected Kevin 50 feet from the car. He landed, unconscious, on the side of the road. Alex remained inside the damaged car.

After Kevin regained awareness, he hurried to the car. Alex's head hung abnormally. He didn't move; he wasn't breathing.

I've killed my son.

A friend who came on the accident scene heard what happened and said, "I believe Alex has gone to be with Jesus."

Minutes later, paramedics took Kevin to the local hospital in an ambulance and a helicopter transported a still-alive Alex to Nationwide Children's Hospital in Columbus, Ohio. Except for a scratch on his hip, the crash left Kevin unscathed—a surprise to doctors and people who had seen the damage. After his release, he went to the children's hospital to find out about his son. Beth met him at the hospital. Although unable to see their son, a doctor showed them an MRI and pointed out his concern. "If he survives, he'll never move below his neck. He'll never breathe on his own. He'll never speak. He'll never eat. It's likely he'll have massive brain damage."

The medical term for Alex's diagnosis was occipital C1 disassociation. That is, he had an internal decapitation—his head and spinal column were no longer attached.

Beth couldn't accept the doctor's report. "You're wrong," she said. "He'll be fine. He'll live and his life will affect thousands of people."

To the surprise of the medical staff, within days Alex's head reattached itself on its own—a medical miracle.

About a month after the accident, specialists planned to operate on two separated vertebrae. They took one more X-ray the morning of surgery.

"We're not going to operate on your son," the doctor told them.

Startled, Kevin asked, "Why not?"

"The vertebrae are back where they belong. We don't know what happened."

Alex came out of his coma after two months. Soon he was smiling and laughing at his younger brother who performed crazy antics at his bedside. The boy still couldn't speak, so they developed a form of communication using mouth signals and facial gestures.

After another month, Alex began to talk. Over time, he shared tidbits of what he had experienced during his time in a coma. He described in detail what happened at the accident scene, including what the firefighters said and the color of clothing they wore. He also told them about things that happened in the hospital while he was unconscious.

"I was really glad when they took you away in the ambulance, Daddy."

"How did you know I was in an ambulance? You were in a helicopter."

"I didn't see you from the helicopter. I saw you from heaven."

Kevin, a trained psychologist, was naturally skeptical. Yet the more Alex revealed, the more he was convinced that his son had spoken the truth. He realized Alex couldn't have made up the stories he told.

Alex talked about seeing angels. At different times, he said, they had been in the room with him. He also said, "Five angels took you out of the car. Four of them carried your body and a fifth one held your head. They set you on the side of the road." The same five angels were with Alex in heaven. "They comforted me."

Alex also said he saw the doctors working on his body. "I wasn't afraid. I was safe because Jesus was with me." He heard the doctors say many bad things about his condition. "They didn't think I would live." He talked about a bolt they attached to his head. (It was a pressure monitor to gauge brain swelling.) He didn't have it when he came out of the coma, further confirming his out-of-body experience.

Alex said that while he was in heaven, he talked with Jesus and the angels. To him, the gates of heaven looked like fish scales. He saw the throne of God and loved the powerful music. "Heaven is God's palace. Everything about it is perfect—beyond words."

God allowed Alex to visit heaven and sent him back to earth to a quadriplegic body, and he is that way today. Yet Alex has spiritual insight and wisdom beyond that of many adults. He wants people to know the truth and have the expectation of heaven when they die. Someday, Alex says, he'd like to be a missionary.

His favorite word to describe heaven is *amazing*. He says, "Heaven is amazing. Heaven is what here was supposed to be."

The day he looks forward to most is the day he returns to that amazing place. "That's home, this isn't. I can't wait to go back."[81]

Not Yet

(LOUISE LANKFORD-DUNLAP)

Being a normal 44-year-old woman with few health problems up to that time, it was a shock to awaken early Mother's Day morning, 1976, feeling weak, nauseated and vomiting a large amount of blood every few minutes.

Scared and alarmed, my husband and I sped to the hospital, six miles away. Doctors there were unable to stop the vomiting or make a diagnosis, so they recommended sending me to Oregon Health and Sciences University in Portland (OHSU). They transported me by ambulance. I continued to grow weaker during the 35-mile ride.

After extensive tests and blood transfusions, in the early hours of Monday morning I underwent exploratory surgery as doctors searched for the source of the bleeding. With so much blood loss—transfusions were unable to keep up—I slipped into unconsciousness.

"We're losing her! Code blue! Code blue!" The doctor shouted into the intercom as I lay on the operating table.

The doctor's voice and face faded, and I felt myself leaving my body. Immediately I entered a frightening dark tunnel. The darkness seemed to have hands that squeezed the life out of me. I was a Christian and a minister, and yet I was troubled. Had I been wrong all these years? Did this mean I was lost?

I burst forth into a light at the end of the tunnel that was more brilliant and brighter than I'd ever seen. It dispelled the darkness and flooded everything with a sweet, peaceful fragrance. A wonderful calming assurance washed over me and drove away my fear.

I had read in the Bible that light was a symbol of God; now I was gazing upon it with excitement and perfect sight. Beyond doubt, this was Jesus, the bright and morning Star.

I saw no form or face, no figure, no streets of gold or heavenly scenes much like what others have described. I saw nothing but that penetrating, resplendent light. That was enough.

The joyful anticipation at being drawn to that light is unrivaled and defies description. Getting closer, I expected at any moment to be with Jesus in heaven.

"Jesus, let me come to You, now."

The thought of leaving my loved ones interrupted my sense of rapture. After that thought, I felt myself being pulled away from the light, back into mortality. Disappointed, I cried out, "Not yet!"

Unknown to me, my family and many members of our congregation had gathered at the hospital for an all-night prayer vigil. "Don't take her, Lord, we need her," they prayed.

During the night, my husband opened his Bible to Psalm 46:5. Although it speaks of Jerusalem, he claimed that promise for me and believed I would live: "God will help her at the break of day" (*NIV*). After I re-entered my body and opened my eyes, the doctor welcomed me with a smile. "You're back! We've found the source of the bleeding and made the repair. You'll soon be fine," he assured me.

I stared at him, hardly able to take in what he was saying.

"You must have swallowed a sharp object; something that severed an artery just below your esophagus. It could have been a piece of eggshell or a nut hull. We've never had a case like this before. With every heartbeat, blood was being pumped into your stomach with barely enough left to keep you alive."

I was alive—and I've lived more than 37 years since that event. Now I understand; God answered the prayers of the congregation that night and said *not yet* to my prayer. He sent me back to continue the work He had in mind for me.

With that experience I gained a lasting and comforting perspective about dying. Death for the redeemed child of God is just a short dark passage into the presence of God and is nothing to be feared.

Louise Lankford-Dunlap is an 81-year-old widow. After more than 50 years in ministry with her husband, she has transitioned from pulpit to print with short inspirational articles, songs and poetry published in books and magazines (loudnherd@aol.com).

The Day I Died

(Pat Laye)

The day I died, I was a normal, happy 18-year-old college student stressing over final semester exams. One minute I was dashing down the dormitory corridor toward the communal bathroom and the next I was in a long, dark tunnel with a blazing white light at the other end.

It happened on a cold Monday morning during exam week. When I attended college, the women's dormitories were on one end of the campus and the men's housing on the far end—as far away from the women as possible.

Our dorms had up to three students to a room, and we had none of the luxuries known today such as private bathrooms or suites with bathrooms. We shared one bathroom area on each floor with 10 showers, 10 toilet stalls, and 10 sinks with lighted mirrors for putting on makeup.

I liked to set my clock for 6:45 to get to the bathroom ahead of the rush, as most of the other women, including my roommate, arose around 7:00 or later. That morning, however, I overslept. I had studied late into the night for an especially hard exam in my weakest subject, algebra. Making a high grade was imperative to keeping my scholarship.

When I woke up and discovered that I had overslept, I grabbed my clothes and dashed down the hall to the bathroom. I heard the other students laughing and chattering as I entered the room.

Just then, I went into a dark area and stood at one end of a tunnel. Intuitively, I knew the tunnel led to heaven. I was walking toward heaven. I wasn't scared; I felt excited. I had been a Christian since I was 12 years old. I felt that my going to heaven was the reward for having lived the best life I could. I wanted to reach the bright blinding light at the end of the tunnel, and I continued walking up through space.

A loud, deep voice called out, "Go back!"

I didn't want to go back. I kept on walking toward the bright light.

"Go back!"

I stopped, even though I didn't understand why I shouldn't continue to walk toward the light. "Why should I go back? I want to enter heaven."

The voice sounded softer and kinder, "Go back."

This time I listened, turned and started down the long, dark tunnel utterly mystified because the urge to go forward was so powerful.

Just then, I heard people talking in excited tones. I thought I was losing my mind. First I had been sent back from heaven, and now I was hearing human voices.

What's wrong with me?

I opened my eyes and stared at the doctor and nurses hovering over me. They had shocked my heart, and it was beating rhythmically again.

I later learned exactly what had happened to me. As I entered the bathroom my heart began beating too fast and erratically. Then it simply stopped.

I fell to the floor, which I didn't remember, and the others in the bathroom assumed I had just fainted.

However, several of those students were physical education majors and nursing majors. They knelt down to check on me, and no one could get a pulse. One student ran to the dorm mother's room to telephone for an ambulance while the other students gave me CPR.

Had I not overslept and been alone in the bathroom, or if I had a private bathroom as dorms do today, I probably wouldn't still be alive.

Since that was a university, the campus had a hospital close by, and the paramedics were on site within three minutes. They took over the CPR and rushed me to the ER, where the medical staff was waiting.

My parents, who lived 350 miles away, were told that I was critical and might not live until they arrived. They were busy packing when the second call arrived that my heart was again beating on its own. Even so, they were advised to come anyway, which they did.

After several days in the hospital, doctors couldn't determine exactly why my heart had stopped. The only issue they could find was a slight thickening of one of my heart valves. They thought perhaps the stress of final exams, the sudden erratic beating of my heart, and the racing down the hallway might have triggered the problem.

"I know that I heard God speaking to me," I told the examining doctor.

He smiled and patted my arm. But I *knew* what I had heard and experienced.

I strongly believed God sent me back to earth for some purpose. Since then I've heard of others who had similar experiences, which reinforces my strong belief in heaven. Many times through the years, I've shared my story with others. I believe God gave me a second chance, and I've tried to encourage others through my writing and in work as a school social worker.

Pat Laye writes inspirational stories for the Chicken Soup books, *Guideposts* and other publications. She is also the author of seven Regency novels.

90 Minutes IN HEAVEN:
The Story of Don Piper

Bad weather caused the Baptist General Convention of Texas conference to end earlier than normal on a Wednesday morning in January 1989. Don Piper was relieved, because that would give him the extra time to prepare for his midweek service at church. The senior minister was out of the country and Don was in charge.

Rather than travel his normal way home, he decided to take a different route. A citation he had received three weeks earlier for not wearing a seatbelt lay on the seat beside him, and reminded him to buckle up.

Cecil Murphey and Twila Belk

Within ten minutes he drove onto a narrow bridge spanning Lake Livingstone. Before Don reached the other end, an 18-wheeler, owned by the Texas Department of Corrections, came toward him, crossed the center line, and hit Don's red Ford head-on. Because of the rate of speed the truck traveled, all nine wheels on the driver's side passed over Don's car, crushing it and leaving it sandwiched between the bridge railing and the tractor trailer.

Four different sets of emergency medical technicians (EMTs) at the accident site conducted tests on Don. They checked for a heartbeat using a portable EKG, and examined Don with other equipment. All tests pointed to the same answer: He was dead.

They covered the wrecked Ford with a waterproof tarp with Don still pinned inside and called for the Jaws of Life to extricate his body from the smashed car. They kept the traffic tied up while they waited for an official to pronounce him dead (as required in Texas).

The instant Don took his last breath on earth, he appeared in perfect condition at heaven's gate where a breathtaking buffet of senses awaited him. A feeling of abiding love enveloped him. Joy permeated the atmosphere. The textures, dazzling colors, sights and sounds surrounding him defied human explanation. Everything glowed with a brilliant light.

A group of people, all of whom he recognized, welcomed him. Those who greeted him were long-dead relatives as well as friends who had died in high school, teachers and people he had known for a long time. Some he hadn't seen in at least 20 years. His dearly loved grandfather was the first person. Don had been with him when he died of a heart attack, and he rejoiced in seeing his grandfather again happy and whole.

Everyone greeted Don with smiles and hugs. Their faces and body language exuded happiness and serenity. More important, they were fully alive. Love emanated from every person surrounding him. As he would realize later, each one of his greeters had played a spiritually significant role in his life.

Those he knew who once had osteoporosis or heart conditions, and others who had lost teeth or hair, all looked incredibly beautiful and perfect. The people he encountered were the same age as when he last saw them, yet age had no meaning because time was irrelevant.

A looming, pearlescent gate—translucent and shimmering—rose above them in the background. The iridescent, shimmering edifice was astonishingly beautiful. Intense brightness radiating from there was even more brilliant than what he had already seen.

As his celestial welcoming committee walked with him toward the gate, the light's intensity increased. With each step Don took, the splendor became stronger in magnitude, and Don sensed that he was being ushered into the presence of God.

The closer Don got to the gate, the more he became aware of heavenly music—an awesome choir rendering never-ending songs of praise and worship, all directed toward God. "Hallelujah!" "Praise to the King!" "Glory to God!" Thousands of joyous songs and melodies filled the air, yet there was no chaos. He could distinguish each song individually. The glorious music flowed as if sung with one voice, and it reverberated through him. He had never before experienced such great joy and peace.

Don continued toward the portal to heaven and paused. He looked inside and stared at streets paved with pure gold. Everything—the lights, the colors, the sights, the sounds—became even more vivid, and the beauty of the place enraptured him.

Completely enamored with all he experienced, Don didn't think of those he had left behind. He realized his family members would one day join him there. He stepped forward to enter, and just as suddenly as his heavenly journey began, it ended.

He was back in his crushed red Ford, covered with a tarp, and weakly singing "What a Friend We Have in Jesus."

While Don delighted in the glories of heaven, he was oblivious to the situation on earth.

⊰⊹⊱

Pastor Dick Onarecker and his wife, Anita, had attended the same conference as Don, even though they hadn't known each other and didn't meet that day. The Onareckers were behind Don and by the time they reached the bridge, the accident had happened and traffic had backed up a long way.

Dick got out of his car, walked to the scene, and talked with a police officer. "I'm a minister. Can I pray with anyone?"

The officer said no. He explained that one man was dead and still inside the car.

Dick pointed to Don's car and said, "What about the person in that car?"

"That man is deceased," the officer said.

Dick felt an overpowering urge to pray for the dead man. It made no sense to him theologically—he didn't pray for dead people—yet he couldn't shake the compelling feeling to pray for him. He told the officers he needed to pray with Don.

"Sir, you don't understand. He's dead," one police officer said. "And he's been that way for a long time."

Dick persisted, but the officer still refused.

Dick said that if they wouldn't let him pray for the man inside the car, he would lie down on the middle of the bridge. "And you'll have to run over me."

The officer relented, but not without warning him about what he'd encounter—an awful site and a mangled body, with blood and glass everywhere.

Dick, who had served in Vietnam, wasn't concerned. He knelt down and crawled under the tarp, laid his hands on Don's lifeless body, and began to pray.

The steering wheel had impaled Don's chest and the roof had crushed his head. The dashboard smashed his left leg, and his limbs were separated and barely hanging on to his body.

The gruesome site only reinforced how strange it was for Dick to pray. Yet he did—and boldly. He prayed specifically for Don's survival and that there would be no internal injuries and no brain damage.

Dick interspersed hymns with his prayers. As he sang "What a Friend We Have in Jesus," a weak voice harmonized with his. Dick left the car in a hurry.

It was at least 90 minutes after the collision.

Surgeons were certain, because of earlier testing at the accident site, that even though Don had survived, he certainly would have brain damage and internal injuries. Subsequent testing at the Level One Trauma Center in Houston, however, showed no brain damage and no internal injuries.

The news baffled medical personnel. It was a miracle not explainable by medical technology.

Don has since undergone 34 surgeries, and he still suffers pain from his massive injuries and the multiple surgeries to correct them.

He didn't speak of his sacred secret for a long time because it was such a personal thing. Now his life-changing messages offer countless others a chance for a meaningful, hope-filled life.[82]

PART 2

QUESTIONS ABOUT
Heaven

What Does the Bible Mean by "Heaven"?

When we try to figure out what the Bible says about heaven, we need to remind ourselves that we're probably asking questions that didn't concern believers in the first century. Those questions evolved after Christianity became the official religion of the Roman Empire. Jeffry Burton Russell states this well:

> No single view of heaven exists in the New Testament, which left many questions unresolved and open to debate in succeeding centuries. The Epistles and gospels say little about a celestial paradise, because the earliest Christian writers were expecting the imminent return of Christ and the end of the world. . . . At the endtime, Christ would unite Jew and Gentile, circumcised and uncircumcised, in the realized Kingdom of God or Kingdom of Heaven.[1]

The *New International Version* lists 422 entries for "heaven" or "heavens" with a variety of meanings, so we have to determine from the context what the writers meant. The most frequently used Hebrew word for heaven in the Old Testament is *samayim* (the heights), which refers to the atmosphere just above the earth. The ancients pictured the world as a three-tiered structure with the place of dead at the bottom, earth in the middle, and heaven above.

For us, heaven is:

· The abode or dwelling place of God and the angels;
· The final destination of all who trust in Jesus Christ;
· The skies above the earth;
· The abode of God;
· A synonym for God's will;
· The capital of God's kingdom; and

• The eternal abode of Christians after the resurrection of all believers.

Several times in the Bible, we read of people looking toward heaven. In Acts 1:9-10, we read that after Jesus' resurrection, "He was taken up into a cloud while they were watching, and they could no longer see him. As they strained to see him rising into heaven, two white-robed men suddenly stood among them. 'Men of Galilee,' they said . . . 'Jesus has been taken from you into heaven, but someday he will return from heaven in the same way you saw him go!' "

Ancient Hebrew had no word for the "universe." The frequent references to heaven express the idea by the term "heaven" and "earth":

• "Is there any god in heaven or on earth who can perform such great and mighty deeds as you do?" (Deut. 3:24)

• "So remember this and keep it firmly in mind: the LORD is God both in heaven and on earth and there is no other." (Deut. 4:39)

• "Look, the highest heavens and the earth and everything in it all belong to the LORD your God." (Deut. 10:14)

The Hebrews believed God was always present and omnipresent, but that heaven was His special place. David said, "Listen to me, my fellow Israelites, my people. I had it in my heart to build a house as a place of rest for the ark of the covenant of the LORD, for the footstool of our God" (1 Chron. 28:2, *NIV*). Isaiah wrote, "This is what the LORD says: 'Heaven is my throne and the earth is my footstool' " (Isa. 66:1).

New Testament writers use this image several times. In the Sermon on the Mount, when Jesus taught against making vows, He urged, "Do not say, 'By Heaven!' Because heaven is God's throne. And do not say, 'By the earth!' because the earth is his footstool" (Matt. 5:34-35). The New Testament uses *ouranos*, a Greek word that refers to the sky or to air:

- "In the beginning, Lord, you laid the foundation of the earth and made the heavens with your hands" (Heb. 1:10).

- "They deliberately forget that God made the heavens by the word of his command and he brought the earth out from the water and surrounded it with water" (2 Pet. 3:5).

In summary, heaven is much more than a place to spend eternity; it is also the place where God "dwells." We don't have to see as if we're viewing through a smoked glass, but it *is* where we can see God face-to-face. We also have the divine assurance, "God's home is now among his people! He will live with them, and they will be his people. God himself will be with them" (Rev. 21:3).

How Can We Explain Heaven?

The Bible doesn't address all our questions. We want specifics, but God has chosen to give us only general responses and, quite frequently, the statements appear in highly symbolic language.

When God tells us about heaven, it's similar to what we tell a pre-schooler who asks, "Where do babies come from?" The answer we give that child will certainly differ from what we would tell a teen. We give explanations that fit his or her ability to grasp. Doesn't it make sense to bear that concept in mind when it comes to our questions about eternal things?

In the questions and answers that follow in this book, we've chosen to remain silent when the Bible is silent. Too much of what we encounter in many contemporary writings stem from emotional responses or logical, rational arguments. These may be correct—or they may be mistaken. Only God knows.

When we learn the truth about heaven in heaven, the questions won't matter. Our attempt in this book is to avoid conjecture and guesswork about the unknown. We stand firmly on the biblical record, but we aren't willing to accept speculation as facts.

If we truly believe in a loving and benevolent God, can't we rest assured in His more-than-adequate provision for every need? Can't we admit that with our flawed and limited minds it's impossible for us to understand what God has prepared for those of us who love Him?

We take the position stated by the apostle Paul in 1 Corinthians 2:9, where, referring to Isaiah 64:4, he writes, "No eye has seen, no ear has heard and no mind has imagined what God has prepared for those who love him."

Cecil Murphey and Twila Belk

What Is Paradise? Is It Different from Heaven?

When the apostle Paul writes of his experience of going to the third heaven in 2 Corinthians 12, he uses the terms "third heaven" and "paradise" (Greek *paradeisos*) interchangeably: "I was caught up to the third heaven fourteen years ago.... I do know that I was caught up to paradise and heard things so astounding that they cannot be expressed in words, things no human is allowed to tell" (vv. 2,4).

Paradeisos is of Persian origin—the Septuagint uses it to translate the word *Eden* (Hebrew *edhen*).[2] The word means "an orchard of pleasure and fruits," a garden, pleasure ground, or simply an orchard. The Hebrew word *Edhen* appears three times in the Old Testament: (1) Song of Songs 4:13, (2) Ecclesiastes 2:5 (gardens), and (3) Nehemiah 2:8 (translated in various ways, although the *NLT* and *NIV* both use "forest").

Jesus uses the word only once when He says to the repentant thief, "I assure you, today you will be with me in paradise" (Luke 23:43).

If we ponder the word as used by both Jesus and Paul and think of the way first-century Christians would have reacted, the word "garden" or "orchard" would have held a powerful meaning for them. It would have made them think of the original Eden in the Bible—a perfect place where God provided for every need.

Jesus and Paul spoke in symbolic language to express the inexpressible—the ultimate joy and providence of God for believers. As Jeffrey Burton Russell says:

> Traditionally, heaven is a place, a sacred space. The sacredness of this space is expressed in metaphors of kingdom, garden, city, or celestial spheres. Jesus refers to it most often as a reign or kingdom, a metaphor of God's sovereignty over all that is. This is coupled with the imagery of God's throne in the center of heaven. Kingdom was the

most common metaphor in the Eastern tradition, city in the Western.

The garden is the most common metaphor. Its origin is in the Hebrew Bible: the garden of the earthly paradise at the beginning of the world. It was linked through the "garden enclosed" of the Hebrew Bible to the Greco-Roman images of . . . the "lovely place."[3]

Russell adds that the enclosed garden "is the original dwelling of Adam and Eve. The imagery closest to that of Genesis is orchard or wood."[4]

What's the Difference Between the Kingdom of God and the Kingdom of Heaven?

"The kingdom of God" and "the kingdom of heaven" probably mean the same thing, although some see the two terms as used differently.

Those who insist they are distinct usually follow the teachings that came from the notes of the *Scofield Reference Bible*, which dominated English-speaking Christian theology from its publication in 1909 until recent years, and which still are dominant among dispensational Christians. Scofield distinguished between the two terms and taught that the kingdom of God is chiefly inward and spiritual. He believed they have much in common, but that the terms will merge when Christ puts all things under His feet.

One way to express this is to say that the "kingdom of heaven . . . is the sphere of a profession which may be real or false," while the kingdom of God is inward and spiritual. People enter the kingdom of God only through the new birth (see John 3:3).[5]

The term "kingdom of God" occurs 68 times in 10 different biblical books, while the "kingdom of heaven" occurs 32 times— and *only* in the Gospel of Matthew. Most scholars assume Matthew used the term "heaven" because he was writing primarily to Jews, and it would have been the way they spoke and thought— they avoided using words for God.

The most obvious way to see that these two terms refer to the same thing is to compare Matthew's use of the word with Luke's, where both writers use the term to make the same point. One example is in Matthew 11:11 and Luke 7:28, which both refer to John the Baptist. Matthew says that the least person in the kingdom of *heaven* is greater than John, while Luke says the least person in the kingdom of *God* is greater.

For those who want to examine places where Mark and Luke use "the kingdom of God" while Matthew prefers "kingdom of heaven," compare these verses:

- Matthew 11:11-12 with Luke 7:28;
- Matthew 13:11 with Mark 4:11 and Luke 8:10;
- Matthew 13:24 with Mark 4:26;
- Matthew 13:31-32 with Mark 4:30-32 and Luke 13:18-19;
- Matthew 13:33 with Luke 13:20-21;
- Matthew 18:3-4 with Mark 10:14-15 and Luke 18:16-17;
- Matthew 22:2 with Luke 13:29.

In each instance, Matthew refers to the "kingdom of heaven," while Mark and Luke write of "the kingdom of God." Given this, the overwhelming view of biblical scholars is that the two terms refer to the same reality.

What Does the Bible Say About Death?

We can't talk about heaven without talking about the one event that sends us there: death.

When Don Piper, author of *90 Minutes in Heaven,* talks to someone who has lost a loved one, he often says, "I'm sorry for your temporary loss." That's an excellent way for us as believers to think about dying—an impermanent separation from our loved ones. For those who are disciples of Jesus Christ, death *is* transitory—even though we have a variety of understandings about what happens immediately after death.

From the human perspective, death means the end of personal life—life as we know it now. We also affirm that death is not the ultimate end, but is the one required action on a journey that leads to resurrection. All of us die, and except for those who will be alive on earth when Jesus returns, it's a universal experience.

But how should we look at death?

The biblical figures we find in the Old Testament certainly struggled with the issue. For them, the blessings of God meant a long life on earth, plenty of children, and fruitful lands. First Samuel 2:4-6, which is part of the prayer of Hannah, seems consistent with belief of that period: "The LORD gives both death and life."

At the beginning of Job's afflictions, he worshiped God and said, "I came naked from my mother's womb, and I will be naked when I leave. The LORD gave me what I had, and the LORD has taken it away. Praise the name of the LORD!" (Job 1:21).

In the Ten Commandments, God told the Israelites to honor their parents and added, "Then you will live a long, full life in the land the LORD your God is giving you" (Deut. 5:16).

Psalm 128 states the attitude of those who followed God before the coming of Jesus Christ:

How joyful are those who fear the LORD—all who follow his ways! You will enjoy the fruit of your labor. How joyful and prosperous you will be! Your wife will be like a fruitful grapevine, flourishing with your home. Your children will be like vigorous young olive trees as they sit around your table. That is the LORD's blessing for those who fear him. May the LORD continually bless you from Zion. May you see Jerusalem prosper as long as you live. May you live to enjoy your grandchildren. May Israel have peace!

Several times in the Old Testament, in translations such as the *King James Version,* we read that someone was "old and full of years." Modern versions translate the phrase "lived a long, full life" (see, for example, Job 42:17). The phrase refers to a life filled with the threefold blessings of prosperity, many children and a long life.

Sometimes ancients spoke of death as evil and something over which humans had no control. We find this in Psalm 89:48, where the psalmist writes, "No one can live forever; all will die. No one can escape the power of the grave." In one of David's songs of praise, he says that God saved him from death much like he saved him from his enemies: "The grave wrapped its ropes around me; death laid a trap in my path" (2 Sam. 22:6). David goes on to say that in his distress, he prayed and God set him free.

At other times, the authors of the Old Testament spoke about being gathered to their fathers, as we find in Genesis 49:33. This passage is translated in different ways, but the meaning is clear:

- "Gathered to his people" (*NIV*);
- "Joined his ancestors in death" (*NLT*);
- "Gathered to his people" (*KJV*).

Biblical authors commonly used *Sheol* to refer to the place of death. Sometimes this word has a neutral tone and simply means the grave as the destination of all humanity (see Gen. 37:35). However, it can also carry a more sinister tone (see Hos. 13:14). It can even refer to separation from the presence of God (see Isa. 38:10-11).

In Psalm 6:5, David writes that the dead can't praise God. Psalm 115:17 states they "go down to silence" (*NIV*) or "have gone into the silence of the grave" (*NLT*). Isaiah writes that they can't hope in God's faithfulness (see Isa. 38:18).

Although ancient Greeks thought of death as ascending to God, Hebrews saw *Sheol* as a descent. In Job 11:8, Zophar says to Job, "Such knowledge is higher than the heavens—and who are you? It is deeper than the underworld—what do you know?" David writes, "Let death stalk my enemies; let the grave [*Sheol*] swallow them alive" (Ps. 55:15). Proverbs 15:24 states, "The path of life leads upward for the wise to keep him from going down to the grave [*Sheol*]" (*NIV*).

In speaking against Babylon, Isaiah writes, "But you are brought down to the grave, to the depths of the pit" (Isa. 14:15, *NIV*). Ezekiel uses the same image of downwardness by using the image of the cedars of Lebanon: "No other trees so well-watered are ever to reach such a height; they are all destined for death, for the earth below, among mortal men, with those who go down to the pit" (Ezek. 31:14, *NIV*). Other similar references include Psalm 64:9 and Ezekiel 32:18.

In the Old Testament, we don't read fully developed ideas of an eternal, blissful place of heaven as we see in the New Testament. The authors often implied something beyond death, but little more, as the following passages reveal:

- "Should I [God] ransom them from the grave? Should I redeem them from death?" (Hos. 13:14)

- "For you will not leave my soul among the dead [*Sheol*] or allow your holy one to rot in the grave. You will show me the way of life, granting me the joy of your presence and the pleasures of living with you forever" (Ps. 16:10-11).

- "For your love for me is very great. You have rescued me from the depths of death [*Sheol*]" (Ps. 86:13).

These statements may refer to victory, or healing from a terminal illness, or some not-quite-defined life beyond death.

During and after the Jews' exile in Babylon, the hope for divine salvation for the righteous brought the issue to the front. The clearest note on the afterlife in the Old Testament appears in Daniel 12:2: "Many of those whose bodies lie dead and buried will rise up, some to everlasting life and some to shame and everlasting disgrace."

In the New Testament, the Christian hope of resurrection doesn't say that the earth gives back the dead, as if the action were a resuscitation of corpses who then return to earthly existence. Rather, resurrection signifies our elevation to a higher, perfected plane of existence—a time when we will experience complete fellowship with God and others.

Resurrection also signifies that we shall live in the new heavens and the new earth, or the New Jerusalem. As John states, "Then I saw a new heaven and a new earth, for the old heaven and the old earth had disappeared . . . And I saw the holy city, the New Jerusalem, coming down from God out of heaven like a bride beautifully dressed for her husband" (Rev. 21:1-2). John continues in this vein in Revelation 21–22, writing in symbolic language, but making it clear enough for readers to see the deep understanding of a life beyond human death.

The New Testament also makes it clear that God gives an earnest, or down payment, to assure of that future. "The Spirit is God's guarantee that he will give us the inheritance he promised and that he has purchased us to be his own people" (Eph. 1:14). The apostle Paul also makes this clear in Romans 8:23: "And we believers also groan, even though we have the Holy Spirit within us as a foretaste of future glory, for we long for our bodies to be released from sin and suffering. We, too, wait with eager hope for the day when God will give us our full rights as his adopted children, including the new bodies he has promised us."

What Will We Do in Heaven?

In heaven, surely our glorified or spiritual bodies will be active, and there's no reason to think our minds won't be used. Without the limitations of sin and disease, it seems reasonable that our minds will be even stronger and more useful.

Think of a new Eden—a return to the innocence and beauty of the original paradise that God created for the human race. Adam and Eve were to take care of the Garden and tend the animals. If we regain access to the "Tree of Life" (which is symbolic), it means that we will live forever.

Paul, preaching at Lystra, said that the nations had been allowed to go their own ways, "but [God] never left them without evidence of himself and his goodness. For instance, he sends you rain and good crops and gives you food and joyful hearts" (Acts 14:17). The argument of some is that if that were true among sinful, wayward souls, how much more God will abundantly give us in the new earth.

Some have appealed to Job 38–39, where God speaks of all the natural wonders and especially about the animals and birds. Those verses hint, some say, that God's new kingdom will include creaturely activity. Furthermore, physical activity seems consistent with everything God does for humanity. He put the couple in the Garden, and at the end of the sixth day of creation, we read:

> Then God blessed them and said, "Be fruitful and multiply. Fill the earth and govern it. Reign over the fish in the sea, the birds in the sky and all the animals that scurry along the ground." Then God said, "Look! I have given you every seed-bearing plant throughout the earth and all the fruit trees for your food. And I have given every green plant as food for all the wild animals, the birds in the sky and the

small animals that scurry along the ground—everything that has life" (Gen. 1:28-30).

Again, it's an appeal to logic, but if God did all of that in the beginning when the human race was sinless, wouldn't it be consistent to have an unblemished world restored?

The book of Revelation speaks of the end of our earthly lives with the song of victory and praise in chapter 19. Some have grabbed that image and made a parody or mockery of heaven being nothing but people sitting on clouds with harps and praises. That's not like anything else in the Bible. Revelation 21 tells us about the new heaven and the new earth and calls it the New Jerusalem:

> I heard a loud shout from the throne, saying, "Look, God's home is now among his people! He will live with them and they will be his people. God himself will be with them. . . . and there will be no more death or sorrow or crying or pain. All these things are gone forever." And the one sitting on the throne said, "Look, I am making everything new!" (vv. 3-5).

If we read those verses through the understanding of first-century believers (most of them converted Jews), we would have immediately thought of Eden. The all-things-new statement by God implies not just the restoration of Eden but also an even better place.

When Do We Receive Our Rewards?

The Greek word for reward is *misthos* and means "to pay for service." That may be a good way to consider rewards for believers.

We need to be clear on one thing: Going to heaven is a *gift*, not a reward. Paul tells us, "God saved you by his grace when you believed. And you can't take credit for this; it is a gift from God. Salvation is not a reward for the good things we have done, so none of us can boast about it" (Eph. 2:8-9).

Once we've received the gift of life, we're eligible to receive divine payment for our commitment and service to Jesus Christ. Nothing in the Bible makes all of us equal. The equality is the gift of entrance; beyond that, God recognizes and honors our unselfish, God-centered activities.

Nowhere in the Bible does it tell us specifically what rewards we'll receive. At one point, Jesus told the 12 apostles that they would rule over the 12 tribes of Israel (see Matt. 19:28). Jesus, however, goes on to say:

> And everyone who has given up houses or brothers or sisters or father or mother or children or property, for my sake, will receive a hundred times as much in return and will inherit eternal life. But many who are the greatest now will be least important then and those who seem least important now will be the greatest then (Matt. 19:29-30).

Those words come at the end of an event when Jesus speaks about those who have wealth. He adds, "It is easier for a camel to go through the eye of a needle than for a rich person to enter the Kingdom of God!" (v. 24). We call the statement hyperbole, because it's exaggerated and clearly impossible. That's the point Jesus is making—none of us can buy our way to heaven or get there because of our wealth on earth.

188 I Believe in Heaven

The New Testament contains many promises of recompense:

- Paul uses the image of building a house with Jesus Christ as the foundation. He urges his readers to build with the right materials. "Anyone who builds on that foundation may use a variety of materials—gold, silver, jewels, wood, hay, or straw. But on the judgment day, fire will reveal what kind of work each builder has done . . . If the work survives, that building will receive a reward. But if the work is burned up, the builder will suffer great loss. The builder will be saved, but like someone barely escaping through a wall of flames" (1 Cor. 3:12-15).

- Jesus says, "God blesses you when people mock you and persecute you and lie about you and say all sorts of evil things against you because you are my followers. Be happy about it! Be very glad! For a great reward awaits you in heaven" (Matt. 5:11-12). He also states, "Store your treasures in heaven, where moths and rust cannot destroy and thieves do not break in and steal" (Matt. 6:20).

- Paul writes, "Work willingly at whatever you do, as though you were working for the Lord rather than for people. Remember that the Lord will give you an inheritance as your reward and that the Master you are serving is Christ" (Col. 3:23-24). He also states, "What gives us hope and joy and what will be our proud reward and crown as we stand before our Lord Jesus when He returns? It is you!" (1 Thess. 2:19).

- Paul makes the point to the Corinthian church that as long as "we live in these bodies we are not at home with the Lord," adding, "So whether we are here in this body or away from this body, our goal is to please him. For we must all stand before Christ to be judged. We will each receive whatever we deserve for the good or evil we have

Cecil Murphey and Twila Belk

done in this earthly body" (2 Cor. 5:6,9-10). He also states, "So, my dear brothers and sisters, be strong and immovable. Always work enthusiastically for the Lord, for you know that nothing you do for the Lord is ever useless" (1 Cor. 15:58).

• Jesus says, "Look, I am coming soon, bringing my reward with me to repay all people according to their deeds" (Rev. 22:12).

• When Jesus instructs the people about fasting, He offers a practical word about their motives—they are to fast so that others aren't aware they are doing it. "Then no one will notice that you are fasting, except your Father, who knows what you do in private. And your Father, who sees everything, will reward you" (Matt. 6:18).

• The Bible makes it clear that it's not only what we do but also the motivation behind our actions. In Matthew 6:1, Jesus warns us not to do our "good deeds publicly, to be admired by others," and adds, "for you will lose the reward from your Father in heaven."

• Jesus also says that when we give to those in need, we're not to call attention to our giving. If we do, "I tell you the truth, they have received all the reward they will ever get" (Matt. 6:2). He then exhorts them, "Give your gifts in private and your Father, who sees everything, will reward you" (v. 4).

When we desire to serve God and not to be praised by others, we earn rewards. That means our reason for action is out of love and not because we want to receive rewards for our efforts.

Many people today assume that those who have prominent names or ministries will stand at the head of the line for rewards. But in Matthew 20:16, Mark 10:31 and Luke 13:30, Jesus states the principle that those who are first in this life will be last in heaven. That's not to be taken literally, but is simply meant to imply that those who seem to be the greatest and most admired Christians may receive their payment by human praise now—and that may be the extent of their divine recompense. Those who seem insignificant may be the most honored.

Jesus said that when people prepare a feast, they shouldn't invite their friends and relatives, "For they will invite you back, and that will be your only reward. Instead, invite the poor, the crippled, the lame, and the blind. Then at the resurrection of the righteous, God will reward you for inviting those who could not repay you" (Luke 14:12-14).

Another way to look at rewards is to focus on faithfulness. No matter what our spiritual gifts are (and according to 1 Corinthians 12, all of us are gifted), God judges us on our faithfulness in using what we have.

Paul makes this clear when he compares himself to Apollos and says they're both servants of God: "Now it is required that those who have been given a trust must prove faithful" (1 Cor. 4:2, *NIV*). The apostle goes on to say that he isn't concerned how other humans judge him, because he doesn't even judge himself. "It is the Lord who judges me. Therefore judge nothing before the appointed time; wait till the Lord comes. He will bring to light what is hidden in darkness and will expose the motives of men's hearts. At that time each will receive his praise from God" (vv. 4-5).

In that short passage, the apostle links faithfulness to reward. Only God knows the real faithfulness (or true motivation) for what we do.

What Form Will the Rewards Take?

Here's another question for which the Bible provides no answer. Because we know God and trust that He is loving and all-knowing, we can assume that the ultimate payments—in whatever form they occur—will be greater than anything we can comprehend while we're alive on earth.

In the New Testament, the Bible uses two concepts to speak about the future of believers: crowns and rewards. It seems obvious that crowns aren't physical ornaments that people wear. Common sense says that the use of *crowns* simply explains the idea of victory and achievement. The crown of life (see Jas. 1:12) may refer to the reality of achieving an eternal relationship with God.

For first-century believers, crowns symbolized power and stature. Imagine how a common, poor family who worked hard to provide daily food would feel to hear they will be crowned and live in honor and prosperity.

If we are crowned in heaven, doesn't that help us grasp the idea of a marvelous, overwhelming return on our spiritual investments?

Will There Be Different Punishments in Hell?

The Bible doesn't speak directly to the question of differences in punishment; however, in the parable of the Rich Fool (see Luke 12:35-48), Jesus hints at the answer.

He introduces His story by urging His followers, "Be dressed for service and keep your lamps burning, as though you were waiting for your master to return from the wedding feast" (v. 35). Because Peter and the others were unclear about His instructions, He went on to say, "A faithful, sensible servant is one to whom the master can give the responsibility of managing his other household servants and feeding them" (v. 42).

The point is clear: those who misuse their responsibility and wrong others will be judged according to their deeds. Jesus then distinguishes between two kinds of servants: "A servant who knows what the master wants, but isn't prepared and doesn't carry out those instructions, will be severely punished. But someone who does not know and then does something wrong, will be punished only lightly" (vv. 47-48).

The passage ends with the warning that knowledge brings responsibility. Sin is even more sinful for those who know better and fail. "When someone has been given much, much will be required in return; and when someone has been entrusted with much, even more will be required" (v. 48).

In another passage, Jesus sends His 12 disciples out to proclaim that the kingdom of heaven is near and then instructs them that if people in any of the cities don't welcome them, they're to shake the dust off their feet as they leave. "I tell you the truth, the wicked cities of Sodom and Gomorrah will be better off than such a town on the judgment day" (Matt. 10:15).

Neither of the quoted passages speaks clearly of levels of punishment in hell, but most Christians infer that meaning. The implication is that sinners will be judged by the amount of light and understanding they have. As Gary Habermas and J. P. Moreland state, "This differentiation of punishments provides an equitable means of meaning with various levels of offense."[6]

Are There Different Levels of Heaven?

When people ask this question, they usually want to know whether there is a first, second and third layer of heaven. They take literally the words of Paul in 2 Corinthians 12:2, where he writes, "I was caught up to the third heaven fourteen years ago."

The logic of that statement implies that there must be a first and second heaven. A few have gone on to interpret Paul as saying that only the most spiritual of Christians go into the third or highest heaven (note that there is no seventh heaven mentioned in the Bible).

According to these individuals, ordinary Christians go to the second heaven; and those who barely enter into the special realm (such as the dying thief on the cross) are assigned the first level. There is no proof for that theory.

Most scholars interpret "third heaven" as a way to express the ultimate place of God. In fact, Paul never implies that there are three heavens or even three levels of heaven—the concept probably originated in the nine different levels of heaven and hell presented in Dante's *Divine Comedy*. His book is a work of fiction.

As we point out elsewhere, the Bible speaks of rewards in heaven for believers. In 2 Timothy 4:6-8, Paul writes to his disciple:

> The time of my death is near. I have fought the good fight, I have finished the race, and I have remained faithful. And now the prize awaits me—the crown of righteousness, which the Lord, the righteous judge, will give me on the day of his return. And the prize is not just for me but for all who eagerly look forward to his appearing.

Paul pictures no elitism or special levels. Although there are different degrees of rewards, the Bible doesn't teach different levels of heaven.

As many wise people have said, "When the Bible is silent, we are silent."

What Are the New Heavens and the New Earth?

In several places in the Bible, we read of a new heaven and a new earth. Isaiah makes the first biblical reference with these words from God:

> Look! I am creating new heavens and a new earth and no one will ever think about the old ones anymore. Be glad; rejoice forever in my creation! And look! I will create Jerusalem as a place of happiness. Her people will be a source of joy. I will rejoice over Jerusalem and delight in my people. And the sound of weeping and crying will be heard in it no more (Isa. 65:17-19).

Peter presents a horrific picture of the end of this world:

> The day of the Lord will come as unexpectedly as a thief. Then the heavens will pass away with a terrible noise and the very elements themselves will disappear in fire and the earth and everything on it will be found to deserve judgment. Since everything around us is going to be destroyed like this, what holy and godly lives you should live, looking forward to the day of God. . . . On that day he will set the heavens on fire and the elements will melt away in the flames. But we are looking forward to the new heavens and new earth he has promised, a world filled with God's righteousness (2 Pet. 3:10-13).

Not everyone agrees, but this statement may point to the new world: "God blesses those who are humble, for they will inherit the whole earth" (Matt. 5:5). Because we haven't yet inherited the earth in this life, it must be a promise that God will fulfill in the future.

Perhaps one of the best passages that gives us a brief preview of the new heavens and the new earth is found in Revelation 21–22. Although there are sharp differences in interpreting this book, most see these chapters as a symbolic preview of what lies ahead. For instance, Revelation 21:1-4 reads:

> Then I saw a new heaven and a new earth, for the old heaven and the old earth had disappeared. . . . And I saw the holy city, the New Jerusalem, coming down from God out of heaven like a bride beautifully dressed for her husband. I heard a loud shout from the throne, saying, "Look, God's home is now among his people! He will live with them and they will be his people. God himself will be with them. He will wipe every tear from their eyes and there will be no more death or sorrow or crying or pain. All these things are gone forever.

This is a prophetic picture of the culmination of life on earth and a preview of what awaits believers. Like most of the book, the figures and symbols John used, especially those from the Old Testament, were meant to explain to human minds what we're unable to comprehend now.

For this reason, even as we read these beautiful, inspirational passages, we need to remind ourselves that John wrote the book in the midst of persecution by the Roman government. He used symbolic language that persecutors probably wouldn't grasp to compose words to comfort the believers.

This means we need to be careful in reading into those details. Instead of insisting John's words are literal (though some of them may be), we need to think of the *purpose* of John's words. Specifically, *what was the message the Holy Spirit (working through John) wanted to communicate to first-century believers?*

I stress caution about reading into the details because none of us truly knows what the new heavens and earth will be like. In fact, if we ponder the promises given about the Messiah in the Old Testament, many of them seem strange or obscure when we read about their fulfillment in the New Testament.

For example, Matthew 2:14-15 tells us that Mary, Joseph and baby Jesus lived in Egypt until the death of King Herod, after which time they returned to Israel. Matthew writes, "This fulfilled what the Lord had spoken through the prophet: 'I called my Son out of Egypt.'" The prophecy in the Old Testament reads, "When Israel was a child, I loved him and I called my son out of Egypt" (Hos. 11:1). I doubt that believers would have grasped the fulfillment of this promise had not Matthew written those words.

Nonetheless, we can show from biblical texts that at the end-time as we know it, a new heaven and a new earth will replace our existing heaven and earth. We can also say that heaven—which is the new earth—is a physical place where we will dwell with glorified physical bodies (see 1 Cor. 15:35-58).

The concept that we become spirits who float around in heaven and play harps is not found anywhere in the Bible. The heaven that believers experience will be a new and perfect place prepared by God so we can be perfect and fulfilled. That means the new earth will be free from sin, evil, sickness, suffering and death.

Again, perhaps the best way to think of the new heaven is to compare it to a re-created Garden of Eden—as it was before the curse of sin. Everything was perfect, and there was no sin, no sickness and no death. The first couple cared for the Garden and lived at peace among the animals.

Who Will Go
to Heaven?

There are too many verses to quote them all, but John 3:16 tells us that all who believe won't perish but will have eternal life. The same chapter concludes, "And anyone who believes in God's Son has eternal life. Anyone who doesn't obey the Son will never experience eternal life but remains under God's angry judgment" (v. 36).

In another place, Jesus says, "The time is coming when all the dead in their graves will hear the voice of God's Son, and they will rise again. Those who have done good, will rise to experience eternal life and those who have continued in evil will rise to experience judgment" (John 5:28-29).

When the apostle Paul appears before the Roman governor Felix and defends himself against the false charges raised by the Jewish leaders, he says, "I firmly believe the Jewish law and everything written in the prophets. I have the same hope in God that these men have, that he will raise both the righteous and the unrighteous" (Acts 24:14-15; see also John 5:24; 6:40; 10:28; Rom. 2:6-7; 1 John 2:25).

As Christians, we believe that heaven is our eternal destiny and that only believers will go there. As someone once asked, "If unbelievers aren't interested in God on earth, why would they be interested in heaven after they die?"

When We Die, Do We Immediately Go to Heaven?

When we die, do we simply cease to live, with nothing but our mortal remains to mark our years on earth? Does our invisible soul soar immediately to heaven?

Christians have always insisted that God will resurrect everyone, and those who have loved and obeyed Him will enter into a new quality of life that's endless. That's not an issue. However, Christians disagree on the answer to this question, and there is no solid, irrefutable evidence to resolve the issue.

No one living really knows what happens after death. Christians share a belief in the resurrection, but they aren't in total agreement as to what happens *immediately* after death. Christians stand behind different theories or beliefs.

However, regardless of our theology, we can all make this statement: "We die, and our next *conscious* moment will be in the presence of God." When we use the word "conscious," it refers to one of two possibilities:

1. We're immediately ushered into the presence of God as soon as our hearts stop beating; or

2. We die, our bodies are in the grave, and we have no awareness until the moment of resurrection. Thus, that's the next conscious moment.

(Note that there is a third possibility: an intermediate state of consciousness between the grave and heaven, which we discuss below.)

Colleen McDannell and Bernhard Lange write the following about the beliefs the Jews held during the time of Jesus:

> By the first century, CE, when Christianity first appeared, three Jewish views of the afterlife were prevalent. Out of those three perspectives on what happened after death, a fourth one, the Christian response, emerged. The teachings of the first-century Sadducees, Pharisees, and Essenes . . . furnished Jewish sages, lay people, sectarians, and philosophers with material for debate and speculation . . . We can speculate on the people to whom they appealed. New Testament Christianity derived much of its understanding of eternal life from the sectarian disputes which provided for a rigorous religious life in Roman-ruled Palestine. . . .
>
> The Sadducees were probably upper-class Jews who promoted strict adherence to the Scriptures and voiced a conservative opinion on questions of ritual and belief . . . no works of the Sadducees have been preserved and we have only brief mention of them in the writings of the Jewish historian Josephus (37–100 CE), the New Testament, and their philosophical opponents. Since virtually all ancient sources on the Sadducees were unsympathetic to them, and do not attempt to understand their perspective on death, we can only offer a provisional and somewhat speculative evaluation of why they believed that life ended in death.
>
> According to Josephus, the Sadducees held that "the soul perishes with the body." While other Jews argued for some type of survival, the Sadducees held that the Scripture contained no such assurance. A possible clue to the Sadducean this-worldly spirit and denial of an afterlife might be their participation in the wealthy priestly aristocracy. Tradition attributed to the Sadducees this-worldly attitude . . . According to Paul they found satisfaction in the slogan, "let us eat and drink, for tomorrow we die." Given such a background, we can postulate that they lived

a comfortable life and expected no further compensation for hardship in a future one.[7]

The authors also point out, "Being able to be close to God while living on earth meant they did not have to look forward to death bringing them into contact with the divine . . . [and] assumes that the promise of a full, heavenly existence can occur within one's own lifespan."[8]

The Pharisees tried to reconstruct Judaism "as a culture whose identity was shaped by meticulous observance of religious law." The authors presume the Pharisees believed, along with many prophets of the Old Testament, in the glorious re-establishment of a renewed Israel and the destruction of their enemies. "According to Josephus, they assumed the imperishable nature of the soul with the important qualification that 'the soul of good alone passes into another body.' "[9]

The authors go on to note, "While the Sadducees denied the resurrection of the dead and the Pharisees upheld it, a third Jewish movement adopted a more individualistic perspective on the afterlife. . . . [This group] held that at death the immortal soul ascended into heaven. . . . Some evidence indicates that the Essenes also hoped for freedom from bodily constraints and eventual rest in a heavenly kingdom."[10]

Here are the major beliefs about when Christians go to heaven.

The first belief is that death and resurrection are a singular event. At death, Christians "immediately experience the elevation into eternal life to which the hope of resurrection points."[11]

Advocates of this belief refer to Philippians 1:23, where Paul writes of his dilemma of whether he would rather stay and bless others or die. "I am torn between two desires: I long to go and be with Christ, which would be far better for me." The focus is on "be with Christ," which implies an immediate translation to heaven.

A serious objection is that such experiences constitute personal and individual resurrection—that is, each *person* experiences eternal life and death. This destroys the corporate aspect that all believers will experience resurrection at the same time.

Another objection to believers immediately going to heaven is that they would become ensconced there before they've been judged and rewarded by Jesus Christ. As Paul writes, "We must all stand before Christ to be judged. We will each receive whatever we deserve for the good or evil we have done in this earthly body" (2 Cor. 5:10).

This issue of immediate reward may not seem like a serious objection to some, but what about the counterpart? What about those who won't go to heaven? Logic says that those who are plunged into hell are then punished before they're judged guilty.

A second belief that some people hold is popularly referred to as soul sleep. Pope John XXII (who held office from 1316 to 1334) stated that the human soul doesn't enjoy eternal life until the judgment. He believed that the soul sleeps after death. His successor, Pope Benedict XII (1344–1342), decreed in 1336 that the souls of the righteous enjoy face-to-face contemplation of the divine essence at the moment of death. The souls of the wicked, in contrast, descend to hell, even though they will give an account of their deeds on judgment day.[12]

Martin Luther wrote, "For just as a man who falls asleep and sleeps soundly until morning does not know what has happened to him when he wakes up, so we shall suddenly rise on the Last Day; and we shall know neither what death has been like or how we have come through it." Elsewhere, he offers a similar picture of his own status while waiting for the resurrection: "We are to sleep until he comes and knocks on the grave and says, 'Dr. Martin, get up.' Then I will arise in a moment and I will be eternally happy with him."[13]

Those who hold this belief refer to 1 Thessalonians 4:16, where Paul writes about the return of Jesus Christ: "First, the Christians who have died [literally 'dead in Christ'] will rise from their graves." (Biblical writers use "sleep" to refer to the dead.) Here are verses on which this theological position relies:

> Multitudes who sleep in the dust of the earth will awake: some to everlasting life, others to shame and everlasting contempt (Dan. 12:2, *NIV*).

> And now, dear brothers and sisters, we want you to know what will happen to the believers who have died so you will not grieve like people who have no hope. For since we believe that Jesus died and was raised to life again, we also believe that when Jesus returns, God will bring back with him the believers who have died. We tell you this directly from the Lord: We who are still living when the Lord returns will not meet him ahead of those who have died. For the Lord himself will come down from heaven with a commanding shout, with the voice of the archangel and with the trumpet call of God. First, the Christians who have died will rise from their graves. Then, together with them, we who are still alive and remain on the earth will be caught up in the clouds to meet the Lord in the air. Then we will be with the Lord forever (1 Thess. 4:13-17).

This leads to the third position, which is held by Roman Catholics: those who die are held in an "intermediate state"—there is a continuous existence of the soul without immediate resurrection. In other words, there is a disembodied, personal, conscious existence of the soul between death and the entrance into the eternal state.

This continued personal existence in the form of a disembodied state solves the problem of the continuity of humans between death and resurrection. This position leads to the next question— what it must be like to be in the disembodied state.

The most obvious answer is that there must be a place of bliss and another of torment. Roman Catholic doctrine refers to this as "purgatory." For them, at death Christians enter a place "of purifying suffering, where they are fitted for heaven by the expiation of all remaining guilt."[14]

"Purgatory," from the Latin *purgare*, means to make clean or purify. It refers to the condition or place of temporal punishment for those who have died but aren't entirely free from venial faults, or who have not fully paid the satisfaction due to their transgressions. ("Venial sins" are minor transgressions that wouldn't keep a person out of heaven.) The idea behind this temporary punishment is that God has pardoned their sins, but He also requires satisfaction and will punish them for their failure to do penance in this life. In this way, they won't be cast off eternally from God.[15]

Those who hold this view sometimes refer to the story of the rich man and Lazarus. Jesus told the story, and although most people consider it a parable, some insist that because He names Lazarus (and no other name appears in Jesus' parables), it must be a true account.

In this parable told in Luke 16:19-31, a man lives in luxury while a beggar named Lazarus begs for scraps from the man's table. Both men die, and their situations are reversed. "Finally the poor man died and was carried by the angels to be with Abraham [literally "into Abraham's bosom"]. The rich man also died and was buried and his soul went to the place of the dead [Greek *hades*]. There, in torment, he saw Abraham in the far distance with Lazarus at his side" (vv. 22-23).

The once-rich man is in torment and begs Abraham to send Lazarus to give him a little water. "I am in anguish in these flames" (v. 24). Abraham reminds the man that he had once had everything and Lazarus had nothing. "So now he is here being comforted and you are in anguish. And besides, there is a great chasm separating us. No one can cross over to you from here and no one can cross over to us from there" (vv. 25-26).

For some, that is a literal picture of purgatory.

Most protestant scholars reject the idea of purgatory—even though it has a "certain theological appeal"[16]—as neither the word nor the concept is taught in the Bible. However, for some, it answers the question of the intermediate state after physical death on earth.

In summary, regardless of the lack of information, we who are believers are assured that from the moment we die, our next moment of awareness—our next *conscious* moment—will be in God's presence.

What Happens
to the Wicked?

Hell is probably the most unpopular of all Christian beliefs. Certainly it's one that most of us don't like to consider.

From what little we read in the Bible about the destiny of the wicked, there seems to be degrees of punishment, which is equal with their sinning against their knowledge and understanding.

Most Christians believe that the punishment will be eternal because of verses such as the following:

- "So if your hand or foot causes you to sin, cut it off and throw it away. It's better to enter eternal life with only one hand or one foot than to be thrown into eternal fire with both of your hands and feet" (Matt. 18:8).

- "[Jesus] will come with his mighty angels, in flaming fire, bringing judgment on those who don't know God and on those who refuse to obey the Good News of our Lord Jesus. They will be punished with eternal destruction, forever separated from the Lord and from his glorious power" (2 Thess. 1:7-9).

- "And they will be tormented with fire and burning sulfur in the presence of the holy angels and the Lamb. The smoke of their torment will rise forever and ever and they will have no relief day or night" (Rev. 14:10-11).

Not all Christians agree that the punishment will be literal fire, arguing that it wouldn't affect spirits such as Satan and demons. Regardless, the Bible is clear that the punishment of unbelievers doesn't end.

Those who argue against eternal punishment point to the words translated as "everlasting" and "eternal." In the original Greek the words literally denoted an age or a long period of time, because the Greek had no such words for eternity.

The reasons for holding to eternal punishment are because in Matthew 25:46, the same Greek word (*kolasin*) describes the duration of believers and the punishment of the wicked. If one is without end, so must be the other. Elsewhere, Jesus uses terms such as "fire is not quenched" (Mark 9:43, *NIV*) and the "maggots never die" (Mark 9:48).

Louis Berkhof says there are three things we have to consider when we discuss the final state of the wicked. The first is where "the wicked are consigned. In present day theology there is the evident tendency in some circles to rule out the idea of eternal punishment." He adds, "In modern liberal theology the word 'hell' is generally regarded as a figurative designation of a purely subjective condition, in which [people] find themselves even while on earth and which may become permanent in the future. . . . But there can be reasonable doubt as to the fact that the Bible teaches the continued existence of the wicked."[17] Berkhof cites Matthew 24:5, 25:30,46 and Luke 16:19-31 to support his argument.

We must always remember that the Bible was written by people to explain words and concepts *in their own culture*. This is why the place of torment is called *gehenna,* which comes from the Hebrew word for "valley" or "land."

The New Testament also used *hinnom,* which was a valley southwest of Jerusalem where idolaters sacrificed their children to the god Moloch. It was a despised region, and fires constantly burned there to consume the waste from Jerusalem. Thus, it became the symbol of the place of eternal torment (see Matt. 10:28; 23:33; Luke 12:5).

Matthew 18:9 refers to the *geennan tou puros* (the gehenna of fire), and there is a lake of fire listed in Revelation 20:14-15. (The lake of fire is a contrast to the sea of glass that was like crystal, re-

ferred to in Revelation 4:6.) Other terms for this place are translated as:

- Prison (see 1 Peter 3:19);

- Abyss (see Luke 8:31);

- Hades, the unseen world, the place of dead, the dead and
  the grave (see Matt. 11:23; Luke 10:15; Acts 2:27; Rev. 1:18).

Darkness—the absence of light—is another description of hell.
The Bible also speaks of those who won't go to heaven as be-
ing *outside* (see 2 Thess. 1:9) or being *cast into hell* (see Luke 12:5). In
truth, no human knows exactly what constitutes the eternal punishment of the wicked. Here are the possibilities:

- Total absence of God's favor;

- Endless disturbance of life, because peoples' lives had
  been dominated by sin;

- Pain and suffering in body and soul;

- Some subjective punishment, such as pangs of conscience,
  anguish, despair, weeping and gnashing of teeth (see
  Matt. 8:12; 13:50; Mark 9:43-44,47-48; Luke 16:23,28;
  Rev. 14:10; 21:8).

Jesus warns, "Don't be so surprised! Indeed, the time is coming when all the dead in their graves will hear the voice of God's
Son and they will rise again. Those who have done good will rise
to experience eternal life and those who have continued in evil will
rise to experience judgment" (John 5:28-29).

Matthew writes, "But many Israelites—those for whom the
Kingdom was prepared—will be thrown into outer darkness, where
there will be weeping and gnashing of teeth" (8:12).

Paul writes, "But he will pour out his anger and wrath on those
who live for themselves, who refuse to obey the truth and instead
live lives of wickedness" (Rom. 2:8).

There are two views of *limited punishment* that appear in modern Christianity. Some denominations, such as Seventh-day Adventists, hold that after a period of punishment, God will annihilate the wicked. That is sometimes referred to as "conditional immortality." When this term is used, advocates say that humans are mortal and God gives the gift of eternal life to believers. At death, the wicked cease to exist in any form.

The other view is universalism, which has been a growing attitude among Christians during the past decade. Rob Bell popularly expressed this idea in *Love Wins*.

Although most Christians still reject the idea that punishment will be limited in duration, the universalists' position is that God will eventually reconcile all things to Himself. Morton Kelsey argues, "To say that men and women after death will be able to resist the love of God forever seems to suggest that the human soul is stronger than God."[18] Others insist that God will eventually succeed in His purpose of winning everyone to Himself.

Most serious Christians don't believe that hell is a place where God spitefully and actively tortures the wicked forever and ever. The position is that according to the Bible, the people have made their choice to separate themselves from God; and thus their torment means banishment from heaven and all the beauty and perfection it stands for. The wicked will live in mental and physical anguish.

Habermas and Moreland quote Leon Morris, a New Testament scholar, who states the position of most evangelicals today:

> Peter told [Cornelius] that God is no respecter of persons, "But in every nation he who fears him and works righteousness is acceptable to him" (Acts 10:35). This surely means that people are judged by the light they have, not by the light they do not have. We remember, too, that Paul says, "It is accepted of a man according to what he has and not according to what he does not have" (2 Corinthians 8:12). Long ago Abraham asked, "Shall not the Judge of

all the earth do right?" (Genesis 18:25) and we must leave it there. We do not know what the fate of those who have not heard the gospel will be. But we do know God, and we know that he will do what is right.[19]

There are some who speak of a second chance after death. Hebrews 9:27-28 states, "And just as each person is destined to die once and after that comes judgment, so also Christ died once for all time as a sacrifice to take away the sins of many people." However, nowhere in the Bible is there any support for a second chance after this life is over.

What Is Hell?

In discussing hell, Christians tend to hold four major views, as shown by William Crockett in his book *Four Views on Hell.*[20]

The first is the *orthodox* view. This is the belief that punishment for the wicked is everlasting and that it is punitive, not redemptive. Because the Bible reveals that God is a God of love and grace, a tension has developed between the concepts of a loving God and a righteous God who demands absolute justice of the wicked. Strict orthodoxy provides a literal everlasting punishment for the wicked.

The second view of hell is that it is *metaphorical;* in other words, it is somewhat non-literal and less specific than the orthodox view. Usually, those who hold this view concede that the wicked will never be redeemed and restored to a place of blessing in eternity, but the scriptural accounts of their suffering and divine judgment are taken in a less-than-literal understanding.

A third view—that of the Roman Catholic Church—sees hell as *purgatorial.* As previously discussed, in this view hell has an antechamber called purgatory, a place of divine cleansing from which some, at least, will eventually emerge as redeemed and be among the blessed of God. Generally speaking, this view requires that all must go through a period of purgation in which their unconfessed sins are judged and punishment inflicted. Though it may be extensive and continue over a period of time, ultimately, many will be restored to a place of grace and bliss, though others will be damned eternally.

The fourth view of hell is as a *conditional* or temporary situation for the wicked. This view has been advocated by many who find a contradiction between the doctrines of everlasting punishment and of a God of love and grace. They explain that hell is either temporary, in the sense that immortality is conditional and only the righteous will be raised, or that it is redemptive, in the sense that whatever suffering there may be after this life because of sin will end up in the wicked being redeemed and restored to a

I Believe in Heaven

place of blessing. Conditional immortality or annihilation lessens the severity and the extent of everlasting punishment, while in universalism, all are eventually saved.

Crockett states that he could have provided "almost endless" quotations from early Christian writers up to the present who had different views of hell. Some believed in eternal punishment, and some didn't. He goes on to say that the only value to his citing them would be to show that "there has always been a diversity of opinion."[21]

The importance of the above statement is to point out that serious Christians from the earliest days have disagreed about hell. For the past 2,000 years, godly people have held such disparate views *and* have insisted the Bible reflects their views.

Will There Be Time in Heaven?

The Bible speaks often of time, but it's not clear that those verses *prove* there will be time in heaven.

For example, some refer to Revelation 6:10-11, where martyred souls cry out and ask God, "How long before you judge the people who belong to this world?" In this passage "how long" has a time reference; but that's hardly proof. Again, we have to remember that the book of Revelation was written to provide encouragement for persecuted saints of the first century. They would naturally ask such questions.

Revelation 7:15 speaks of those who died that "stand in front of God's throne and serve him day and night in his Temple." There is also the reference to the tree of life "bearing twelve crops of fruit, with a fresh crop each month" (Rev. 22:2).

The counter argument, again, is that God speaks to humans in time language because we are on earth and need words and symbols we can grasp. When the dead ask questions such as "how long?" or "when?" it is a way for God to communicate to His troubled, persecuted people that He has not forsaken or forgotten them.

On earth, we need hours, days, months and seasons to make sense of our daily world. Paul's metaphor speaks well here: "When I was a child, I spoke and thought and reasoned as a child. But when I grew up, I put away childish things. Now we see things imperfectly, like puzzling reflections in a mirror, but then we will see everything with perfect clarity. All that I know now is partial and incomplete, but then I will know everything completely, just as God now knows me completely" (1 Cor. 13:11-12).

Paul makes a strong statement about our incompleteness and likens us to children. Isn't it possible that *time* may be part of the language God uses to speak to us in our "partial and incomplete" knowledge? Furthermore, why would we *need* time in the New Jerusalem?

Most of us readily acknowledge that God's time isn't the same as ours. God works in a different dimension—far beyond anything we can understand or anticipate. Consequently, the words of the Bible are directed at our limited comprehension.

Another way to look at the issue is to realize there is no past or future with God. God sees only now—and the divine *now* takes in our past, present and future.

We also have human witnesses. Don Piper, after his 90 minutes in heaven, has often said that time doesn't exist there. His is not a lone voice. A common statement among people who have had near-death experiences is that not only was there an absence of time, but also that their "whole life flashed before them." Doesn't that imply they saw the total of their lives in a few human moments? Although this is not possible here on earth, why would heaven have such limitations?

If God knows (not *knew*) the future before the creation of the world, why would time be an issue?

Here is one verse that makes this assertion clear. Paul writes, "Even before he made the world, God loved us and chose us in Christ to be holy and without fault in his eyes. God decided in advance to adopt us into his own family by bringing us to himself through Jesus Christ" (Eph. 1:4-5).

Most of us have seen pictures of the all-seeing eye, such as the one represented on the backside of the dollar bill. I see it this way:

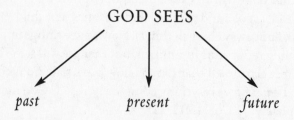

GOD SEES

past   *present*   *future*

While we must live in the time of past that has now moved to the present and is going into the future, God already sees everything in ways that are beyond our comprehension.

Here's another way to look at time: If the transition from death to resurrection means a passage from human time to divine time, at death, we enter into God's eternal *now*. Eternity isn't billions and trillions of years that we can count (or would want to count). Doesn't it obliterate time in the past and in the future? When we die, we enter into God's now.

Can Our Dead Loved Ones See Us Now?

Despite the fact that many find comfort in believing their loved ones look down on them, there's no biblical assurance that they do.

There are also no biblical references that say they don't.

The Bible doesn't specifically say whether people in heaven can look down on those of us who are still on the earth. While it is highly unlikely that they can, the common response in favor of their seeing us comes from those who want to feel the comfort of a departed loved one looking after them. This isn't a theological question, but one that involves the loss of loved ones and a yearning to feel connected to them.

A few people refer to Hebrews 12:1, which follows the famous faith chapter of heroes: "Therefore, since we are surrounded by such a huge crowd of witnesses to the life of faith, let us strip off every weight that slows us down, especially the sin that so easily trips us up."

However, the obvious point of the verse is *not* that a large group of people in heaven are watching everything we do, but that we have the *examples* from the lives (and deaths) of believers from Abel to those of the first century who trusted God.

They set the standard for us, but it doesn't say they're watching. Because of the faith and diligence of Christians who went before us, we should be inspired to follow their example.

If our loved ones are conscious in heaven and look down on us, wouldn't they see things that would cause them pain and anguish? If there is no unhappiness in heaven, how could they see and not be touched? If they look down from heaven and see the pain and suffering of their loved ones, would it still be heaven?

In addition, whatever they are doing in heaven, are they not removed from the cares and anguish of earth? Wouldn't the ability to see activity below ruin that perfection of heaven? If they are

224 I Believe in Heaven

free from sin and experience God's presence in heaven, surely there is more than enough to captivate their attention.

Could We Be Happy in Heaven if Our Loved Ones Are in Hell?

If heaven is a place of perfection and utter joy, there must be some way that the awfulness of hell won't detract from the glories we experience in heaven. Our present limitations make it impossible for us to understand how that can be true.

When we talk about the joy of heaven and think about our loved ones possibly being eternally punished in hell, many ask how it could be heaven for those individuals (and probably all of us). That concern has challenged many people.

The Bible doesn't offer a specific answer, but there are passages containing bits of information that supply a significantly substantial answer to the perceived problem.

We have to acknowledge that a number of things about the eternal order go beyond our ability to comprehend. We assume that's why the Bible writers used metaphorical or symbolic language. For example, Revelation 21:4 promises that God "will wipe every tear from their eyes and there will be no more death or sorrow or crying or pain. All these things are gone forever." We don't believe that God literally wipes every single tear from every person, but we certainly understand (and are encouraged) by the meaning. Certainly, the persecuted believers of John's day would have rejoiced in reading such words.

From those few words, we understand the symbolism that God will eliminate sadness—all of it. If it were the case that sorrow over lost loved ones destroys the bliss of heaven, then there would be no heaven for many of the redeemed, because the Lord's people have had family members—whether local or extended members, or friends—who have died outside the sphere of salvation.

Cecil Murphey and Twila Belk

If we trust a loving, benevolent God to bring us into a place of perfect happiness, won't God make it totally joyful? God is a being of supreme love, which is intrinsic to His very nature (see for example, 1 John 4:7-8, which states, "Love comes from God . . . for God is love"). Our comprehension of divine love can't begin to grasp the depth of the divine heart and plan.

However, even though we read of the love that's beyond human understanding, we also need to remind ourselves of the language used about those who reject our Savior. Jesus said, "But many Israelites—those for whom the Kingdom was prepared—will be thrown into utter darkness, where there will be weeping and gnashing of teeth" (Matt. 8:12). This same expression also appears in Matthew 22:13, 24:51, 25:30 and Luke 13:28.

We may feel repelled by the language, but we must rest with the acknowledgment that the love of God and the justice of God are both at work. We can't comprehend how saints in heaven can live in perfection while sinners in hell suffer eternal damnation. (Even those who believe in some form of universalism or annihilation of the wicked usually acknowledge a period of punishment for their sins before total annihilation.)

Whether temporal or eternal, it doesn't settle the question about those in heaven and separation from their loved ones. Surely the God of heaven will do the righteous and just thing for all concerned. Our minds may not be able to comprehend how it can be done, but that doesn't mean God can't or won't do it.

God will judge aright, and all angels, saints and martyrs will praise Him for it. It seems inescapable that along with them, we'll approve the judgment of those who have refused God's grace. In heaven, we will see with a new and far better perspective. Second Corinthians 1:3 reminds us that "God is our merciful Father and the source of all comfort."

Isn't that comforting enough?

Will We Have
a Different Body
in Heaven?

Modern Christians aren't the first to ask what we'll look like after the resurrection.

Within 30 years after Jesus' ascension, the apostle Paul received this question, and he answered, "Christ has been raised from the dead. He is the first of a great harvest of all who have died" (1 Cor. 15:20). Older translations refer to Jesus as the "firstfruits," which has an important theological emphasis. When Moses gave the law to the people, one of the requirements involved giving the first-fruits—the first produce from their fields and orchards—to God. They were taken to the priests, who were God's representatives.

The initial fruit of harvest was always meant as a dedication to God. Moses writes, "I also give you the harvest gifts brought by the people as offerings to the LORD—the best of the olive oil, new wine and grain. All the first crops of their land that the people present to the LORD belong to you" (Num. 18:12-13).

Deuteronomy 26:2-3 commands, "Put some of the first produce from each crop you harvest into a basket and bring it to the designated place of worship . . . Go to the priest in charge at that time and say to him, 'With this gift I acknowledge to the LORD your God that I have entered the land he swore to our ancestors he would give us.' "

Leviticus 23:9-11 points out that the waving of the sheaf of the first grain harvest before the Lord served to consecrate the whole harvest that followed. Similarly, the resurrection of Christ is referred to as the firstfruit of those who have died and will become the assurance that all who trust Him will be resurrected. As the firstfruit—the beginning of the fulfillment of resurrection for all of us—He is given to God. That implies there will be a bountiful harvest afterward.

Paul's response in 1 Corinthians 15:20 is a way of saying to us, "What Jesus was, we will be." First John 3:2 reads, "Dear friends, we are already God's children, but he has not yet shown us what we will be like when Christ appears. But we do know that we will be like him." So, to understand what our bodies will be like in heaven, we have to examine the accounts in the Bible of where Jesus appeared to His followers after His resurrection.

Following Jesus' resurrection, we have two distinct accounts where Jesus appeared to followers and they did not immediately recognize Him. The first takes place on Sunday morning, the day of the resurrection. Mary Magdalene discovered that Jesus' tomb was empty and stood crying. "She turned to leave [the tomb] and saw someone standing there. It was Jesus but she didn't recognize him. . . . She thought he was the gardener" (John 20:14-15). After Jesus called her by name, she recognized Him.

Notice she recognized Him *only after He called her by name.* The implication is that Jesus' appearance was different.

Luke 24:13-34 tells the other story of Jesus walking alongside two disciples who were traveling to the village of Emmaus. They did not recognize Him until they sat down to eat and He blessed the bread. The Bible says, "Suddenly, their eyes were opened and they recognized him" (v. 31).

Later, "The two from Emmaus told their story of how Jesus had appeared to them as they were walking along the road, and how they had recognized him as he was breaking the bread" (v. 35).

When God raised Jesus from the dead, He demonstrated a power sufficient to resurrect our bodies as well. In His resurrected body, Jesus talked with His disciples and ate food with them (see John 21:1-14).

These accounts tell us that Jesus could fit within earthly dimensions and also transcend them. Before His death, Jesus promised that He would not leave His disciples to be orphans but would come to them (see John 14:18).

From these accounts, we can surmise that our resurrection bodies will retain our identities and that others will recognize us, although we'll possess greater capabilities than we have with our present earthly bodies.

In 1 Corinthians 15, the apostle devotes a section to our resurrection bodies. Beginning with verse 35, He answers the question of what our bodies will be like. He calls it a foolish question and points to the fact that in nature, seeds go into the ground, die and produce a plant. "Then God gives it the new body he wants it to have" (v. 38).

Paul goes on to say, "The glory of the heavenly bodies is different from the glory of the earthly bodies" (v. 40). He paints our bodies as weak and broken, but "they will be raised in strength. They are buried as natural human bodies, but they will be raised as spiritual bodies" (vv. 43-44).

Paul compares the first Adam with his natural body with the "last Adam" (Christ). "Earthly people are like the earthly man and heavenly people are like the heavenly man. Just as we are now like the earthly man, we will someday be like the heavenly man" (vv. 48-49).

We can state clearly that we will have bodies, but not our earthly ones. As Paul concludes, "What I am saying, dear brothers and sisters, is that our physical bodies cannot inherit the Kingdom of God. These dying bodies cannot inherit what will last forever" (v. 50).

Will We Recognize Others in Heaven?

Will we know each other in heaven? That's a common question. The answer seems obvious. How else could it be heaven if we wandered throughout eternity not recognizing those whom we loved in this life? We will be the same, yet wonderfully different, because we'll be transformed by the grace of God and the results of sin will no longer mar our lives.

Nothing in the Bible implies that we won't recognize others. In fact, we have hints that we *will* know each other. In this life, we're blocked by human limitations; but in heaven, the imperfections of age, sickness, weakness and disease will be removed. The mark and the proclivity toward sin will be erased. The result will be that those in heaven, while retaining their personality, will shed all marks of human weakness.

We have no indication that heaven abolishes human personality. In that day, the assumption is that we will know each other completely, far beyond our limited knowing in this life. Age and the passage of time won't matter.

Some occasionally ask about our age in heaven, but it's an unanswerable question. If time has no consequence, our age won't matter. Besides, we have no idea what our heavenly bodies will look like. They surely won't show the damage of wear through human aging. We have to assume that our lack of information is because of our inability to understand the answer.

Heaven, by definition, is a realm unlike the world in which we live. God could tell us everything we want to know, but the answers wouldn't always make sense to us. One way we know this is to think about Jesus and His first followers. For three years, He repeatedly told His 12, intimate followers that He was the Christ, but they couldn't comprehend. Only *after the resurrection* did they finally and fully grasp what that meant.

Cecil Murphey and Twila Belk

How can we possibly understand heaven or what lies ahead of us? We have the assurance that it will be better than the best we've experienced on earth. That should take away our concerns.

Someone has well said, "For the children of God, heaven will be the ultimate family reunion, a place where we will have no difficulty recognizing our loved ones who have gone on before us."

We know from the implied teachings that we will all be changed "in the blink of an eye" (1 Cor. 15:52) and that we'll have bodies suited for our life that has no ending.

Do Babies Who Die Go to Heaven?

No one knows the answer to this question.

Most of what we hear is an emotional argument rather than a biblical one. There is absolutely no statement in the Bible that refers to infants who die. We often hear the term "limbo," which is a doctrine in the Roman Catholic Church to account for the dead who cannot clearly be assigned to heaven or hell.

The idea is controversial even among Catholics, and most Protestants don't accept limbo. In fact, throughout the history of the Roman Catholic Church, the idea of limbo has been much discussed and debated by theologians. Think of it as referring to an intermediate place between heaven and hell, outside of the presence of God but free from the torment associated with hell.

Limbo is a Latin word that literally means "hem" or "border." Catholics use the word in two senses. This first is to describe a temporary place or state of those who were believers but were unable to go to heaven until Christ died, was resurrected and went to heaven. The second way to explain limbo is that only those who accept God's gift of salvation *and are baptized* may enter heaven.[22]

The second use, which is familiar to most people, is that limbo refers to the permanent place or state of *unbaptized* children or others who may have believed but weren't baptized before their deaths.

The problem involves the question of what we call "original sin." That is, all humans are born with the taint or mark of sin. We don't become sinners when we do something wrong; we come *into* this world as sinners—and that's clearly backed up in many biblical passages. Paul quotes a number of verses from the Psalms to prove that all are sinners. For example, "No one is righteous—not even one" (Rom. 3:10). He continues the argument in the rest of the chapter.

Christians have always held that we must forsake sin and trust Jesus Christ to enter into heaven, which is what makes the question about infants who die so troubling.

There are two strong answers that address this issue of what happens to those who die in infancy. The first (and probably the more popular) is that if a child dies before reaching the "age of accountability," God considers that child innocent. No one has ever clearly defined "age of accountability," and it also has to take into account those who are mentally deficient and unable to understand the distinctions between right and wrong. Thus, it's not purely an age question.

It's also not addressed anywhere in the Bible. In fact, those who disagree point out that there is no age of innocence, only an age of understanding of one's sinfulness.

The second position, which was taught by many of the reformers and Puritan leaders, is that the promise of salvation for infants is *only* for the children of Christians. The biblical support for this view comes from 1 Corinthians 7:14: "For the unbelieving husband has been sanctified through his wife, and the unbelieving wife has been sanctified through her believing husband. *Otherwise your children would be unclean, but as it is, they are holy*" (NIV, emphasis added).

The first view really doesn't answer the question and, for many, the second seems harsh.

I (Cecil Murphey) am theologically trained and was a part-time teacher in a Bible college for 18 years. I'm a former pastor and missionary to Kenya. I point to that background to state that I've been asked the question many times during my professional career. Although I don't know the answer, I believe the grace and benevolence of God is far, far greater than we humans can imagine and that it's one of the many things God hasn't chosen to reveal to us.

My answer won't be sufficient for everyone, but I find comfort in these words: "The LORD our God has secrets known to no one. We are not accountable for them, but we and our children are accountable forever for all that he has revealed to us, so that we may obey all the terms of these instructions" (Deut. 29:29).

The verse means that God holds us responsible for what we know, and the rest is in His hands. My faith allows me to trust God without knowing the answer.

Will There Be Animals in Heaven?

The Bible offers no clear answer to this question either.

We need to remind ourselves that having household pets wasn't part of ancient Hebrew or Christian culture. Cats aren't mentioned in the Bible. Dogs were scavengers, and biblical pictures of them show that concept. In fact, references to dogs are nearly always negative and derisive:

- God tells the Israelites, "You must be my holy people. Therefore, do not eat any animal that has been torn up and killed by wild animals. Throw it to the dogs" (Exod. 22:31).

- When David confronts Goliath, the giant is insulted and sneers, "Am I a dog? . . . Come over here and I'll give your flesh to the birds and wild animals!" (1 Sam. 17:43-44).

- The prophet Ahijah prophesies against King Jeroboam and says, "The members of Jeroboam's family who die in the city will be eaten by dogs and those who die in the field will be eaten by vultures. I, the LORD, have spoken" (1 Kings 14:11).

- A similar message is for King Baasha, which Jehu repeats (see 1 Kings 16:4).

- The Lord gives Elijah a message to evil King Ahab: "Wasn't it enough that you killed Naboth? Must you rob him, too? Because you have done this, dogs will lick your blood at the very place where they licked the blood of Naboth!" (1 Kings 21:19).

The portrayal of dogs is no better in the New Testament:

- Jesus tells a story about a rich man and a beggar named Lazarus. He says the dogs would come and lick his sores (see Luke 16:21).

- Paul warns, "Watch out for those dogs, those people who do evil, those mutilators who say you must be circumcised to be saved" (Phil. 3:2).

- In describing the new heavens and new earth, John writes of the blessedness of those who will be in the New Jerusalem. Then he says, "Outside the city are the dogs—the sorcerers, the sexually immoral, the murderers, the idol worshipers and all who love to live a lie" (Rev. 22:15).

The word "dogs" is clearly a derogative term for the wicked. But it also shows the common understanding during biblical times: Dogs weren't household pets. Given this, why would there be any reference to dogs in heaven? It would have been repugnant to ancient believers.

Isaiah writes of the day when "the wolf and the lamb will lie together; the leopard will lie down with the baby goat. The calf and the yearling will be safe with the lion . . . the cow will graze near the bear. The cub and the calf will lie down together. The lion will eat hay like a cow" (11:6-7).

Some have seen that as a promise of having pets in heaven. Perhaps so; however, the entire passage is written in poetic language in terms that a primitive culture would understand. Natural enemies would live in harmony. Although some may take this literally, more likely it's a metaphor or picture of what life will be *like* in heaven.

Many are emotionally attached to pets on earth, so they're unable to think of pure joy and happiness without their animal companions. However, there is no definitive answer about the presence or absence of pets in eternity.

One answer is clear: When we live in the New Jerusalem, our lives will be perfect, flawless and filled with joy. If we need our pets to enjoy and maintain perfect happiness, we can be assured that God will provide them.

Do Christians Believe in Reincarnation?

To answer this question, we need to define the word "reincarnation." This idea, also called the transmigration of souls, teaches the cyclic return of a soul after physical death to live another life in a new body. The soul is born again . . . and again.

No place in Jewish or Christianity theology is there any indication of belief in reincarnation. The teaching of reincarnation is built on the concept of self-improvement—if we do good in this life, we come back in a higher state. Conversely, if we do evil, we move lower down the ladder.

The clear Christian teaching is that we live this life, and on the day of final judgment, those of us who are believers will enter into God's eternal kingdom, the New Jerusalem, and we'll be rewarded there for the deeds we did in this life.

And only then.

In traditional Hindu thinking, the reborn soul comes back in another state, either in a higher form of life (as a reward) or a lesser one (as punishment). Good people continue to move upward into a higher form of life until they move out of the reincarnation cycle. Those who have more bad deeds than good, come back as some lower form of life, such as a snake or a toad. Modern Westerners who embrace reincarnation seem to ignore the reward or punishment and claim to come back as another human being regardless of their previous behavior.

Serious Christians have always rejected reincarnation.

Groups such as Unity School of Christianity, the Theosophical Society and Edgar Cayce's Association for Research and Enlightenment advocate the cycle of souls. The late Jeanne Dixon (1904–1997) popularized the Western version of reincarnation through Ruth Montgomery's book *A Gift of Prophecy*. Later, celebrities like Shirley MacLaine also popularized reincarnation.

Estimates are that as many as 25 percent of Americans believe in some form of reincarnation.

A few advocates insist that Christians believed in reincarnation until the sixth century, when it was suppressed. There is no proof of that statement.

In an article by Joseph P. Gudel, Robert M. Bowman Jr. and Dan R. Schlesinger titled "Reincarnation—Did the Church Suppress It?"[23] the authors point out that Church fathers such as Justin Martyr (c. AD 100–150) made it clear that he did not believe in any form of reincarnation. They refute the charge that Clement of Alexandria (c. AD 155–220) taught reincarnation.

Origen (c. AD 185–254) is the Church father most often cited by reincarnationists as teaching their doctrine; however, the three authors provide lengthy proof that he actually *opposed* the doctrine. The same is true with Jerome (c. AD 345–419), who is occasionally cited as favoring the transmigration of souls.

The authors state, "Not only did none of the church fathers embrace reincarnation . . . but they explicitly rejected the notion as wholly contrary to the Christian faith." From there they list a number of church fathers who held anti-reincarnation ideas. They conclude, "None of the church fathers commonly recognized as orthodox during the first five centuries of the church held to reincarnation. Reincarnation was certainly not suppressed by the church in the sixth century or at any other time. It has been explicitly rejected by church leaders since the middle of the second century and never taken seriously as a belief that might be adopted by Christians."[24]

Those who hold to reincarnation attempt to prove their position by quoting from the Bible. One text they often use is John 3:3. This is the significant place where evangelicals point out that Jesus said,

"Unless you are born again, you cannot see the Kingdom of God." They grab the words "born again" to support reincarnation; however, the term literally means "born from above" (also repeated in v. 7). The Greek does not support their views.

But wasn't John the Baptist the reincarnated Elijah? That's where most reincarnation believers base their arguments. After all, Matthew 17:10-13 reads, "His disciples asked [Jesus], 'Why do the teachers of religious law insist that Elijah must return before the Messiah comes?' Jesus replied, 'Elijah is indeed coming first to get everything ready. But I tell you Elijah has already come, but he wasn't recognized and they chose to abuse him. And in the same way they will also make the Son of Man suffer.' Then the disciples realized he was talking about John the Baptist."

Jesus refers to the prophet Malachi's final words when he speaks of a time of great judgment: "Look, I am sending you the prophet Elijah before the great and dreadful day of the Lord arrives" (Mal. 4:5). Elijah would prepare the way for the Messiah.

Luke 1:17 clarifies that John came "with the spirit and power of Elijah," but he wasn't a reincarnation of Elijah. The Old Testament is clear that Elijah filled the role as one who pointed the way to God, just as John did for Jesus.

Another helpful passage occurs in Luke 9:7-8. Herod had killed John the Baptist, and "when Herod . . . heard about everything Jesus was doing, he was puzzled. Some were saying that John the Baptist had been raised from the dead. Others thought Jesus was Elijah or one of the other prophets risen from the dead."

If there had been any idea of reincarnation, wouldn't there be a hint? As it is, the people believed in resurrection but not in reincarnation.

In addition, if John the Baptist had been a reincarnation of Elijah, wouldn't John himself have known? Yet we have that clarified in the first chapter of John's Gospel. John declared he wasn't the Messiah, but also said he wasn't Elijah.

" 'Well, then, who are you?' they asked. 'Are you Elijah?' 'No,' he replied" (John 1:21). When pressed, John said, "I am a voice shouting in the wilderness, 'Clear the way for the Lord's coming!' "

(v. 23). Any Jew would have understood he was referring to Isaiah's prophecy: "Listen! It's the voice of someone shouting, 'Clear the way through the wilderness for the LORD! Make a straight highway through the wasteland for our God!'" (Isa. 40:3).

The end of the John quotation makes it clear that the people saw John as a then-modern version of Elijah, not the reincarnated prophet.

In Luke 1:17, the answer is plain. The angel Gabriel appears to Zechariah to tell him about his to-be-born son, John (who will be known as John the Baptist). "He will be a man with the spirit and power of Elijah. He will prepare the people for the coming of the Lord." John will come with the same zeal as the prophet but he won't be the reincarnation of Elijah.

Another significant passage to which the advocates of reincarnation point is John 9:1-3. This is the story of a man born blind. The disciples asked, "Why was this man born blind? Was it because of his own sins or his parents' sins?" (v. 2).

Some Jewish theologians of Jesus' day believed that it was possible to sin while in the womb. They quoted Genesis 4:7, where God told Cain, "Sin is crouching at the door." This is one of those verses that no one seems able to explain satisfactorily. What makes this about sin in the womb? Is the womb the "door of the uterus"? Cain was an adult by that time.

Some of the Jews were influenced by Plato and the Greeks, who believed in reincarnation. They also thought that a person's affliction—even if he or she was born that way—could come from sin that had been committed before the person was born.

Jesus swept away the question by saying, "It was not because of his sins or his parents' sins" (John 9:3).

On this issue, the position of Christians is that there is absolutely no evidence in the Bible for the transmigration of souls.

This is also a place to quote Hebrews 9:27-28 again: "And *just as each person is destined to die once* and after that comes judgment, so also Christ died once for all time as a sacrifice to take away the sins of many people" (emphasis added).

Will We Be Sexual Beings in Heaven?

This question gets asked in many ways, such as, "Will there be romantic relationships? Will my spouse and I still be together?"

The question seems to arouse many to affirm that sexual relationships will be part of heaven. One man who had been married for nearly 40 years before his wife died insisted that if there was no sex in heaven, he would be vastly disappointed. His statement shows an inadequate concept of heaven. Whatever the answer, God will make heaven better and more wonderful than anything we can expect. If that's true, how could any of us be disappointed with heaven?

One man, who had buried two wives, asked, "If there's sex in heaven, to which wife would I belong?"

This, again, is one of the issues that people respond to emotionally and in human, present-life terms. God created human beings with a sexual nature. But what if heaven is absolutely different?

Do we dare to impose our thinking and feelings on earthly life to express what life will be with Jesus Christ in the new heavens and the new earth? Isn't it better to remain silent where the Bible is silent? The best answer to the question is, "We don't know."

Even so, Luke 20:27 contains an interesting teaching by Jesus when confronted by the Sadducees with an obvious attempt to find a way to make a fool of Him: "Then Jesus was approached by some Sadducees—religious leaders who say there is no resurrection from the dead." Their convoluted question went like this:

Teacher, Moses gave us a law that if a man dies, leaving a wife but no children, his brother should marry the widow and have a child who will carry on the brother's name. Well, suppose there were seven brothers. The oldest one married and then he died without children. So the second brother married the widow, but he also died. Then the third brother married her. This continued with all seven of them, who died without children. Finally, the woman also died. So tell us, whose wife will she be in the resurrection? For all seven were married to her! (vv. 28-33).

It appears that the Sadducees' question was aimed at making the belief in a resurrection seem ridiculous. But Jesus told them not to think of heaven in terms of this earth, because it will be quite different. He said, "Marriage is for people here on earth. But in the age to come, those worthy of being raised from the dead will neither marry nor be given in marriage. And they will never die again. In this respect they will be like angels. They are children of God and children of the resurrection" (vv. 34-36).

Because of Jesus' words, the answer seems to be that sexual relationships won't be part of heaven. And if it's truly heaven, it won't be anything we'll miss, because we're assured that life will be perfect in every way.

Aren't Jesus' words satisfactory?

What Are Near-death Experiences?

As mentioned in part 1, the term "near-death experience" was coined by Dr. Raymond Moody and popularized by his book *Life After Life*, first published in 1975. Habermas and Moreland state, "The evidence for near-death experiences includes corroborated reports and some limited scientific means of testing and systematizing them . . . by enumerating four different types of evidence."[25]

The first type of evidence comes from individuals who were *almost dead*. We know of many instances where the dying "were able to view individuals, events, or circumstances around them, or even in other places, with amazing accuracy after coming close to dying or being pronounced clinically dead."[26]

Some of the events people described took place while they were comatose. Things happened that the near-death individual could not have known, even if they had been conscious.

Habermas and Moreland present several reported instances. One was of a young girl named Katie who almost drowned in a pool. She was resuscitated and given a 10 percent chance of surviving. Three days later, she recovered and told amazing events that took place "even though she was 'profoundly comatose,' with her eyes closed during the entire time."[27]

Katie said she met Jesus and "followed" her family. She told them what her mother had prepared for the evening meal, how her father had reacted, and the boys her brother and sister played with—all things she couldn't have known. Her family confirmed each detail.

The second type of evidence comes from those who report a near-death experience *after their hearts stop*. Habermas and Moreland quote sources that state that six minutes is the maximum duration of clinical death in which the brain cortex can fully recover.[28]

They tell of a boy, 11 years old, who suffered from cardiac arrest in the hospital and had no heartbeat for 20 minutes. Like many who went through near-death experiences, he accurately described the medical procedures, the locations and colors of the instruments, and even the genders of the medical personnel and their conversations.[29]

A third type of evidence comes from individuals who report near-death experiences *after the brain stops*. These are patients who have registered a *total absence* of brain waves. Habermas and Moreland report on cardiologist Fred Schoonmaker's 18-year study of 1,400 cases of people who reported near-death experiences. More than 50 of these took place with flat EEG readings, with periods that ranged from 30 minutes to three hours. The authors note, "Many of the patients reported incidents that were also corroborated by others."[30]

A fourth type of evidence comes from individuals who report *they saw friends and loved ones whom they didn't know had died*. Individuals report having seen or visited with loved ones whom they now knew were dead, even though no one told them. In a number of instances, no one present had yet heard about the deaths of those individuals. It was only later they learned that these loved ones had died—sometimes at the same hour as the person who saw them in a near-death experience.

One example was a boy named Cory who told his mother that her boyfriend in high school had been crippled in an auto accident and had died. The mother didn't know whether that was true, so she made phones calls and learned that her former beau had died the same day Cory had seen him.

These individuals also report having met deceased people they had never known. One account is of a man who had several near-death experiences and "reported going to hell repeatedly." He became a believer, and "in one of his subsequent experiences, this man found himself in a gorge full of beautiful colors, lush vegetation and light."[31] He met his stepmother and his mother. His birth mother had died when he was 15 months old, and he had never seen a picture of her.

The man's aunt visited later and brought a picture of his mother, standing with several others. "The man had no difficulty picking his mother out of the group, which astounded his father."[32]

According to a 1992 Gallup poll, about 5 percent of Americans have had a near-death experience (about 13 to 15 million people). One site estimates that every day, 774 Americans have a near-death experience.[33] The number is probably larger, because many people don't speak about them, especially those who have experiences where they feel they went to hell before being resuscitated.

What Causes Near-death Experiences?

The short, easy answer is that we don't know. Here are the eight most popular theories on what might cause a near-death experience.

1. Dying-brain Theory

This theory was popularized by Dr. Susan Blackmore in her book *Dying to Live*.[34]

Those who have had near-death experiences tend to follow the same path toward the light and have similar stages on the way, which makes a powerful case for the whole experience being a profound spiritual journey to an afterlife where everyone, from all ages and cultures, is welcome. However, that same evidence, Blackmore says, is also a fundamental part of the argument that these aren't real experiences but a function of the dying brain.

The skeptics claim that all brains die in the same way, which explains why people who have had near-death experiences speak of similar elements. The skeptics say it's not that the dying person is traveling toward a beautiful afterlife, but that the brain's neurotransmitters are shutting down and creating the same illusions for all who are near death.

But why? Why should the dying brain do this, if it is only a highly sophisticated lump of tissue? Are we individuals with personalities and minds that are exclusive to us? Or are we simply bodies controlled by clever brains, each of which works a little differently from the rest, thus making each of us unequal even though there are far more similarities between our brains than there are differences?

Scientists and researchers are divided. Some reduce reports of near-death experiences to nothing more than a series of brain reactions. Few people today deny the reality of these experiences, but they dispute the cause and its meaning. Within the scientific community, there are two major strands of research: one takes the psychological approach and seeks reasons for human beings to behave the way they do or think or possibly to hallucinate; and the other is the straightforward physiological approach, which searches for the part of the brain that malfunctions and causes these episodes to occur.

The depersonalized argument—that near-death experiences are the result of the brain beginning to die—isn't accepted by most researchers because they say, in essence, that they reduce a profound, transforming experience to nothing more than a set of neurotransmitters beginning to fail. A serious counterargument—and not only from Christians—is that if there is no afterlife and near-death experiences are the evidence of a dying brain, why does it bother?

If everything, including the soul and personality, is going to dust and ashes, why does the brain play this last wonderful show for people near death, or facing actual death, who relax into peacefulness and describe their wonderful visions? If near-death experiences are a hallucination, why do many people report hearing words such as, "You have to go back; your work isn't yet finished," or, "It's not time for you to die"? If they are merely hallucinations, how can so many people receive similar hallucinations?

2. Charles Darwin's Theory

This theory states that near-death experiences are a deliberate ploy of the human race to help those left behind adapt to the inevitable end of life. Darwin's simple theory of the survival of the fittest holds that every species struggles to increase its hold on this earth and guarantee the survival of its descendants. His theory, however, doesn't explain why these experiences are erratic, or why we shunted down an evolutionary sidetrack for years by making them something that people were reluctant to talk about. After all, in Darwinian terms, humans are the complete masters of the earth.

3. Hallucination Theory

This theory comes from those who believe (but can't prove) that when dying, the human body secretes endorphins and hormones that act on the central nervous system to suppress pain. This is most popularly known because of the "runner's high," which happens when long-distance runners go through a pain barrier and move into feelings of euphoria. However, endorphins aren't hallucinogens, and they don't recreate a state similar to those who report having near-death experiences.

Researchers who study neurotransmitter receptors do say there is a powerful anesthetic called ketamine that can produce some of the features of a near-death experience, particularly the out-of-body element. Dr. Ronald Siegel from UCLA claims to have reproduced these types of experiences in his laboratory by giving LSD to volunteers.

But other researchers say that although drug-induced hallucinations may have *some resemblance* to near-death experiences, they're not the same. For one thing, drug-induced hallucinations often evoke fearful and paranoid experiences, which is generally not the case in near-death experiences. Drug-induced hallucinations also distort reality, while those who have near-death experiences described them as "hyper-reality."

The question as to whether drugs or medication can cause near-death experiences isn't new, and analysts have done an enormous amount of research into it. Habermas and Moreland quote the results of Osis and Haraldsson, as reported in their book *At the Hour of Death*, in which they say, "Only in a very low percentage of cases could drugs have been relevant. Of the 425 patients with medical data, 61 percent received no drugs, while another 19 percent were given drugs that have no effect on consciousness. . . . Thus, 80 percent . . . were not affected by drugs. This means that only one-fifth were considered to have been influenced by medication."[35]

4. Temporal Lobe Theory

This theory states that *some* features of near-death experiences occur in a type of epilepsy associated with damage to the temporal lobe of the brain. By electrically stimulating this lobe, researchers can mimic some elements of these experiences, such as a person leaving his or her body behind and the life memories flashing past.

These researchers suggest that the stress of being near death may cause the stimulation of that lobe.

Some evidence that supports this theory is found with people who suffered strokes that affected that part of the brain or had tumors in the area. However, the characteristic emotions resulting from this temporal lobe stimulation were fear, sadness and loneliness—quite the opposite of calmness and peace.

Furthermore, even though a chemical mechanism is present in the brain, it doesn't mean near-death experiences themselves are chemical reactions.

5. Lack of Oxygen Theory

This theory holds that a lack of oxygen in the brain or too much carbon dioxide causes near-death experiences. However, this doesn't explain why some patients give full and accurate reports of things that went on around them during their experiences.

Comparisons between those who report near-death experiences and those who have hallucinations produced by oxygen-starved brains show that the latter are chaotic and more like psychotic hallucinations. Confusion, disorientation and fear are typical results, compared with the tranquility, calm and sense of order that people who have near-death experiences report.

The two may have common features, such as the person's sense of wellbeing. Those who have experienced both at different times say that there is an unmistakable difference. Hallucinations, whether deliberately drug-induced or caused by oxygen deprivation, almost always take place while they are conscious, whereas near-death experiences happen during unconsciousness—sometimes when they're so close to death that there is no record of brain activity on an electroencephalograph (the machine that monitors brain waves).

Further, those whose medical conditions take them to the point of death and have near-death experiences don't get there by being oxygen-deprived, or through any medication. That is particularly true of accident victims.

6. Depersonalization Theory

This theory, introduced around 1930, argues that those who are faced with an unpleasant reality of death and illness attempt to replace it with pleasurable fantasies to protect themselves. They depersonalize the experience by removing themselves from their bodies and floating away.

Although this theory is still brought up occasionally, it has been largely pushed aside because a typical feature of those who have a near-death experience is that it is extremely personal with strong spiritual feelings and increased alertness and awareness.

7. Memory of Birth Theory

This theory denies that near-death experiences have any connection with death and insists that they are memories of the person's own birth. A baby being born leaves the womb to travel down a tunnel toward a light. The light at the end is usually love and warmth. What happens at the point of death, they contend, is only a stored memory of what transpired when life began.

There are problems with this theory. Babies being born don't *float at high speeds* down a tunnel, but are pushed along *with difficulty* by their mothers' contractions.

Furthermore, the theory has no explanation for the person meeting with friends and relatives who have died. The "Being of Light" is supposed to be the doctor (or midwife) in the delivery room, yet many babies are born without any professionals present.

Another point against the theory is that infants' nervous systems aren't sufficiently developed to assimilate and store memories of the birth process. Those who argue for this theory say that the feelings of peace and bliss are a memory of the peace of the womb the person felt when the mother met all of his or her physical needs and there were no stresses or strains.

And yet, being born isn't always a pleasant experience for babies; it leaves them crying as if in agony. In contrast, near-death experiences are usually the most pleasurable experience individuals can have.

8. Afterlife Theory

This theory says that it's difficult (if not impossible) to explain near-death experiences in terms of the physical working brain. Many researchers no longer feel they need to prove that these experiences happen, but rather the skeptics have to prove that they don't.

This is the position we take in this book. We see it as evidence not only of life beyond death but also eternal life after our sojourn on earth. In addition, we label those who have reported dying (or who believed their spirits or souls left their bodies) and have returned to their bodies as being "near death." That is, they did not have the lasting, final death that is inevitable for all humans.

What Typically Happens in Near-death Experiences?

"Heaven is real. Wouldn't it be wonderful to know that? Can you imagine how you would feel with certain knowledge of life beyond death?"

Those are the first words of Mally Cox-Chapman's book *The Case for Heaven*.[36] She tells about a group of church members who listened to a talk about heaven.

A police officer, Dorothy Young, insisted there is a heaven because she had been there. She explained that after miscarrying her fourth child, she was in the hospital when "she felt a cold, dark chill pass over her" and "was surrounded by a warm, bright light. . . . She felt happier than she ever had before. . . . She heard the sound of a baby crying deep in the Light. She was given to understand that her stillborn daughter was going to stay in the Light and that she was fine."[37]

After she finished her story, the people sat in silence, because Dorothy wasn't a stranger but was well known to them. Cox-Chapman says Dorothy was the calm dispatcher at the police station, the person whom everyone called when there was a crisis.

The author also makes the point that every listener "had to decide if her story was trustworthy. Each had to wonder what it meant." As Dorothy's own pastor said afterward, "I've never really paid much attention to near-death experiences . . . and now Dorothy's telling hers and I'm thinking, 'This is really important.'"[38]

That simple beginning illustrates the attitudes and experiences that many share.

As the stories in part 1 of this book relate, for nearly 40 years stories have spread about people dying on the operating table and having a strange experience, especially of hearing the medical staff say something like, "We've lost her." Only minutes later, the person "returns" to his or her body and survives.

For a long time, most people remained skeptical of such accounts—and some do even today. Many stay skeptical until someone they know well tells them of such an experience. Then they, like members of Dorothy's congregation, have to decide whether to believe the account.

In the past, we've often thought of something called the "moment of death." Research and experience makes it clear that it's a transition or passage and not strictly moving from one moment of life into the next moment of death.

To complicate the concept of death and near-death, such accounts come from those who have had near-death experiences. Because these are self-reported, their experiences cannot be objectively verified, and it can't be proven whether they left their bodies and went to heaven. Furthermore, some individuals have reported similar near-death experiences, but without a sense of being dead.

Skeptics dismiss such experiences by insisting that drugs, oxygen deprivation, or disassociation caused it. They cite the theories discussed in the previous question—temporal lobe stimulation, endorphin surge, anesthesia and even memories of birth as the reasons for the experiences. They also say there are various *triggers* for near-death experiences.

Because we begin with the bias in favor of near-death experiences being genuine and a foretaste of eternity, here are a few of the arguments we use against the doubters:

- Anesthesia during surgery cuts down on the likelihood of patients' remembering a near-death experience. Medications such as Valium are usually added to the anesthesia to create amnesia during the operation.

• A trigger isn't the experience itself. (Therapists use the word "trigger" to refer to a stimulus that causes or generates particular responses.)

Despite the criticisms mentioned above, researchers from every continent have concluded that such experiences are authentic, though they may disagree on how to interpret them.

Many people who have had near-death experiences have entered their names into the database of the International Association of Near-Death Studies (IANDS).[39] As we show elsewhere, these individuals report common characteristics, such as a feeling of being out of their bodies, going through a dark tunnel and entering into the light.

Not all of those who report having these experiences state they were positive.

What About Those Who Say They Went to Hell?

It's not only Christians who report having near-death experiences; those who belong to various religious and secular groups world-wide also report them. Most of these reports come from individuals who speak of the bliss and happiness they experienced while out of their body.

But this is not true in every case. Some people report going to hell. It's impossible to give an accurate number as to how many people have these types of experiences, because they tend not to talk about what happened to them.

Don Piper says that when he speaks at churches and civic groups and afterward does signings for his books about heaven, it's not unusual for individuals to ask to speak to him privately and tell him about their experiences. Because he's open about what happened to him, many speak of their terror and admit they rarely feel comfortable in telling others.

Several experts on near-death experiences say that those who aren't religious are changed and many of them become believers just from the blissful experience.

Our assumption is that many of those who speak of experiencing hell see it as a warning. Many become believers as a result of such powerful and frightening experiences.

Doesn't the Bible Speak of "Once to Die"?

Hebrews 9:27 troubles many Christians when they hear stories such as Don Piper's that he died and went to heaven. On a personal note, I (Cecil Murphey) was the ghostwriter for *90 Minutes in Heaven,* and that is certainly one of the many questions I faced before I agreed to write his book.

Here's the troublesome passage: "And just as each person is destined to die once and after that comes judgment, so also Christ died once for all time as a sacrifice to take away the sins of many people" (Heb. 9:27-28).

Before answering this question, we need to ask what Hebrews 9:27 actually means. The point of emphasis in this passage is that humans *ultimately die one time* and afterward they face judgment; Jesus died one time as a sacrifice for sin.

The context is about Jewish high priests having to offer sacrifices for sin year after year because animal sacrifices couldn't cover human sin. The writer of Hebrews points out that because of the effectual death of Jesus, there is no further sacrifice needed.

The intention of the passage isn't to speak against those who have died and returned. It's certainly not setting forth a doctrinal statement about human death as much as it's stating a simple fact: humans ultimately die one time just as Jesus died one time. Humans die a natural death, while Jesus died a special death that benefits all of us.

Let's also look at the Bible as a whole. If Hebrews 9:27 was meant as a statement that people die one time and thus near-death experiences can't be real, a primary rule of hermeneutics (interpretation of the Bible) says that we need a clear statement to establish any doctrine. We can find several statements about the efficacy of Jesus' death, or that God loves all of us, but Hebrews 9:27, by itself, fails to meet that test.

There's also contrary evidence.

1. The Account of Enoch

Most scholars assert that Enoch did not die a human death. Here's the passage:

> When Enoch was 65 years old, he became the father of Methuselah. After the birth of Methuselah, Enoch lived in close fellowship with God for another 300 years and he had other sons and daughters. Enoch lived 365 years, walking in close fellowship with God. Then one day he disappeared, because God took him (Gen. 5:21-24).

The *New International Version* translates verse 24 this way: "Enoch walked with God; then he was no more, because God took him away."

In the verses before and after the story of Enoch, the writer refers to people dying, so "God took him" wasn't a euphemism for death. For example, in the verse just before the mention of Enoch (v. 20), it says Jared died. Immediately after Enoch, we read of Methuselah's 969 years, "and then he died."

2. The Account of Elijah

We also can't overlook the account of Elijah. In one story told in the Bible, Elijah and his protégé, Elisha, are walking together. Elijah says to his follower, "Tell me what I can do for you before I am taken away" (2 Kings 2:9). The younger man asks for a double portion of Elijah's spirit and to become his successor. Here's the rest of the account:

> As they were walking along and talking, suddenly a chariot of fire appeared, drawn by horses of fire. It drove between the two men, separating them and Elijah was carried by a whirlwind into heaven. Elisha saw it and cried out, "My father! My father! I see the chariots and charioteers of Israel!" And as they disappeared from sight, Elisha tore his clothes in distress (vv. 11-12).

A few verses later, Elisha meets with a "group of prophets from Jericho [who] saw from a distance what happened," and they want to search for the missing prophet. Elisha tells them not to, but they continue begging "until they shamed him into agreeing . . . So fifty men searched for three days but did not find Elijah. Elisha was still at Jericho when they returned. 'Didn't I tell you not to go?' he asked" (vv. 15-18).

Despite their days of searching, they found no body, which believers through the centuries have accepted as Elijah going heavenward without death.

3. The Son of the Shunammite Woman

In this story, told in 2 Kings 4:20-36, a boy died and his mother went to Elisha for help. From the context, it's obvious that the boy had been dead for some time. The Bible states that after Elisha and his servant, Gehazi, arrived at the house, "The child was indeed dead, lying there on the prophet's bed" (v. 32). Elisha lies on top of the boy, breathes into his mouth, and "the child's body began to grow warm again!" (v. 34). The boy sneezes seven times and opens his eyes (v. 35).

4. Paul Went to the Third Heaven/Paradise

In 2 Corinthians 12:1-7, Paul relates he was "caught up to the third heaven." This probably didn't mean he passed through two lower heavens, but is a way of expressing the ultimate—it's like saying the highest, supreme heaven. It's quite possible that Paul had a near-death experience, although his account contains details and rich language not normally associated with them.

Consequently, authorities through the centuries have acknowledged that Paul died, went into the highest heaven, and saw and experienced many things beyond human words. God sent him back with a "thorn in the flesh." No one knows the meaning of the thorn, but most scholars assume it was a physical ailment.

The implication of the passage is that whatever happened to Paul, it was more than a near-death experience.

5. The Son of the Widow of Nain

There's also the story of the son of the widow of Nain. The Gospel of Luke records that Jesus and His disciples went to the village of Nain, where:

> A funeral procession was coming out as [Jesus] approached the village gate. The young man who had died was a widow's only son and a large crowd from the village was with her. When the Lord saw her, his heart overflowed with compassion. "Don't cry!" he said. Then he walked over to the coffin and touched it and the bearers stopped. "Young man," he said, "I tell you, get up." Then the *dead boy* sat up and began to talk! And Jesus gave him back to his mother. Great fear swept the crowd and they praised God, saying, "A mighty prophet has risen among us and God has visited his people today" (Luke 7:12-16, emphasis added).

If the young man had only a near-death experience, it must have lasted longer than those recorded by modern-day people.

Right after that event, John the Baptist sent his followers to ask Jesus if He were the Messiah. Jesus had performed many miracles in their midst and told them to report to John what they had seen. "The blind see, the lame walk, the lepers are cured, the deaf hear, *the dead are raised to life*" (Luke 7:22, emphasis added).

6. Lazarus Was Dead for Four Days

According to John 11, Lazarus had been dead two days before Jesus heard about it, and two more days passed before Jesus went to the tomb. "When Jesus arrived at Bethany, he was told that Lazarus had already been in his grave for four days" (v. 17).

When Jesus first heard of the sad event, He said that their friend Lazarus had "fallen asleep" and He had to go and awaken the man. His disciples took His words to mean that Lazarus was quite ill (possibly a coma) and would get better. "They thought Jesus meant Lazarus was simply sleeping, but Jesus meant Lazarus had died. So he told them plainly, 'Lazarus is dead'" (John 11:13-14).

I don't think the statement of death can be any stronger.

The account ends with these words: "Then Jesus shouted, 'Lazarus, come out!' And the *dead man* came out, his hands and feet bound in graveclothes, his face wrapped in a headcloth. Jesus told them, 'Unwrap him and let him go!' " (11:43-44, emphasis added).

7. The Account of Eutychus

In this story, Paul gathered with elders in an upper room in Troas. This would be his last time with them:

> Paul was preaching to them and since he was leaving the next day, he kept talking until midnight. The upstairs room where we met was lighted with many flickering lamps. As Paul spoke on and on, a young man named Eutychus, sitting on the windowsill, became very drowsy. Finally, he fell sound asleep and dropped three stories *to his death below*. Paul went down, bent over him and took him into his arms. "Don't worry," he said, "he's alive!" . . . the young man was taken home unhurt and everyone was greatly relieved (Acts 20:7-12, emphasis added).

In each of the seven examples above, the most natural and obvious meaning is that four of them literally died, and the Bible states that. (Paul's story doesn't say the young man died, but scholars generally agree that's the implication of the passage.) They are brought back to life. There is, however, nothing to imply that those five people didn't ultimately die like all human beings; however, two of them, Elijah and Enoch, didn't die. God took them out of this world.

Thus, the obvious answer is that Hebrews 9:27 can't be taken as a point of doctrine because there are too many clear statements to the contrary.

If Hebrews 9:27 sets forth a rigid doctrine, God Himself broke it for Elijah, Enoch, Lazarus, Paul, the widow's son and Eutychus.

Here's one more verse from the Bible. What did the writer of Hebrews (who had already written 9:27) mean in 11:35 when he wrote about the torture and persecution of believers: "Women received their loved ones back again from death"?

What Are the Aftereffects of Near-death Experiences?

For those who have a positive experience, the aftereffects of a near-death experience are significant. Most come back and assert such things as an assurance of heaven as well as a sense of loving and being loved.

Some who were agnostics or atheists become believers. One writer says, "They are not necessarily more saintly. The difference is that they see their lives as opportunities for spiritual growth."[40]

According to the International Association of Near-Death (IAND), about 80 percent of those who have had a near-death experience claim their lives were forever changed. A pattern of surprising dimensions emerged. These individuals didn't return just with a renewed zest for life and a more spiritual outlook; they showed specific psychological and physiological differences on a scale never before faced by them. This is as true with children as it is with teenagers and adults.

Here are a few of the aftereffects as reported from various studies:

- They no longer feared death.
- Some went through serious bouts of depression because they couldn't stay in heaven.
- They became more generous and charitable than they had been before their experience.
- Afterward, they initiated and maintained more satisfying relationships.
- Unresolved issues from childhood tended to resurface in their lives.
- They became less competitive, faced less stress and enjoyed life more.

- They became convinced that their lives had a purpose.
- Many spoke of loving and accepting others more readily.
- Their shift in behavior often confused (and threatened) family members, especially when a formerly aloof, uncaring individual became loving and thoughtful.
- Marriages sometimes failed because of the dramatic personality shift of the person who had the experience.
- After a near-death experience, individuals tended to be more aware of the present moment—of living in the now. They weren't disposed to make future plans.
- They used the language of place freely. They spoke of "going there" and "coming back." They often described the beauty of trees, grass and flowers. They raved about the quality of the light and the fragrances that were new to them.
- They believed that what happened to them was real.[41]

Responding to such aftereffects takes time. Research indicates that the first three years tend to be the most confusing for people, almost as if they still have not fully returned.

According to the International Association of Near-Death Studies, those who have near-death experiences come from every lifestyle and include the common experience of "dying" during surgery, as well as being seriously injured, involved in an accident, or attempting suicide.[42] As previously stated, most reported experiences are positive—from the pleasant to the blissful. However, a few report negative experiences and feel guilty, remorseful, fearful, confused, or isolated.

The immediate reactions range from people not considering the experience significant to being intensely preoccupied with what happened to them. IAND also reports that changes in their beliefs range from mild to extreme.

When these individuals talk about what happened to them, they typically "describe their experience in their own cultural context. A truck driver said he shot through a tailpipe toward a brilliant light. A young mother called the Beings she met the "Spirit

People" when she first recounted her experience; six months later, she had joined a church and was referring to them as Jesus and the angels.[43]

Mally Cox-Chapman records the experience of Marianne Helms, who lived in Geneva, Switzerland, for many years. In 1985, she had a severe allergic reaction to a bee sting in Kansas. She reported feeling lifted from her body and sent toward a shining white light. Marianne traveled up through trees like those that line the roads of Western Europe.

As previously mentioned, near-death experiences occur in people of every religion, and even those without any. Christians often refer to Jesus, a loved one, or a biblical figure. Jews call the beings "angels." Others refer to a "being of light" or someone "filled with light." Such descriptions don't imply a human figure, and the individuals usually make a point of saying so.

Even Christians who see Jesus can't describe Him or explain how they knew who He was. Usually their answer is, "I just knew." They may describe Jesus as being perfect and dressed in white. When some individuals were asked if Jesus were Jewish or Caucasian, they seemed unable to answer. "I don't remember," most of them said.

They can't put the description into words, but they often speak of feeling incredibly loved. Some report Jesus telling them such things as, "It's not your time yet" or "You have to go back."

Cox-Chapman makes an interesting comment. In *The City of God,* one of the great texts of Christian mysticism, Augustine takes the original assurance of Jesus that not a hair on the head of those who are granted eternal life shall perish to conclude that at the time of resurrection, the body will appear in its ideal state. Saint Augustine's thinking is out of fashion currently, because he believed in the resurrection of the flesh. But it is worth noting that throughout the literature of near-death studies, deceased loved ones appear healthy and physically whole.[44]

Research on those who attempted suicide has shown an interesting and amazing result. Cox-Chapman refers to the work of Bruce Greyson, editor of the *Journal of Near-Death Studies,* who researched the effect of these experiences on suicide patients. Instead of encouraging them to make another attempt on their lives, Greyson's work indicated that a near-death experience had the opposite effect, and the survivors came to believe that life was precious and meaningful.[45]

In another place, Cox-Chapman refers again to Greyson, who said that people can go through years of therapy and make few changes, but those who have had near-death experiences sometimes go through radical personality shifts overnight.[46]

What Are the Characteristics of Near-death Experiences?

Raymond Moody, the pioneer of near-death experiences, lists nine traits that are characteristic of such episodes. Others have identified as many as 13. Moody's list is as follows:

1. A sense of being dead
2. Peace and painlessness
3. Out-of-body experience
4. The tunnel experience
5. People of light
6. The being of life
7. The life review
8. Rising rapidly into the heavens
9. Reluctance to return[47]

In addition, individuals often say that in near-death experiences "time is greatly compressed and nothing like the time we keep with our watches." Moody quotes one woman as saying, "You could say it lasted one second or that it lasted ten thousand years and it wouldn't make any difference how you put it."[48]

Although only about one-third of those who approach death report any such experiences, Moody and others stress that no two near-death experiences are identical, even though there are similar patterns in adults as well as children.

Here is an explanation of common reports from various sources on these experiences from Moody and others who work in this field.

1. They Have a Feeling of Being Outside Their Bodies

This is the most common initial experience, and people often speak of hovering overhead. Sometimes they describe in detail what they saw, heard or what happened. Some people born blind were able to see while they were out of their body. Again, they often hear the medical personnel say, "We've lost her," as they rise above the scene and watch what's happening below them.

They see their own bodies on the operating table. Even though they're out of their physical bodies, they seem to have a sense of having some kind of body, unlike their physical ones. Some have called it an energy field.

Dr. Michael Sabom, in his book *Light and Death*, observes that they commonly experience being out of their body while at the same time not believing this is possible. They preface their descriptions with disclaimers such as, "I know this sounds crazy, but . . ."[49]

Moody also says that individuals who have near-death experiences break space barriers—if they "want to go somewhere, they can often just think themselves there." He mentions that resuscitated patients "were able to leave the operating room to observe relatives in other parts of the hospital." He refers to a woman who saw her child in the waiting room wearing "mismatched plaids."[50]

One woman said she heard her brother-in-law talk with business associates who asked him why he was in the hospital. He said that he was supposed to leave town on business, but he expected his sister-in-law to die so he was sticking around so he could be a pallbearer.[51] Later, he confirmed her words.

2. They Have No Pain and a Sense of Peace

Many report feeling no pain and having a sense of peace. Sometimes they refer to heightened senses. Some expressed an initial reaction of fear, but it disappears and they feel joy, peace and are often intensely happy.

One person said, "It just seemed so much more real than anything I had ever experienced in my entire life."

Another said, "All I felt was love, joy, happiness and every wonderful emotion you could find all at once."[52]

3. They Pass into or Through a Tunnel

Individuals report moving through a dark space or tunnel and having a sense of timelessness as they move forward. Although the tunnel is the most common, some have spoken of stairways going upward. Others speak of a whooshing sound or humming. The reports vary, but the people move rapidly through a passageway toward intense light.

Others speak of a floating experience in which they rise rapidly into heaven. Some have later spoken about having seen the earth from outer space or that they were transported beyond the stars.

4. They Encounter a Brilliant Light

They encounter brilliant light. Some refer to it as white, golden, or magnetic, and others stress that as they entered into an indescribable light, they felt loved.

5. They Meet People of Light

Many meet people of light. The people they meet aren't always ordinary people, but whoever they are, they make the person feel loved. Despite the brilliance of such beings—which they refer to being as something brighter than anything on earth—it's interesting to point out that no one reported their eyes hurting or feeling blinded by the intensity.

Again, most Christians refer to that person as Jesus, though they can't express what He looked like. They report that they intuitively recognized Him without anyone telling them. Others don't claim to have seen God or Jesus but only a being they sensed as being holy. They're so attracted to that being of light they want to stay forever.

Some also report having seen special pets or guides or angels.

6. They See Loved Ones Who Have Died

They often meet a loved one or a family member who had died. They recognize the individuals, but their bodies are filled with that

indescribable light. Some refer to being in a pastoral scene or looking at a beautiful city from a hill.

A few times people have seen the departed ones standing on
one side of a river or creek—reaching out toward them and calling
them by name.

7. They Learn It's Not Their Time

Even though these individuals want to stay, they aren't allowed. They
may hear Jesus or a family figure they encounter say, "It's not your
time." They know they have to return. Although a few sources say
individuals are happy to return, almost all accounts of near-death
experiences refer to their reluctance, sadness or even depression.

8. They Review Their Lives

They see and re-experience major (or sometimes trivial) events of
their lives. Some claim to have seen their entire lives unfold in a
kind of three-dimensional panoramic view of everything they've
ever done.

Those who report the total-life review say it happens instanta-
neously. Not everyone reports the life review, but those who do
speak of being aware of wrong, unkind, selfish things they did to
others and of feeling momentarily sad.

They also are in awe of the good things they've done and feel
elated or peaceful. Those who report both say they learn that love
is the most important thing in life. They also have a sense of the life
changes they need to make.

Knowing and understanding usually come together at that moment. They know how the universe works—they may not be able to
explain or remember *how*—but afterward they're aware that they
understood at that time.

9. They Reach a Boundary

The individuals reach a place where they can't go forward, and they
must stop. They might face a river, a cliff, or a huge fence. Regardless, they seem to know they can't go beyond that point.

10. Some Have a Choice

Some report that Jesus or the person they knew gave them the choice of staying or returning. They want to stay, but feel they have to go back for their children, parents or some significant task. Sometimes they experience a feeling of unfinished business, but usually their reluctance is because of the supreme peace and love they feel.

After the event, some are angry for having been brought back. Many report those who have gone through a near-death experience say to their doctors, "If this ever happens again, let me go." Many return with a renewed spirituality and a hunger for God. Raymond Moody makes this significant comment:

> There is one common element in all near-death experiences: they transform the people who have them. In my twenty years of intense exposure to NDEers, I have yet to find one who hasn't had a very deep and positive transformation as a result of his experience. I don't mean to imply that NDE turns persons into syrupy, uncritical Pollyannas. . . . It helps them grapple with the unpleasant aspects of reality in an unemotional and clear-thinking way—a way that is new to them.[53]

Moody says that he consulted scholars and clinicians who interviewed people who spoke of such experiences. They all concluded that all of these individuals became better people because of their experience.[54]

What Is "Nearing Death Awareness"?

The term "nearing death awareness" is a fairly new term, coined by Maggie Callanan, a hospice nurse. In her book *Final Gifts,* she writes of her experiences with dying patients, many of whom have an awareness of spiritual beings such as Jesus or an angel as well as loved ones who have died. Some see bright lights.

Many dying patients review their lives and come to a more complete understanding of the meaning of life. The process for the dying is more gradual than for those who have near-death experiences. Often for days before they die, hospice patients speak of a light in the distance, or they talk to deceased loved ones, sometimes for weeks before death, saying they are not ready to leave yet.

Nearing death awareness is part of the dying process. The dying person may seem to look into the distance and talk with people who are not physically present, or they may make friends and family members uncomfortable by talking about their plans for going on a trip.

What they see differs from what appears to observers, who often assume the person is expressing confused ramblings, making incoherent statements, exhibiting unusual behavior, or making references with no personal context. The dying may use symbolic language to describe an inner experience or event that others don't comprehend.

These individuals often say that someone they loved who has died is coming for them or is in the room. The statements, once family members understand them, show what the person needs in order to die peacefully. It's not uncommon for them to tell of the time of their death or to let go only after a certain event or condition takes place.

According to the IANDS website:

- Near-death awareness can occur without the sudden shift in physical condition as is common with near-death experiences.

- Meeting deceased relatives is common for those with near-death awareness.

- The purpose of near-death awareness in terminal illnesses seems to be to prepare the person for death, whereas the purpose of a near-death experience is often to teach the person how to live better.

- The terminally ill may have near-death experiences while in a coma or an unresponsive state. However, people experience near-death awareness while they are fully conscious. They can usually stop talking with a deceased relative and immediately pay attention to whatever is going on around them.

- Visitations differ from hallucinations, because those who experience hallucinations can't suspend their hallucinatory reality to talk with people in their room.

- Living relatives or friends don't appear to the dying. Sometimes they report being with someone whom the family believes is alive, but they learn that the person recently died. If the dying are reassured that their experiences are normal for that stage of life, they can feel great comfort from such encounters.[55]

What Do Individuals Do as They Approach Death?

Individuals approaching death sometimes consciously review their lives, often in great detail. This is true even of people who have previously shown little interest in self-examination. Those tasks primarily involve relationships.

The dying often look for themes in their lives, perhaps for the first time. They try to identify what they've learned and what they've contributed to the world in which they live. Sometimes they are surprised at their conclusions.

Forgiveness is frequently a major concern. The dying often realize the necessity of forgiving and being forgiven to complete their unfinished business of life.

They begin to say good-bye to life and let go of things, one at a time. They also let go of roles they've played, activities that once were important and, finally, they release significant relationships.

Two days before a friend of mine died, she said to me, "I'm resigning from life, and it's a time of great joy."

In Maggie Callanan's lecture at the 1993 annual conference of the International Association of Near-death Studies, she told the story of Su, a Chinese woman who accepted her terminal condition. Her husband had died several years earlier. She said she could see him standing at the foot of her bed, waiting for her.

One day, she was agitated when Maggie arrived. Su asked the hospice nurse why her sister had joined her husband at the foot of the bed. Maggie asked Su if her sister was still alive. Su said she was, but that she lived in China. Su had not seen her for many years.

Maggie didn't try to discredit the vision or solve Su's agitation with medication. Instead, she took Su's daughter, who was there in the room with them, aside and asked her what Su's vision might mean. The daughter told her that Su's sister had died the week before, but the family wanted to protect Su from the news when she herself was so ill.

With Maggie's encouragement, the family shared the news. Su's agitation subsided.

A group of hospice nurses was once asked at their regular Monday morning meeting if they had shared similar experiences. The nurses were specifically urged to say if they felt Callanan had embellished or glamorized the truth. As it turned out, many of the nurses had read Callanan's book *Final Gifts*. When they started hearing the story of Su, almost every nurse smiled and nodded in confirmation. Most had similar stories to tell.

The hospice nurses have found that the perceived presence of deceased family members is a source of solace for dying patients. One hospice nurse recounted the time a woman dying of throat cancer was visited daily over several weeks by her twin sister who had died of the same disease two years earlier.

When the dying woman first announced the next morning what she had discussed with her sister, the daughter thought she was hallucinating and that the medications had caused bad side effects. She complained to the hospice nurse.

During the two-week period before her mother died, however, the daughter came to believe that the conversations had a basis in reality. The sisters had both been painters, and her mother said they discussed favorite paintings and ways to render light. The daughter found that the conversations helped her understand that her mother was comfortable about wherever she was going.

Another hospice nurse described a patient who was severely demented with Alzheimer's disease and who had already had several strokes. The patient thought she still lived in the South and talked as though it were several decades earlier. She was unable to recognize family members caring for her or call them by name.

The day before she died, however, she regained her ability to talk coherently. She called her niece to show her the light that she saw and to describe the deceased family members who were gathered at the top of the room. She mentioned each family member by his or her name and relationship to her.[56]

What Should We Consider When Communicating with the Dying?

Here is a brief list of what we should consider doing when speaking with a person who is dying:

- Be straightforward and honest, but let them lead the way.

- Understand they may talk about going on a journey or going home as a metaphor for preparing to die.

- Be sensitive about how close they want you to sit to them, how much company they want, and how much talking is comfortable for them. People vary widely on this matter, and it is important to ask each one what is comfortable for him or her.

- Recognize that people's skin seems to become more sensitive as they approach death. Even gentle stroking may be irritating at such times. Merely holding their hand gently may be the most comfortable.

- Understand that as they approach death, they may withdraw as part of the process of saying good-bye to this life and all that it has meant. They may be unable to focus or absorb what is going on around them or with family members, and they may not want to visit as much with loved ones as they did before. It's important not to have your feelings hurt but to understand that this may be a necessary part of their preparation for death.

Cecil Murphey and Twila Belk

- Recognize that the dying often have the ability to choose the actual moment of death. For this reason, it is not uncommon for people to die when their loved ones are out of the room, even for the briefest of times, to spare them. It appears as if some people who are dying find it easier to let go when they are alone. Family members who don't understand this often feel unnecessarily guilty under such circumstances.

- Remember that terminally ill people may remain close to death for a long period of time if they are waiting for a significant relative or friend to come to the bedside. They may hang on in order to complete unfinished business with them.

- Understand that many dying people like to have someone with them, but they may not wish to (or be able to) interact very much. Your quiet presence may be all that they want.

- Allow them to talk about their near-death awareness and any near-death experiences if they have occurred, but know that not every dying person shares such experiences. There are no studies yet that explain why some people have them and others don't.

- Know that most dying people can be kept quite comfortable. If your loved one appears to be uncomfortable, please notify their health care provider.

- Know that this last stage of life often provides the most powerful interactions that loved ones will have during their entire lifetime.[57]

Can a Deceased Loved One Actually Appear to a Person?

To answer this question, we first have to recognize that the Bible makes no reference to the bodily appearance of those who are dead. Jesus, who was resurrected, is the only instance.

The Bible condemns any attempt to interact with the dead. Such verses as Leviticus 19:31; Deuteronomy 18:9-12; Isaiah 8:19—and others—command against such a practice.[58]

In 1 Samuel 28:3-25, King Saul disguised himself and went to a medium (or witch) who lived at Endor. He did this in spite of the fact that God had commanded the Jews never to seek necromancers or mediums. King Saul assured her that she wouldn't be killed for her dark magic and said, "Call up Samuel" (v. 11).

Samuel appeared and rebuked the king for "calling" him back (see v. 15). He told Saul that he had become an enemy of God and that God would take the kingdom from him and give it to David the next day. He also said, "And you and your sons will be with me" (v. 19), which meant they would die. That's exactly what happened.

A second point to recognize is that those who work with the dying say that it is not uncommon for those who are grieving to *feel* or *sense* the presence of their recently deceased loved ones who seem to be checking in on them. They may hear words, see their image, smell a familiar aroma such as a favorite shaving lotion, or merely sense their presence.[59] (However, the Bible still commands against *seeking* the dead.)

Some people may need some kind of closure with loved ones, even if they don't ask for it. Isn't it possible that a loving gracious God might send them a temporary reminder or awareness of a person they loved very much?

Last Words of the Famous and Infamous

"Father, I entrust my spirit into your hands." —Jesus Christ (Luke 23:46)

"Lord Jesus, receive my spirit. . . . Lord, don't charge them with this sin!" —Stephen, the first Christian Martyr (Acts 7:59-60)

"I believe, Lord, and confess. Help my unbelief!" —Peter the Great (1672–1725)

"I die before my time, and my body will be given back to the earth to become food for worms. Such is the fate of him who has been called the great Napoleon. What an abyss lies between my deep misery and the eternal kingdom of Christ!" —Napoleon Bonaparte (1769–1821)

"It is beautiful!" —Elizabeth Barrett Browning (1806–1861)

"If I am to be saved, it is not as a prince, but as a sinner." —Edward Augustus (1767–1820), father of Queen Victoria

"It is very beautiful over there." —Thomas Alva Edison (1847–1931)

Sir Francis Newport (1620–1708), head of the English Infidel Club, said, "Do not tell me there is no God for I know there is one, and that I am in his angry presence! You need

not tell me there is no hell, for I already feel my soul slipping into its fires! Wretches, cease your idle talk about there being hope for me! I know that I am lost forever."[60]

The famous nineteenth-century evangelist Dwight L. Moody (1837–1899) said to his family, "Earth recedes. Heaven opens before me. If this is death, it is sweet! There is no valley here. God is calling me, and I must go." Moody's son tried to tell his father that he had been dreaming, to which Moody replied, "I am not dreaming, I have been within the gates. I have seen the children's faces." His last words were, "This is my triumph; this is my coronation day! It is glorious!"

Atheist David Hume (1711–1776) cried, "I am in flames!" Those with him said his desperation was a horrible scene.

Voltaire (1694–1778) died a terrible death. His nurse reported his saying, "For all the money in Europe I wouldn't want to see another unbeliever die!" "All night long," the nurse said, "he cried for forgiveness."

John Newton (1725–1807), a former slave trader who wrote "Amazing Grace," said, "I am still in the land of the dying; I shall be in the land of the living soon."

Sir Thomas Scott (1535–1594), president of the English Lower House, said, "Until this time, I thought that there was no God, neither Hell. Now I *know* and *feel* that there are both and I am delivered to perdition by the righteous judgment of the Almighty."

A Chinese Communist, who witnessed the last words of many Christians delivered to their execution, said to a pastor, "I've seen many of you die. Christians die differently. What is their secret?"

Karla Faye Tucker Brown (1959–1998), executed for murder, said, "I am going to be face to face with Jesus now. . . . I will see you all when you get there . . . I will wait for you."

US President Andrew Jackson (1767–1845) said, "Do not cry—be good children and we will all meet in heaven."

Archbishop of Canterbury Thomas à Becket (1118–1170) stated, "I am ready to die for my Lord, that in my blood the Church may obtain liberty and peace."

Politician and writer Joseph Addison (1672–1719) said, "See in what peace a Christian can die."

Jan Hus (aka John Hus or John Huss) (1369–1415) was a reformer before the Protestant Reformation. When asked to recant to save his own life, he said, "God is my witness that the things charged against me I never preached. In the same truth of the gospel which I have written, taught and preached, drawing upon the sayings and positions of the holy doctors, I am ready to die today." Hus was burned at the stake and his ashes thrown into the Rhine River.[61]

Thomas Cranmer (1489–1556), Archbishop of Canterbury, became a Protestant and defied the Pope. After being tortured, he recanted and should have been set free. However, Queen Mary, desiring to make an example of him, condemned him to be burned at the stake. He repented of his recantation and was sentenced to die by fire at the stake. He held up his right hand (the hand that had signed his confession) and called it his "unworthy right hand." As the flames began to burn, he cried out, "Lord Jesus, receive my spirit. . . . I see the heavens open and Jesus standing at the right hand of God."[62]

Hugh Latimer (c. 1487–1555), the Bishop of Worcester and later chaplain to King Edward VI, was burned at the stake along with Nicholas Ridley. Latimer cried out, "Play the man, Master Ridley; we shall this day light such a candle, by God's grace, in England, as I trust shall never be put out."[63]

Polycarp (c. AD 70–168), disciple of the apostle John, said at his death, "Eighty and six years I have served him [which indicates that he lived 86 years after his conversion]. How then can I blaspheme my King and Savior? Bring forth what thou wilt." Polycarp was burned at the stake for refusing to burn incense to the Roman Emperor.[64]

ENDNOTES

Part 1: Stories and Testimonies of Heaven

1. "Tamara Laroux Shot Herself, Went to Hell, then to Heaven and Back!" 700 Club Interview, February 23, 2011. http://www.youtube.com/watch?v=HGQDkCi-OIY; http://www.cbn.com/700club/guests/bios/tamara_laroux022111.aspx; and www.lifechange intl.com. Tamara and her husband are ordained ministers and members of the American Association of Christian Counselors.

2. Rosemary Trible is the author of *Fear to Freedom: What If You Did Not Have to Be So Afraid?* and founder of Fear 2 Freedom, a global nonprofit organization dedicated to redeeming and restoring lives wounded by sexual abuse (see www.fear2freedom.org). She is married to former United States Congressman and Senator Paul Trible, who currently serves as President of Christopher Newport University in Newport News, Virginia.

3. Rev. J. L. Scott, *Scenes Beyond the Grave: Trance of Marietta Davis* (Dayton, OH: Stephen Duel Publisher, 1859). http://archive.org/stream/scenesbeyondgrav00davi#page/n13/mode/2up=(pp vii–viii).

4. Greg Taylor, *Death Before Life After Life*. http://darklore.dailygrail.com/samples/DL3-GT.pdf.

5. Ibid., p. 56.

6. Ibid., p. 52.

7. Ibid., p. 55.

8. Ibid., p. 57.

9. Ibid., p. 59.

10. Ibid.

11. Ibid.

12. "Rwandan Genocide," Wikipedia. http://en.wikipedia.org/wiki/Rwandan_Genocide.

13. "Emanuel Tuwagirairmana," NearDeath.com. http://www.near-death.com/forum/nde/000/45.html.

14. Ibid.

15. Ibid., pp. 59-61.

16. Ibid., p. 62.

17. "True Near Death Experiences," Bible Probe. http://bibleprobe.com/nde.htm; http://LightshipMinistries.Org.

18. Ken R. Vincent and John C. Morgan, "An 18th Century Near-Death Experience: The Case of George de Benneville," *Journal of Near-Death Studies,* Fall 2006, vol. 25, no. 1, pp. 35-48.

19. David Servant, "True Near Death Experiences: The Resurrection of Pastor Daniel Ekechukwu," Bible Probe for Christians and Messianic Jews. http://bibleprobe.com/ekechukwu.htm.

20. C. G. Jung, *Memories, Dreams, Reflections* (New York: Vintage, 1963), p. 289.

21. Ibid., pp. 290-291.

22. Ibid., p. 291.

23. Ibid., p. 293.

24. Ibid.

25. Clare Dunne, *Carl Jung: Wounded Healer of the Soul* (London: Continuum, 2000), p. 200. Carl Gustav Jung (1875–1961), a Swiss psychotherapist and psychiatrist, founded analytical psychology. His revolutionary concepts are commonly accepted today, such as

individuation, extraversion and introversion personality types, archetypes and the collective unconscious. His work influenced not only psychiatry but also religious thinking.

26. A video version of this story is available from Dean Braxton Ministries at http://www.deanbraxton.com/dean-braxton-videos/ and http://www.cbn.com/media/player/index.aspx?s=/mp4/SW141v1_WS&search=heavenhell&p=1&parent=3&subnav=false.

27. P. M. H. Atwater, *Beyond the Light: What Isn't Being Said About Near Death Experience: From Visions of Heaven to Glimpses of Hell* (New York: Birch Lane Press, 1994).

28. "The Vision of Paul the Apostle," *From the Ante-Nicene Fathers*, vol. X (The Gnostic Society Library: Christian Apocrypha and Early Christian Literature). http://www.gnosis.org/library/visionpaul.htm.

29. "Vision of the Blessed Ezra," Ancient Writings. http://www.zyworld.com/cosmic creeper/OTpseudigigrapha/visionezra.htm.

30. Eileen Gardiner, *Medieval Visions of Heaven and Hell* (Oxford, UK: Routledge, 1993), taken from a letter from St. Boniface (Winfrid) to Abbess Eadberga, Abbess of Thanet. http://books.google.com/books?id=zOYvNNIyjN0C&pg=PR7&dq=This+vision+of+the+otherworld+appears+in+a+letter+from+St.+Boniface+%28Winfrid%29+to+Abbess+Eadberga,+abbess+of+Thanet,&source=gbs_selected_pages&cad=3#v=onepage&q=This%20vision%20of%20the%20otherworld%20appears%20in%20a%20letter%20from%20St.%20Boniface%20%28Winfrid%29%20to%20Abbess%20Eadberga%2C%20abbess%20of%20Thanet%2C&f=false.

31. Ibid.

32. Ibid. See also "Visio Karoli Grossi," Wikipedia, http://en.wikipedia.org/wiki/Visio_Karoli_Grossi.

33. "A NDE (Actually Died) Experience of Yensen," Talk Jesus. http://www.talkjesus.com/testimonials/43209-nde-actually-died-experience-yensen.html.

34. Dr. Carol Zaleski, *Otherworld Journeys* (New York: Oxford University Press, Inc., 1987). http://www.near-death.com/medieval.html.

35. Augustine Calmet, *Phantom World* (1850). http://www.djmcadam.com/curma.html.

36. Carol Zaleski, *The Life of the World to Come: Near-Death Experience and Christian Hope* (New York: Oxford University Press, 1996), pp. 30-31.

37. Ibid., p. 32.

38. Despite Zaleski's assertions, many of the true accounts of modern near-death survivors talk about hell—and the dread they experience.

39. Ibid., pp. 32-33.

40. Ibid.

41. "The Incredible Vision of St. Drythelm," Classical Christianity. Taken from *Ecclesiastical History*, Book 5.12. http://classicalchristianity.com/2011/10/29/the-incredible-vision-of-st-drythelm/. This is recorded in many places, including http://www.therealpresence.org/eucharst/misc/PHP/purg_sb_venerable.pdf.

42. Ibid.

43. Ibid.

44. "A Healing Evangelist of Power and Spiritual Integrity," Mel Montgomery Communications International (MMCI). http://www.brothermel.org/audio-video/74.

45. Kenneth E. Hagin, *I Believe in Visions* (Tulsa, OK: Faith Library Publications, 1994), p. 5.

46. Ibid.

47. Ibid., p. 6.

48. Ibid., p. 7.

49. Ibid.

50. Ibid., p. 9.

51. Ibid.

52. Ibid., p 11.

53. Ibid.

54. As quoted from *The Life Beyond Death* by Arthur Ford as told to Jerome Ellison (G. P. Putnam, New York: 1971), pp. 201-225 in *Afterlife: The Other Side of Death* by Morton T. Kelsey (New York: Crossroad, 1979), p. 265.

55. Ibid.

56. Ibid., p. 266.

57. Ibid.

58. Ibid., p. 267.

59. Ibid.

60. Ibid.

61. Ibid.

62. Rory Fitzgerald, "As I Lay Dying a Voice Said: 'Let's Go,' " *Catholic Herald*. http://www.catholicherald.co.uk/features/2012/04/09/as-i-lay-dying-a-voice-said-lets-go/.

63. Ibid.

64. Ibid.

65. Ibid.

66. Ibid.

67. http://www.howardstorm.com/. This story is also told a number of other places such as http://www.near-death.com/storm.html.

68. Julie Papeivis is a speaker and the author of *Go Back and Be Happy* (Monarch Books, 2008). She also works part-time as a community relations advisor for a top Chicago law firm. See www.gobackandbehappy.com.

69. Adapted from "Oprah and Neurosurgeon Eben Alexander: Proof of Heaven," Interview by Oprah Winfrey, aired December 2, 2012. http://www.oprah.com/own-supersoul-sunday/Oprah-and-Neurosurgeon-Eben-Alexander-Proof-of-Heaven.

70. Eben Alexander, M.D., *Proof of Heaven: A Neurosurgeon's Journey into the Afterlife* (New York: Simon & Schuster, 2012). http://www.lifebeyonddeath.net.

71. "Eben Alexander (Author)," Wikipedia. http://en.wikipedia.org/wiki/Eben_Alexander_(author).

72. Ibid.

73. Freddie Vest's story is told on video at http://www.cbn.com/media/player/index.aspx?s=/mp4/AR99v2_WS.

74. Marvin Besteman with Lorilee Craker, *My Journey to Heaven: What I Saw and How It Changed My Life* (Grand Rapids, MI: Revell/Baker Publishing Group, 2012).

75. See www.reaganministries.org and http://www.youtube.com/watch?v=vQ8TEGMj-jc.

76. Barbara McVicker Dye and Tom, her husband, work with mentally challenged and handicapped people at their church in Ohio. They're also involved in the bus ministry. She enjoys praying for others and is grateful for good friends.

77. John Bunyan, *Visions of Heaven and Hell*, part 2. Excerpt found on His Sheep, Art and Sue Renz, Global Missionary Church Ministries. http://hissheep.org/messages/visions_of_heaven_and_hell_2.html.

78. Linda Evans Shepherd is an author and speaker who has spoken nationally and internationally for 20 years. She is president of Right to the Heart, a Christian ministry, and ministers to women authors and speakers through Advanced Writers and Speakers Association. She reaches out to hurting and suicidal people in her ministry's blog, www.ThinkingAboutSuicide.com. See also www.sheppro.com.

79. Mary C. Neal, MD, *To Heaven and Back: A Doctor's Extraordinary Account of Her Death, Heaven, Angels and Life Again* (Colorado Springs, CO: Waterbrook Press, 2012).

80. Todd Burpo with Lynn Vincent, *Heaven Is For Real: A Little Boy's Astounding Story of His Trip to Heaven* (Nashville, TN: Thomas Nelson, 2010).

81. Kevin and Alex Malarkey, *The Boy Who Came Back from Heaven: A Remarkable Account of Miracles, Angels and Life Beyond This World* (Carol Stream, IL: Tyndale House Publishers, 2010).

82. Don Piper with Cecil Murphey, *90 Minutes in Heaven: A True Story of Death and Life* (Grand Rapids, MI: Revell/Baker Publishing Group, 2004).

Part 2: Questions About Heaven

1. Jeffrey Burton Russell, *A History of Heaven* (Princeton, NJ: Princeton University Press, 1997), pp. 40-41.

2. The Greek translation of the Old Testament, sometimes referred to as LXX.

3. Russell, *A History of Heaven*, p. 13.

4. Ibid.

5. Scofield Reference Notes, Matthew 6. http://www.biblestudytools.com/commentaries/scofield-reference-notes/matthew/matthew-6.html.

6. Gary R. Habermas and J. P. Moreland, *Beyond Death: Exploring the Evidence for Immortality* (Wheaton, IL: Crossway Books, 1998), p. 283.

7. Colleen McDannell and Bernhard Lange, *Heaven: A History* (New Haven, CT: Yale Note Bene, 2001), p. 20.

8. Ibid., p. 21.

9. Ibid., p. 20.

10. Ibid., p. 21.

11. Stanley J. Grenz, *Theology for the Community of God* (Grand Rapids, MI: William B. Eerdmans, 1994), p. 589.

12. Ibid., p. 589.

13. Ibid., p. 590.

14. Ibid., p. 591.

15. Kevin Knight, "Catholic Doctrine" New Advent, 2009. http://www.newadvent.org/cathen/12575a.htm.

16. Ibid.

17. Louis Berkhof, *Systematic Theology* (Grand Rapids, MI: William B. Eerdmans, 1996), p. 735.

18. Morton T. Kelsey, *Afterlife: The Other Side of Dying* (New York: Crossroad, 1985), p. 251.

19. Gary R. Habermas and J. P. Moreland, *Beyond Death: Exploring the Evidence for Immortality* (Wheaton, IL: Crossway Books, 1998), p. 312.

20. William Crockett, editor, *Four Views on Hell* (Grand Rapids, MI: Zondervan Publishing House, 1992), pp. 12-13.

21. Ibid., p. 14.

22. Kevin Knight, "Limbo," New Advent. http://www.newadvent.org/cathen/09256a.

23. Joseph P. Gudel, Robert M. Bowman Jr. and Dan R. Schlesinger, "Reincarnation—Did the Church Suppress It?" Issues, Etc., *Christian Research Journal*, 1987. http://www.mtio.com/articles/aissar14.htm.

24. Ibid.

25. Habermas and Moreland, *Beyond Death: Exploring the Evidence for Immortality*, pp. 156-157.

26. Ibid.

27. Habermas and Moreland, *Beyond Death: Exploring the Evidence for Immortality*, p. 159.

28. Ibid.

29. Ibid.

30. Habermas and Moreland, *Beyond Death: Exploring the Evidence for Immortality*, p. 160.

31. Ibid., pp. 162-163.

32. Ibid., p. 163.

33. Alan Hippleheuser, "Near-death Experiences (NDEs) 101: How Many People Have NDEs?" http://www.examiner.com/article/near-death-experiences-ndes-101-how-many-people-have-ndes.

34. Susan J. Blackmore, *Dying to Live: Near-Death Experiences* (Amherst, NY: Prometheus Books, 1993).

35. Habermas and Moreland, *Beyond Death: Exploring the Evidence for Immortality,* p. 184.

36. Mally Cox-Chapman, *The Case for Heaven: Near-Death Experiences as Evidence of the Afterlife* (New York: G. P. Putnam's Sons, 1997), p. 1.

37. Ibid., pp. 1-2.

38. Ibid., p. 2.

39. The International Association for Near-death Studies (IANDS) is found at http://www.iands.org/home.html.

40. Cox-Chapman, *The Case for Heaven: Near-Death Experiences as Evidence of the Afterlife,* p. 10.

41. "Aftereffects of Near-death States," International Association for Near-death Studies. http://iands.org/about-ndes/common-aftereffects.html#a3.

42. International Association for Near-death Studies. http://www.iands.org/home.html.

43. Cox-Chapman, *The Case for Heaven: Near-Death Experiences as Evidence of the Afterlife,* p. 17.

44. Ibid., p. 41.

45. Ibid., p. 119.

46. Ibid., p. 162.

47. Raymond A. Moody with Paul Perry, *The Light Beyond* (New York: Bantam Books, 1988), pp. 18-19.

48. Ibid., p. 14.

49. Dr. Michael Sabom, *Light and Death* (Grand Rapids, MI: Zondervan Publishing House, 1998), p. 202.

50. Moody, *The Light Beyond,* p. 14.

51. Ibid., p. 15.

52. Jeffrey Long with Paul Perry, *Evidence of the Afterlife* (New York: HarperOne, 2010), p. 8.

53. Moody, *The Light Beyond,* p. 27.

54. Ibid.

55. Pamela M. Kircher MD, Maggie Callanan RN, et al, "Near-death Experiences and Nearing Death Awareness in the Terminally Ill," IANDS. http://www.iands.org/about-ndes/nde-and-the-terminally-ill.html.

56. Pamela M. Kircher, M.D., Maggie Callanan, RN, CRNG and the IANDS Board of Directors, "Near-Death Experiences and Nearing Death Awareness in the Terminally Ill" (IANDS). http://www.iands.org/about-ndes/nde-and-the-terminally-ill.html.

57. Ibid.

58. "Necromancy" claims to communicate with the dead by summoning their spirit as an apparition or by raising them bodily. The purpose of divination is usually to foretell future events, as in the story of King Saul.

59. Pamela M. Kircher, M.D., Maggie Callanan, RN, CRNG and the IANDS Board of Directors, "Near-Death Experiences and Nearing Death Awareness in the Terminally Ill" (IANDS). http://www.iands.org/about-ndes/nde-and-the-terminally-ill.html

60. The rest of these come from http://www.powerpointparadise.com/heaven/grave/last word.htm.

61. "Jan Hus," Wikipedia. http://en.wikipedia.org/wiki/Jan_Hus.

62. "Thomas Cranmer," Wikipedia. http://en.wikipedia.org/wiki/Thomas_Cranmer.

63. "Hugh Latimer," quoting from John Foxe's *Acts and Monuments.* http://en.wikipedia.org/wiki/Hugh_Latimer.

64. "Polycarp," Wikipedia. http://en.wikipedia.org/wiki/Polycarp.

ACKNOWLEDGMENTS

We're grateful to Stan Jantz and the others at Regal for asking us to write this book. Mark Weising's editing and Jackie Medina's promotion deserve praise. Because of Wanda Rosenberry's keen eye in proofing, our book is better. Thanks to Deidre Knight, our hardworking literary agent, for always looking out for our interests, and to Gail Smith for her help with research.

A number of people contributed their personal stories for this book and we appreciate their help.

Cec Murphey: Despite my wife's declining health, Shirley enthusiastically encouraged me in writing this book. Our daughter, Cecile Hege, took over many household tasks during this period and gave me more time to work on this book.

Twila Belk: It wasn't easy, but my husband, Steve, kept me grounded on earth while my mind and heart were in heaven and wanted to stay there. I'm grateful to our wonderful Lord for the hope of heaven. I long for the day I'll see Him face-to-face.

DO YOU *Believe* GOD HEALS TODAY?

I Believe in Healing
ISBN 978-0-8307-6553-9
ISBN 0-8307-6553-0

The Bible is full of miracle stories, but some Christians today aren't sure whether God's healing power is available in the same way. In *I Believe in Healing*, you'll read these stories and others from the Bible, history and today—stories that can't be explained by natural means, reminding us that God is the same yesterday, today and forever:

- Lost voice restored
- Crippling effects erased
- Cancer cells disappear
- Blind eyes regain sight
- Paralyzed legs walk
- Short limbs grow

These testimonies of God's power and compassion can strengthen your faith and inspire you to trust Him during times of sickness or injury. You'll also find biblical answers to the most common questions about healing, as well as a brief historical overview of the Church's long history with healing and miracles.

Available at Bookstores Everywhere!

Go to **www.regalbooks.com** to learn more about your favorite Regal books and authors. Visit us online today!

Regal

God's Word for Your World™

www.regalbooks.com

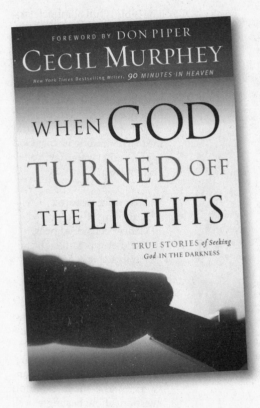